Volvo & Daf Owners Workshop Manual

by J H Haynes
Member of the Guild of Motoring Writers
and A K Legg T Eng (CEI), AMIMI

Models covered
Volvo 66, September 1975 to 1978, 1289 cc
Volvo 343, September 1976 to 1978, 1397 cc
Daf 55, February 1968 to September 1972, 1108 cc
Daf 66, September 1972 to August 1975, 1108 cc
Daf 66, September 1973 to August 1975, 1289 cc
Covers all Saloon, Coupé, Estate and Marathon models with Variomatic transmission

Does not cover manual gearbox models of Volvo 343

ISBN 0 85696 293 7

Printed in England

HAYNES PUBLISHING GROUP
SPARKFORD YEOVIL SOMERSET ENGLAND
distributed in the USA by
HAYNES PUBLICATIONS INC
861 LAWRENCE DRIVE
NEWBURY PARK
CALIFORNIA 91320
USA

Acknowledgements

Special thanks are due to A.B. Volvo for the supply of technical information and certain illustrations. The Champion Sparking Plug Company supplied the illustrations showing the various spark plug conditions. The bodywork repair photographs used in this manual were provided by Lloyds Industries Limited who supply 'Turtle Wax', 'Dupli-color Holts', and other Holts range products.

Lastly, thanks are due to all those people at Sparkford who helped in the production of this manual, particularly Brian Horsfall and Leon Martindale who carried out the mechanical work and took the photographs respectively, Lee Saunders who planned the layout of each page, and Hugh Mayes who edited the text.

About this manual

Its aim

The aim of this manual is to help you get the best value from your car. It can do so in several ways. It can help you decide what work must be done (even should you choose to get it done by a garage), provide information on routine maintenance and servicing, and give a logical course of action and diagnosis when random faults occur. However, it is hoped that you will make full use of the manual by tackling the work yourself. On simpler jobs it may even be quicker than booking the car into a garage, and having to go there twice, to leave and collect it. Perhaps most important, a lot of money can be saved by avoiding the costs the garage must charge to cover its labour and overheads.

The manual has drawings and descriptions to show the function of the various components so that their layout can be understood. Then the tasks are described and photographed in a step-by-step sequence so that even a novice can do the work.

Its arrangement

The manual is divided into ten Chapters, each covering a logical sub-division of the vehicle. The Chapters are each divided into consecutively numbered Sections and Sections into paragraphs (or sub-sections), with decimal numbers following on from the Section they are in, eg 5.1, 5.2, 5.3 etc.

It is freely illustrated, especially in those parts where there is a detailed sequence of operations to be carried out. There are two forms of illustrations: figures and photographs. The figures are numbered in sequence with decimal numbers, according to their position in the Chapter: eg, Fig. 6.4 is the 4th drawing/illustration in Chapter 6. Photographs are numbered (either individually or in related groups) the same as the Section or sub-section of the text where the operation they show is described.

There is an alphabetical index at the back of the manual as well as a contents list at the front.

References to the 'left' or 'right' of the vehicle are in the sense of a person in a seat facing towards the front of the vehicle.

Whilst every care is taken to ensure that the information in this manual is correct no liability can be accepted by the authors or publishers for loss, damage or injury caused by any errors in, or omissions from, the information given.

Introduction to
the Daf/Volvo 55, 66 and 343

The models covered by this manual are available in two or three door versions, and are powered by Renault engines adapted to incorporate the automatic-type clutch.

The belt-driven variomatic transmission is unique as far as popular cars are concerned, and has always been of interest to motorists who want a small automatic car which is reliable and reasonably priced.

The transmission is basically the same for all models although later models have been modified slightly.

The practical body construction together with the well proven engine, and the unique transmission arrangement, have made these models an attractive alternative within the small car market.

Contents

Volvo 343

Daf 66 Estate

General dimensions, weights, and capacities

Overall length
Daf 55, Daf 66 models . . . . 152.75 in (3.88 m)
Volvo 66 models . . . . 153.94 in (3.91 m)
Volvo 343 models . . . . 164.96 in (4.19 m)

Overall width
Daf 55 models . . . . 60.62 in (1.54 m)
Daf 66 models . . . . 59.84 in (1.52 m)
Volvo 66 models . . . . 59.45 in (1.51 m)
Volvo 343 models . . . . 65.35 in (1.66 m)

Overall height
Daf 55 models . . . . 54.33 in (1.38 m)
Daf 66 Saloon and all Volvo models . . . . 56.69 in (1.44 m)
Daf 66 Marathon Coupé models . . . . 53.54 in (1.36 m)

Wheelbase
Daf 55, Daf 66 models . . . . 88.58 in (2.25 m)
Volvo 66 models . . . . 100.39 in (2.55 m)
Volvo 343 models . . . . 94.48 in (2.40 m)

Track

	Front	Rear
Daf 55 standard models	50.39 in (1.28 m)	49.21 in (1.25 m)
Daf 55 Marathon models	51.57 in (1.31 m)	48.81 in (1.24 m)
Daf 66 standard models	51.57 in (1.31 m)	48.81 in (1.24 m)
Daf 66 Marathon models	51.18 in (1.30 m)	48.42 in (1.23 m)
Volvo 66 DL models	51.57 in (1.31 m)	48.81 in (1.24 m)
Volvo 66 GL models	51.18 in (1.3 m)	48.42 in (1.23 m)
Volvo 343 models	53.15 in (1.35 m)	54.33 in (1.38 m)

Kerb weight
Daf 55 Saloon and Coupé models . . . . 1753 lb (795 kg)
Daf 55 Marathon models . . . . 1742 lb (790 kg)
Daf 66 Saloon L models . . . . 1797 lb (815 kg)
Daf 66 Saloon SL models . . . . 1801 lb (817 kg)
Daf 66 Marathon Saloon models . . . . 1856 lb (842 kg)
Daf 66 Marathon Coupé models . . . . 1861 lb (844 kg)
Daf 66 Marathon Estate models . . . . 1918 lb (870 kg)
Daf 66 Coupé models . . . . 1704 lb (733 kg)
Volvo 66 2 door DL models . . . . 1797 lb (815 kg)
Volvo 66 3 door DL models . . . . 1863 lb (845 kg)
Volvo 66 2 door GL models . . . . 1845 lb (837 kg)
Volvo 66 3 door GL models . . . . 1911 lb (867 kg)
Volvo 343 models . . . . 2079 lb (943 kg)

Maximum payload
All except Volvo 343 models . . . .   760 lb (354 kg)
Volvo 343 models . . . .   1007 lb (457 kg)

Towing capacity
Daf 55 and Daf 66 models . . . .   926 lb (450 kg)
Volvo 66 DL models . . . .   1323 lb (600 kg)
Volvo 66 GL and all 343 models . . . .   1543 lb (700 kg)

Roof rack load
All models (maximum) . . . .   110 lb (50 kg)

Turning circle
Daf 55, Daf 66, and Volvo 66 models . . . .   374 in (9.5 m)
Volvo 343 models . . . .   362 in (9.2 m)

Engine oil capacity
1108 cc and 1289 cc engines . . . .   5.3 pints (3.0 litres)
1397 cc engine . . . .   6.1 pints (3.5 litres)

Transmission oil capacity
Primary . . . .   0.75 pints (430 cc)
Secondary . . . .
Daf 55 models . . . .   0.4 pints (230 cc)
All other models . . . .   1.4 pints (800 cc)

Cooling system capacity
Daf 55, Daf 66, and Volvo 66 models . . . .   8.5 pints (4.8 litres)
Volvo 343 models . . . .   9.7 pints (5.5 litres)

Fuel tank capacity
Daf 55 models . . . .   8.36 galls (38.0 litres)
Daf 66 and Volvo 66 models . . . .   9.38 galls (42.0 litres)
Volvo 343 models . . . .   9.89 galls (45.0 litres)

Buying spare parts and vehicle identification numbers

Buying spare parts

Spare parts are available from many sources, for example: Daf/Volvo garages, other garages and accessory shops, and motor factors. Our advice regarding spare part sources is as follows:

Officially appointed Daf/Volvo garages – This is the best source of parts which are peculiar to your car and are otherwise not generally available (eg complete cylinder heads, transmission components, badges, interior trim etc). It is also the only place at which you should buy parts if your car is still under warranty – use of non Daf/Volvo components may invalidate the warranty. To be sure of obtaining the correct parts it will always be necessary to give the storeman your car's vehicle identification number, and if possible, to take the 'old' part along for positive identification. Remember that many parts are available on a factory exchange scheme – any parts returned should always be clean! It obviously makes good sense to go straight to the specialists on your car for this type of part for they are best equipped to supply you.

Other garages and accessory shops – These are often very good places to buy materials and components needed for the maintenance of your car (eg oil filters, spark plugs, bulbs, fan belts, oils and grease, touch-up paint, filler paste etc). They also sell general accessories, usually have convenient opening hours, charge lower prices and can often be found not far from home.

Motor factors – Good factors will stock all of the more important

components which wear out relatively quickly (eg clutch components, pistons, valves, exhaust systems, brake cylinders/pipes/hoses/seals/shoes and pads etc). Motor factors will often provide new or reconditioned components on a part exchange basis – this can save a considerable amount of money.

Vehicle identification numbers

Although many individual parts, and in some cases sub-assemblies, fit a number of different models it is dangerous to assume that just because they look the same, they are the same. Differences are not always easy to detect except by serial numbers. Make sure therefore, that the appropriate identity number for the model or sub-assembly is known and quoted when a spare part is ordered.

The engine number is located on a metal plate fixed to the left-hand side of the cylinder block in front of the distributor.

The chassis number is stamped on the right-hand side of the scuttle (Daf models), or engine bulkhead (Volvo models), within the engine compartment.

The vehicle identification plate is located in the engine compartment on the left-hand scuttle (Daf 66 models), right-hand scuttle (Volvo 66 models), or front panel (Volvo 343 models).

Additionally, on Volvo models, a *service data plate* is located below the left-hand door lock.

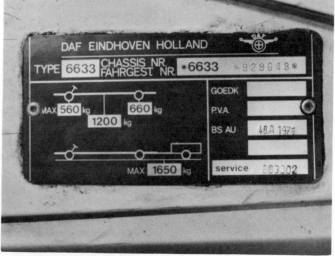

Engine number plate

Identification plate (typical)

Tools and working facilities

Introduction

A selection of good tools is a fundamental requirement for anyone contemplating the maintenance and repair of a motor vehicle. For the owner who does not possess any, their purchase will prove a considerable expense, offsetting some of the savings made by doing-it-yourself. However, provided that the tools purchased are of good quality, they will last for many years and prove an extremely worthwhile investment.

To help the average owner to decide which tools are needed to carry out the various tasks detailed in this manual, we have compiled three lists of tools under the following headings: *Maintenance and minor repair, Repair and overhaul,* and *Special.* The newcomer to practical mechanics should start off with the *Maintenance and minor repair* tool kit and confine himself to the simpler jobs around the vehicle. Then, as his confidence and experience grows, he can undertake more difficult tasks, buying extra tools as, and when, they are needed. In this way, a *Maintenance and minor repair* tool kit can be built-up into a *Repair and overhaul* tool kit over a considerable period of time without any major cash outlays. The experienced do-it-yourselfer will have a tool kit good enough for most repair and overhaul procedures and will add tools from the *Special* category when he feels the expense is justified by the amount of use to which these tools will be put.

It is obviously not possible to cover the subject of tools fully here. For those who wish to learn more about tools and their use there is a book entitled *How to Choose and Use Car Tools* available from the publishers of this manual.

Maintenance and minor repair tool kit

The tools given in this list should be considered as a minimum requirement if routine maintenance, servicing and minor repair operations are to be undertaken. We recommend the purchase of combination spanners (ring one end, open-ended the' other); although more expensive than open-ended ones, they do give the advantages of both types of spanner.

Combination spanners - 10, 11, 13, 14, 17 mm
Adjustable spanner - 9 inch
Engine sump/gearbox/rear axle drain plug key (where applicable)
Spark plug spanner (with rubber insert)
Spark plug gap adjustment tool
Set of feeler gauges
Brake adjuster spanner (where applicable)
Brake bleed nipple spanner
Screwdriver - 4 in long x $\frac{1}{4}$ in dia (flat blade)
Screwdriver - 4 in long x $\frac{1}{4}$ in dia (cross blade)
Combination pliers - 6 inch
Hacksaw, junior
Tyre pump
Tyre pressure gauge
Grease gun (where applicable)
Oil can
Fine emery cloth (1 sheet)
Wire brush (small)
Funnel (medium size)

Repair and overhaul tool kit

These tools are virtually essential for anyone undertaking any major repairs to a motor vehicle, and are additional to those given in the *Maintenance and minor repair* list. Included in this list is a comprehensive set of sockets. Although these are expensive they will be found invaluable as they are so versatile - particularly if various drives are included in the set. We recommend the $\frac{1}{2}$ in square-drive type, as this can be used with most proprietary torque wrenches. If you cannot afford a socket set, even bought piecemeal, then inexpensive tubular box spanners are a useful alternative.

The tools in this list will occasionally need to be supplemented by tools from the *Special* list.

Sockets (or box spanners) to cover range in previous list
Reversible ratchet drive (for use with sockets)
Extension piece, 10 inch (for use with sockets)
Universal joint (for use with sockets)
Torque wrench (for use with sockets)
'Mole' wrench - 8 inch
Ball pein hammer
Soft-faced hammer, plastic or rubber
Screwdriver - 6 in long x $\frac{5}{16}$ in dia (flat blade)
Screwdriver - 2 in long x $\frac{5}{16}$ in square (flat blade)
Screwdriver - 1$\frac{1}{2}$ in long x $\frac{1}{4}$ in dia (cross blade)
Screwdriver - 3 in long x $\frac{1}{8}$ in dia (electricians)
Pliers - electricians side cutters
Pliers - needle nosed
Pliers - circlip (internal and external)
Cold chisel - $\frac{1}{2}$ inch
Scriber (this can be made by grinding the end of a broken hacksaw blade)
Scraper (this can be made by flattening and sharpening one end of a piece of copper pipe)
Centre punch
Pin punch
Hacksaw
Valve grinding tool
Steel rule/straight edge
Allen keys
Selection of files
Wire brush (large)
Axle-stands
Jack (strong scissor or hydraulic type)

Special tools

The tools in this list are those which are not used regularly, are expensive to buy, or which need to be used in accordance with their manufacturers' instructions. Unless relatively difficult mechanical jobs are undertaken frequently, it will not be economic to buy many of these tools. Where this is the case, you could consider clubbing together with friends (or a motorists' club) to make a joint purchase, or borrowing the tools against a deposit from a local garage or tool hire specialist.

The following list contains only those tools and instruments freely available to the public, and not those special tools produced by the vehicle manufacturer specifically for its dealer network. You will find occasional references to these manufacturers' special tools in the text of this manual. Generally, an alternative method of doing the job without the vehicle manufacturer's special tool is given. However, sometimes, there is no alternative to using them. Where this is the case and the relevant tool cannot be bought or borrowed you will have to entrust the work to a franchised garage.

Valve spring compressor
Piston ring compressor
Balljoint separator
Universal hub/bearing puller
Impact screwdriver
Micrometer and/or vernier gauge

Carburettor flow balancing device (where applicable)
Dial gauge
Stroboscopic timing light
Dwell angle meter/tachometer
Universal electrical multi-meter
Cylinder compression gauge
Lifting tackle (photo)
Trolley jack
Light with extension lead

Buying tools

For practically all tools, a tool factor is the best source since he will have a very comprehensive range compared with the average garage or accessory shop. Having said that, accessory shops often offer excellent quality tools at discount prices, so it pays to shop around.

Remember, you don't have to buy the most expensive items on the shelf, but it is always advisable to steer clear of the very cheap tools. There are plenty of good tools around at reasonable prices, so ask the proprietor or manager of the shop for advice before making a purchase.

Care and maintenance of tools

Having purchased a reasonable tool kit, it is necessary to keep the tools in a clean serviceable condition. After use, always wipe off any dirt, grease and metal particles using a clean, dry cloth, before putting the tools away. Never leave them lying around after they have been used. A simple tool rack on the garage or workshop wall, for items such as screwdrivers and pliers is a good idea. Store all normal spanners and sockets in a metal box. Any measuring instruments, gauges, meters, etc, must be carefully stored where they cannot be damaged or become rusty.

Take a little care when tools are used. Hammer heads inevitably become marked and screwdrivers lose the keen edge on their blades fom time to time. A little timely attention with emery cloth or a file will soon restore items like this to a good serviceable finish.

Working facilities

Not to be forgotten when discussing tools, is the workshop itself. If anything more than routine maintenance is to be carried out, some form of suitable working area becomes essential.

It is appreciated that many an owner mechanic is forced by circumstances to remove an engine or similar item, without the benefit of a garage or workshop. Having done this, any repairs should always be done under the cover of a roof.

Wherever possible, any dismantling should be done on a clean flat workbench or table at a suitable working height.

Any workbench needs a vice: one with a jaw opening of 4 in (100 mm) is suitable for most jobs. As mentioned previously, some clean dry storage space is also required for tools, as well as the lubricants, cleaning fluids, touch-up paints and so on which become necessary.

Another item which may be required, and which has a much more general usage, is an electric drill with a chuck capacity of at least $\frac{5}{16}$ in (8 mm). This, together with a good range of twist drills, is virtually essential for fitting accessories such as wing mirrors and reversing lights.

Last, but not least, always keep a supply of old newspapers and clean, lint-free rags available, and try to keep any working area as clean as possible.

Spanner jaw gap comparison table

Jaw gap (in)	Spanner size
0·250	$\frac{1}{4}$ in AF
0·275	7 mm AF
0·312	$\frac{5}{16}$ in AF
0·315	8 mm AF
0·340	$\frac{11}{32}$ in AF; $\frac{1}{8}$ in Whitworth
0·354	9 mm AF
0·375	$\frac{3}{8}$ in AF
0·393	10 mm AF
0·433	11 mm AF
0·437	$\frac{7}{16}$ in AF
0·445	$\frac{3}{16}$ in Whitworth; $\frac{1}{4}$ in BSF
0·472	12 mm AF
0·500	$\frac{1}{2}$ in AF
0·512	13 mm AF
0·525	$\frac{1}{4}$ in Whitworth; $\frac{5}{16}$ in BSF
0·551	14 mm AF
0·562	$\frac{9}{16}$ in AF
0·590	15 mm AF
0·600	$\frac{5}{16}$ in Whitworth; $\frac{3}{8}$ in BSF
0·625	$\frac{5}{8}$ in AF
0·629	16 mm AF
0·669	17 mm AF
0·687	$\frac{11}{16}$ in AF
0·708	18 mm AF
0·710	$\frac{3}{8}$ in Whitworth; $\frac{7}{16}$ in BSF
0·748	19 mm AF
0·750	$\frac{3}{4}$ in AF
0·812	$\frac{13}{16}$ in AF
0·820	$\frac{7}{16}$ in Whitworth; $\frac{1}{2}$ in BSF
0.866	22 mm AF
0.875	$\frac{7}{8}$ in AF
0·920	$\frac{1}{2}$ in Whitworth; $\frac{9}{16}$ in BSF
0·937	$\frac{15}{16}$ in AF
0·944	24 mm AF
1·000	1 in AF
1·010	$\frac{9}{16}$ in Whitworth; $\frac{5}{8}$ in BSF
1·023	26 mm AF
1·062	$1\frac{1}{16}$ in AF; 27 mm AF
1·100	$\frac{5}{8}$ in Whitworth; $\frac{11}{16}$ in BSF
1·125	$1\frac{1}{8}$ in AF
1·181	30 mm AF
1·200	$\frac{11}{16}$ in Whitworth; $\frac{3}{4}$ in BSF
1·250	$1\frac{1}{4}$ in AF
1·259	32 mm AF
1·300	$\frac{3}{4}$ in Whitworth; $\frac{7}{8}$ in BSF
1·312	$1\frac{5}{16}$ in AF
1·390	$\frac{13}{16}$ in Whitworth; $\frac{15}{16}$ in BSF
1·417	36 mm AF
1·437	$1\frac{7}{16}$ in AF
1·480	$\frac{7}{8}$ in Whitworth; 1 in BSF
1·500	$1\frac{1}{2}$ in AF
1·574	40 mm AF; $\frac{15}{16}$ in Whitworth
1·614	41 mm AF
1·625	$1\frac{5}{8}$ in AF
1·670	1 in Whitworth; $1\frac{1}{8}$ in BSF
1·687	$1\frac{11}{16}$ in AF
1·811	46 mm AF
1·812	$1\frac{13}{16}$ in AF
1·860	$1\frac{1}{8}$ in Whitworth; $1\frac{1}{4}$ in BSF
1·875	$1\frac{7}{8}$ in AF
1·968	50 mm AF
2·000	2 in AF
2·050	$1\frac{1}{4}$ in Whitworth; $1\frac{3}{8}$ in BSF
2·165	55 mm AF
2·362	60 mm AF

A Haltrac hoist and gantry in use during a typical engine removal sequence

Jacking and towing

When changing a roadwheel, the jack supplied to the car may be used at the four jacking points below the bodysills. When servicing the car a more substantial jack should be used at the same points, but before working under the car, always supplement the jack with axle-stands or wooden blocks positioned beneath the bodyframe.

Towing eyes are provided at the front and rear of most models.

Jack and jacking point

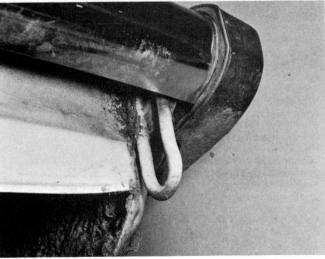

Rear towing eye

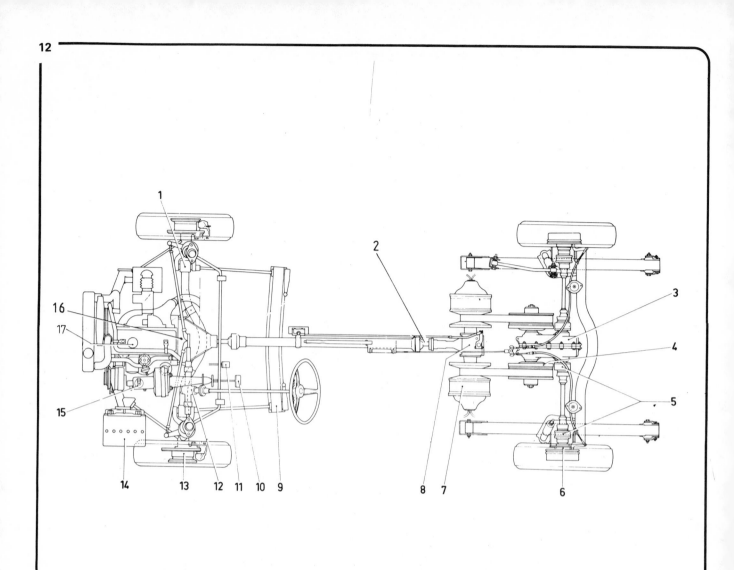

Recommended lubricants and fluids

Component or system	Lubricant or fluid specification
Torsion bar bush (1)*	Lithium based grease
Propeller shaft splines (2)	Lithium based grease
Secondary transmission unit gearcase (3)	SAE 80 Hypoid
Secondary transmission unit pulleys (4)	ATF fluid
Constant velocity joint (5)	Lithium based grease
Rear wheel bearings (6)	Lithium based grease
Primary transmission unit pulleys (7)	ATF fluid
Primary transmission gearcase (8)	SAE 80 Hypoid
Torsion bar rear bearing (9)*	Lithium based grease
Brake pedal pivot (10)	Engine oil
Accelerator pedal pivot (11)	Engine oil
Steering gear (12)	Lithium based grease
Front wheel bearings (13)	Lithium based grease
Battery terminals (14)	Petroleum jelly
Brake fluid (15)	SAE J 1703 or DOT 3
Spigot bearing (16)	Lithium based grease
Engine oil (17)	SAE 20 W 50

Not applicable to Volvo 343 models

Routine maintenance

Maintenance is essential for ensuring safety, and desirable for the purpose of getting the best in terms of performance and economy from your car. Over the years the need for periodic lubrication – oiling, greasing and so on – has been drastically reduced, if not totally eliminated. This has unfortunately tended to lead some owners to think that because no such action is required, components either no longer exist, or will last forever. This is a serious delusion. It follows therefore that the largest initial element of maintenance is visual examination.

Every 250 miles (400 km) travelled or weekly – whichever comes first

Steering
Check the tyre pressures, including the spare wheel
Examine tyres for wear or damage
Check steering for smooth operation

Brakes
Check reservoir fluid level
Check brakes for efficiency, adjust if necessary

Lights, wipers and horn(s)
Check all bulbs, front and rear
Check that the wipers and horn(s) work correctly
Check windscreen washer fluid level and jets

Engine
Check the sump oil level and top-up if required
Check the radiator coolant level and top-up if required
Check the battery electrolyte level and top-up to the level of the plates with distilled water as needed

---

Every 6000 miles (10 000 km) or six monthly – whichever comes first

Check disc pads and/or brake shoes for friction material wear
Check brake hydraulic system for leaks, damaged pipes etc
Check operation of brake servo (when fitted)
Check operation of handbrake and adjust if necessary
Examine the depth of the tyre treads
Check front wheel alignment and adjust if necessary
Check front hub bearing adjustment
Check for wear in steering gear, balljoints, and the condition of rubber bellows, dust excluders and flexible couplings
Examine exhaust systems for corrosion and leakage
Check the shock absorbers for wear and leakage
Check and lubricate the throttle and choke controls
Lubricate the bonnet and door hinges sparingly
Lubricate the heater controls
Change engine oil and renew oil filter element
Check the clutch lining thickness (not Daf 55 models)
Check the engine for oil and water leaks
Check the variomatic transmission for oil leaks and drivebelt wear and

Windscreen washer reservoir

Fuel tank filler cap location (Daf 66 models)

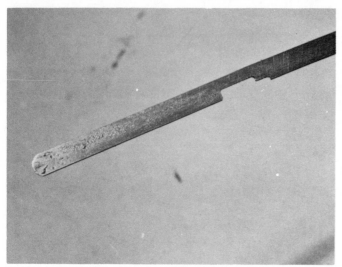

Engine oil dipstick markings (Daf 66 model shown)

Topping-up the engine oil

examine the mountings
Check the transmission disc gap and adjust if necessary
Check the primary and secondary transmission oil levels and top-up if necessary
Check the brake, vacuum, and fuel lines for damage
Check the halfshaft rubber bellows for damage
Clean and adjust spark plugs
Clean and adjust contact breaker points and lubricate
Adjust valve clearances
Check fan drivebelt tension and adjust if necessary
Check ignition timing and adjust if necessary
Adjust the idling speed
Check the transmission vacuum control micro-switch adjustment

---

Every 12 000 miles (20 000 km) or annually – whichever comes first

---

Renew the air cleaner element
Change the primary and secondary transmission oil
Inspect wiper blades and renew if necessary
Check security of seat belts and anchorages

Renew contact breaker points and plugs
Check all suspension bushes and balljoints and renew if necessary
Clean the crankcase ventilation hoses
Check antifreeze strength and top-up if necessary
Clean battery terminals and apply petroleum jelly

Every 24 000 miles (40 000 km) or two yearly – whichever comes first

---

Check torque of all engine, transmission and suspension nuts and bolts
Drain, flush and refill cooling system with antifreeze mixture
Clean fuel pump filter and carburettor filter (where fitted)
Check engine compression

Every 48 000 miles (50 000 km)

Drain brake hydraulic system of old fluid, renew all rubber seals and refill system with clean fluid
Check underbody for rust or corrosion and apply new protective sealant where necessary

Chapter 1 Engine

Contents

Specifications

Engine general

Type .... Four-cylinder in-line, overhead valve
Displacement:
    Daf 55, Daf 66/1100, Volvo 66/1100 .... 67.61 cu in (1108 cc)
    Daf 66/1300, Volvo 66/1300 .... 78.66 cu in (1289 cc)
    Volvo 343 .... 85.25 cu in (1397 cc)
Bore:
    1108 cc engine .... 2.756 in (70 mm)
    1289 cc engine .... 2.874 in (73 mm)
    1397 cc engine .... 2.992 in (76 mm)
Stroke:
    1108 cc engine .... 2.835 in (72 mm)
    1289 cc and 1397 cc engines .... 3.031 in (77 mm)
Firing order .... 1 - 3 - 4 - 2
Compression ratio:
    1108 cc and 1289 cc engines .... 8.5 to 1
    1397 cc engine .... 9.5 to 1
BHP (DIN 70020):
    Daf 55 .... 50 hp at 5000 rpm
    Daf 66/1100 .... 53 hp at 5000 rpm
    Daf 66/1300 .... 57 hp at 5200 rpm
    Volvo 66/1100 .... 47 hp at 5000 rpm
    Volvo 66/1300 .... 57 hp at 5200 rpm
    Volvo 343 .... 70 hp at 5500 rpm

Cylinder head

Material .... Aluminium alloy
Valve seat angle .... 45°

Valves

Seat width:
Inlet . . . . 0.055 in (1.4 mm)
Exhaust . . . . 0.064 in (1.7 mm)
Stem clearance in guide:
Inlet . . . . 0.00038 to 0.00272 in (0.010 to 0.069 mm)
Exhaust . . . . 0.000787 to 0.003307 in (0.020 to 0.084 mm)
Valve spring free length . . . . 1.661 in (42.2 mm)
Tappet clearance in block . . . . 0.00051 to 0.00185 in (0.013 to 0.047 mm)
Valve clearances:
Cold . . . . Inlet 0.006 in (0.15 mm) Exhaust 0.009 in (0.20 mm)
Hot . . . . Inlet 0.007 in (0.18 mm) Exhaust 0.010 in (0.25 mm)
Valve timing (at cold valve clearance) – Daf 55 models:
Inlet valve opens . . . . 10° BTDC
Inlet valve closes . . . . 34° ABDC
Exhaust valve opens . . . . 46° BBDC
Exhaust valve closes . . . . 10° ATDC
Valve timing (at valve clearance of 0.04 in (1.0 mm) – Daf 66 and
Volvo 66 models:
Inlet valve opens . . . . 0°30' ATDC
Inlet valve closes . . . . 36° ABDC
Exhaust valve opens . . . . 38° 30' BBDC
Exhaust valve closes . . . . 5° BTDC
Valve timing (at valve clearance of 0.04 in (1.0 mm) – Volvo 343
models:
Inlet valve opens . . . . 4° ATDC
Inlet valve closes . . . . 39° ABDC
Exhaust valve opens . . . . 42° BBDC
Exhaust valve closes . . . . 3° 30' ATDC

Camshaft

Journal diameter (except 1289 cc engine) . . . . 1.493 to 1.494 in (37.925 to 37.950 mm)
Journal diameter (1289 cc engine) . . . . 1.494 to 1.495 in (37.960 to 37.975 mm)
Endfloat . . . . 0.002 to 0.004 in (0.06 to 0.11 mm)

Cylinder liners and pistons

Liner projection above cylinder block (except Volvo 343
models . . . . 0.002 to 0.005 in (0.05 to 0.12 mm)
Size of gaskets available . . . . 0.003 in (0.07 mm), 0.004 in (0.10 mm), 0.005 in (0.13 mm)
Mean piston clearance . . . . 0.0197 to 0.0276 in (0.050 to 0.070 mm)
Piston rings:
Compression 2
Oil scraper 1
Piston ring gap (compression) . . . . 0.011 to 0.018 in (0.3 to 0.45 mm)
Piston ring clearance in groove:
Top compression . . . . 0.001 to 0.002 in (0.030 to 0.058 mm)
Centre compression . . . . 0.0009 to 0.002 in (0.024 to 0.050 mm)
Oil scraper . . . . 0.0005 to 0.002 in (0.015 to 0.06 mm)
Piston ring gap (oil scraper) . . . . 0.03 to 0.09 in (0.76 to 2.29 mm)

Connecting rods

Crankpin endplay (Daf 55 and 66/1100) . . . . 0.004 to 0.009 in (0.11 to 0.246 mm)
Crankpin endplay (Daf 66/1300, Volvo 66 and Volvo 343) . . . . 0.012 to 0.022 in (0.31 to 0.57 mm)

Crankshaft

Main bearing running clearance . . . . 0.001 to 0.003 in (0.030 to 0.071 mm)
Endplay (except Volvo 343) . . . . 0.002 to 0.007 in (0.05 to 0.19 mm)
Endplay (Volvo 343) . . . . 0.002 to 0.009 in (0.045 to 0.23 mm)

Lubrication

Oil capacity (excluding oil filter):
1108 cc and 1289 cc engines . . . . 5.3 pints (3.0 litres)
1397 cc engine . . . . 6.1 pints (3.5 litres)
Filter capacity . . . . 0.44 pints (0.25 litre)
Oil pump:
Gear endplay . . . . 0.0008 to 0.003 in (0.020 to 0.080 mm)
Oil pressure at idling . . . . 14.2 to 21.3 lbf in^2
Release valve spring free length . . . . 1.811 in (46.0 mm)

Torque wrench settings

	lbf ft	Nm
Cylinder head bolts	40 to 47	55 to 65
Connecting rod big-end nuts	28 to 32	40 to 45
Flywheel bolts	32 to 36	45 to 50
Main bearing cap bolts	40 to 47	55 to 65
Crankshaft pulley bolt	51 to 58	70 to 80
Oil pump housing and cover bolts	5 to 8	7 to 10

Sump bolts	5 to 8	7 to 10
Oil drain plug	14 to 18	20 to 25
Oil pressure switch	14 to 18	20 to 25
Camshaft sprocket bolt	19 to 23	27 to 32
Rocker shaft pedestal bolts	11 to 14	15 to 17
Timing chain tensioner bolts	5 to 8	7 to 10
Front engine mounting (engine side)	18 to 20	25 to 27
Front engine mounting (bearer side)	30 to 34	42 to 47
Rear engine mounting (engine side)	13 to 14	18 to 20
Rear engine mounting (bearer side)	30 to 34	42 to 47
Timing cover bolts	5 to 8	8 to 12
Camshaft flange bolts	5 to 8	8 to 12

1 General description

The engine is of 4 cylinder, in-line overhead valve type. The crankshaft has five main bearings, the centre main bearing incorporates thrust washers which control the crankshaft endfloat. Replaceable wet cylinder liners are fitted. The camshaft is chain driven from the crankshaft and is supported in four bearings. A spring or hydraulic type timing chain tensioner is fitted. The inclined valves are operated by rockers mounted on a rocker shaft. The cylinder head is cast in aluminium alloy.

A semi-closed crankcase ventilation system is employed, and crankcase gases are drawn from the rocker cover via a hose to the air cleaner and inlet manifold.

Lubrication is provided by a gear type oil pump driven from the crankshaft and located in the crankcase. Engine oil is fed through an externally mounted full-flow filter to the engine oil gallery and then to the crankshaft, camshaft, and rocker shaft bearings. A pressure relief valve is incorporated in the oil pump.

2 Major operations possible with engine in car

The following operations can be carried out without having to remove the engine from the car:

(a) Removal and servicing of the cylinder head
(b) Removal of the sump
(c) Removal of the liner and piston/connecting rod assemblies (through top of block)
(d) Removal of the timing cover, chain and gears
(e) Removal of the oil pump
(f) Renewal of the engine mountings

3 Major operations only possible after removal of engine

The following operations can only be carried out after removal of the engine from the car:

(a) Removal of the camshaft and followers
(b) Renewal of crankshaft main bearings
(c) Renewal of crankshaft rear oil seal
(d) Removal of the flywheel

4 Engine – removal

1 Remove the bonnet as described in Chapter 10.

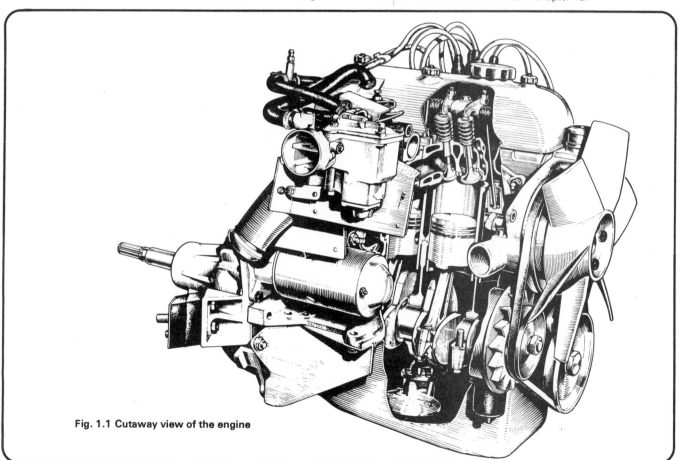

Fig. 1.1 Cutaway view of the engine

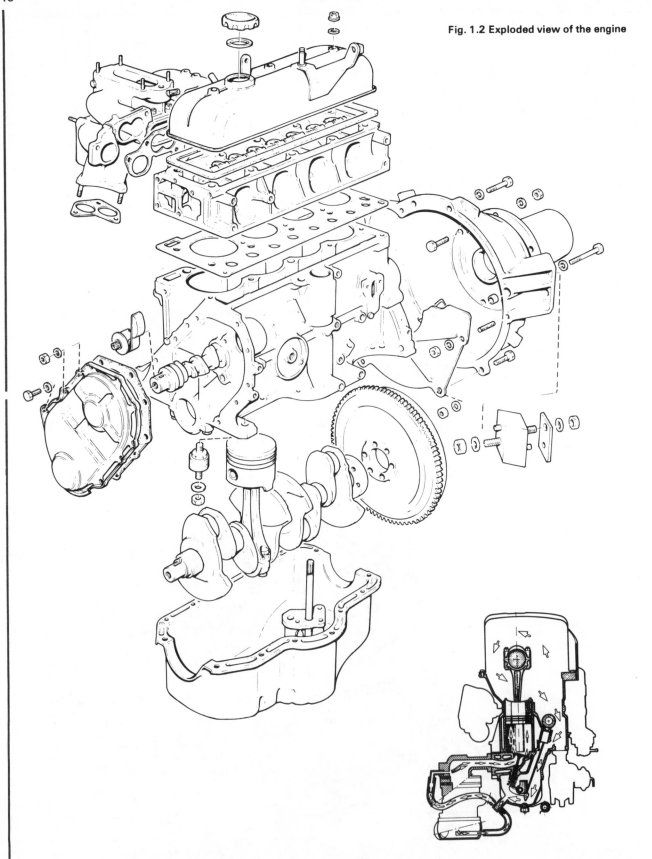

Fig. 1.2 Exploded view of the engine

Fig. 1.3 Crankcase ventilation system (Volvo 343 models)

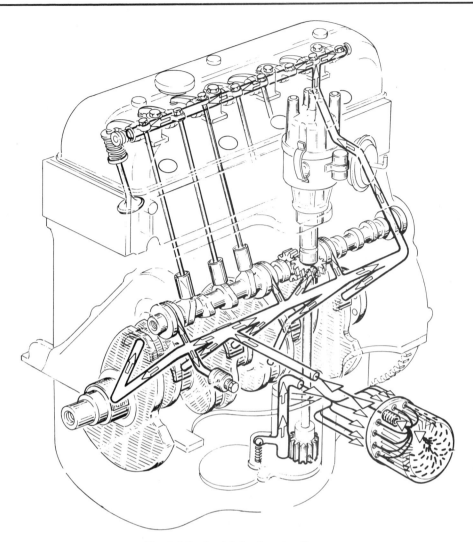

Fig. 1.4 Engine lubrication circuit

2 Disconnect the battery negative lead.

3 Remove the spare wheel and drain the cooling system as described in Chapter 2.

4 Drain the engine oil and remove the engine guard panels where fitted.

5 Remove the radiator as described in Chapter 2.

6 Detach the exhaust pipe from the manifold and clutch housing mountings and tie to one side.

7 Unscrew and remove the engine front and rear mounting nuts (photos).

8 Detach the engine earth lead, then disconnect the leads from the starter motor and vacuum control micro-switch when fitted.

9 Detach the vacuum hose(s) and heater hoses and the air filter hose, including the declutching cylinder hose on Volvo 343 models (photo).

10 Disconnect the leads from the alternator or dynamo, oil temperature sender, water temperature sender and coil.

11 Disconnect the throttle and choke cables, then detach the fuel line(s) from the fuel pump and plug them to prevent ingress of foreign matter.

12 On Volvo 343 models remove the air filter assembly as described in Chapter 3; on all other models disconnect the air cleaner hose.

13 Fit chains or slings securely to the engine and, using a suitable hoist, lift the engine from the mountings then move it forwards to disengage the propeller shaft splines; make sure that the shaft stays engaged with the transmission.

14 Swing the engine in a clockwise direction (viewed from above) then slowly lift it from the engine compartment, at the same time checking that all connections are detached (photo).

15 Once the engine sump is high enough pull the hoist forwards and lower the engine onto a workbench.

5 Engine – dismantling general

1 It is best to mount the engine on a dismantling stand, but if this is not available, stand the engine on a strong bench at a comfortable working height. Failing this, it will have to be stripped down on the floor.

2 During the dismantling process, the greatest care should be taken to keep the exposed parts free from dirt. As an aid to achieving this thoroughly clean down the outside of the engine, first removing all traces of oil and congealed dirt.

3 A good grease solvent will make the job much easier, for, after the solvent has been applied and allowed to stand for a time, a vigorous jet of water will wash off the solvent and grease with it. If the dirt is thick and deeply embedded, work the solvent into it with a strong stiff brush.

4 Finally, wipe down the exterior of the engine with a rag and only then, when it is quite clean, should the dismantling process begin. As the engine is stripped, clean each part in a bath of paraffin or petrol.

5 Never immerse parts with oilways in paraffin (eg crankshaft). To clean these parts, wipe down carefully with a petrol dampened rag. Oilways can be cleaned out with wire. If an air-line is available, all parts can be blown dry and the oilways blown through as an added precaution.

6 Re-use of old gaskets is false economy. To avoid the possibility of trouble after the engine has been reassembled *always* use new gaskets throughout.

4.7A Front engine mountings and radiator mountings

4.7B Rear engine mounting

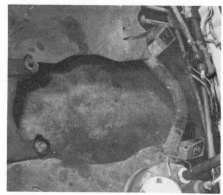

4.7C Engine mounting locations

4.9 Engine heater hose clips

4.14 Removing the engine (Daf 66 model shown)

6.2 Coil mounting on the cylinder block

7.2 Rocker shaft location

7.3 Removing the pushrods

7.5 Lifting the cylinder head from the engine

8.2A Compressing the valve springs

8.2B Removing valve spring and retainer

8.6 Removing a valve

7   Do not throw away the old gaskets, for sometimes it happens that an immediate replacement cannot be found and the old gasket is then very useful as a template. Hang up the gaskets as they are removed.

8   To strip the engine, it is best to work from the top down. When the stage is reached where the crankshaft must be removed, the engine can be turned on its side and all other work carried out with it in this position.

9   Wherever possible, refit nuts, bolts and washers finger tight from wherever they were removed. This helps to avoid loss and muddle. If they cannot be refitted then arrange them in such a fashion that it is clear from whence they came.

6   Ancillary components – removal

1   With the engine removed from the car the externally mounted ancillary components should now be removed before dismantling begins.

2   The following is a suggested sequence of removal, detailed descriptions are to be found in the relevant Chapters of this manual:

(a) Dynamo or alternator (Chapter 8)
(b) Clutch assembly (Chapter 5)
(c) Manifolds and carburettor (Chapter 3)
(d) Engine mounting rubbers
(e) Oil filter (see Section 10)
(f) Distributor and spark plugs (Chapter 4)
(g) Fuel pump (Chapter 3)
(h) Water pump and thermostat (Chapter 2)
(i) Starter motor (Chapter 8)
(j) Coil (Chapter 4) (photo)

7   Cylinder head – removal

If the head is to be removed with the engine still in the car, first carry out the following operations:

(a) Disconnect the battery negative terminal
(b) Drain the cooling system
(c) Remove the manifolds complete with carburettor
(d) Disconnect the spark plug HT leads
(e) Disconnect the temperature sender lead
(f) Remove the drivebelt, fan, and pulley
(g) Disconnect all hoses

1   Unscrew the rocker cover retaining nuts and remove the rocker cover and gasket.

2   Unscrew the two retaining nuts and bolts and lift the rocker shaft and rocker from the cylinder head (photo).

3   Remove the pushrods keeping them in order for replacement in their original positions (photo).

4   Unscrew each of the cylinder head bolts half-a-turn at a time in the reverse order to that shown in Fig. 1.21.

5   With all the bolts removed, lift the cylinder head from the block (photo). If it is stuck, tap it upwards using a block of wood and a hammer. On no account insert a lever into the gasket joint.

6   Remove the cylinder head gasket. **Note**: *the crankshaft must not be rotated with the head removed, otherwise the liners will be displaced.*

8   Cylinder head – dismantling

1   Extract the circlip from the end of the rocker shaft then remove the springs,rocker arms, and pedestals keeping each component in its original fitted sequence.

2   Remove the valve from the cylinder head. Compress each spring in turn with a valve spring compressor until the two halves of the collets can be removed (photo). Release the compressor and remove the spring, spring retainer, and thrust washer (photo).

3   If when the valve spring compressor is screwed down, the valve spring retaining cap refuses to free to expose ths split collet, do not continue to screw down on the compressor but gently tap the top of the tool directly over the cap with a light hammer. At the same time hold the compressor firmly in position with one hand to avoid it jumping off.

4   It is essential that the valves are kept in their correct sequence unless they are so badly worn that they are to be renewed. Numbering

from the front of the cylinder head, exhaust valves are 1–4–5–8 and inlet valves 2–3–6–7

5   The valve springs and collets should also be kept in their correct sequence as the inlet and exhaust valve components differ.

6   Insert the cylinder head and push the valves out (photo).

9   Sump – removal

The sump can be removed with the engine in the car but Volvo 343 models first carry out the following operations:

(a) Detach the front anti-roll bar from the crossmember
(b) Disconnect the steering shaft from the steering gear, then remove the mounting bolts and pull the steering gear downwards

1   Drain the engine oil.

2   Unscrew and remove all the sump bolts and withdraw the sump from the engine.

3   If the sump is stuck tight, run a blunt knife around the gasket to release it.

10   Oil pump and oil filter – removal

If the oil pump is to be removed with the engine still in the car first remove the sump as described in Section 9.

1   Unscrew and remove the retaining bolts and withdraw the oil pump from the block, at the same time disengaging the shaft from the drivegear (photo).

2   The oil filter is simply removed by unscrewing it; place a small container below it to catch any oil which may be spilled. If difficulty is experienced use a strap or cord in a tourniquet manner to free it.

3   Discard the filter element.

11   Timing cover, gears, and chain – removal

If the timing cover, gears and chain are being removed with the engine in the car, first carry out the following operations:

(a) Remove the radiator (Chapter 2)
(b) Remove the fan/alternator drivebelt (Chapter 2)

1   Unscrew and remove the crankshaft pulley bolt (photo). To do this use a wide blade screwdriver to jam the flywheel ring gear. If the engine is still in the car it will first be necessary to remove the starter motor (Chapter 8).

2   Withdraw the crankshaft pulley using two levers if necessary placed behind the pulley at opposite points.

3   Unscrew and remove the timing cover securing bolts and withdraw the cover and its gasket.

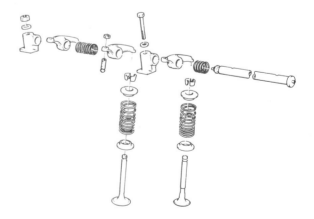

Fig. 1.5 Rocker shaft and valve components

10.1 Oil pump location

11.1 The crankshaft pulley bolt location

11.4 Removing the timing chain tensioner

12.1 Removing the distributor drive gear

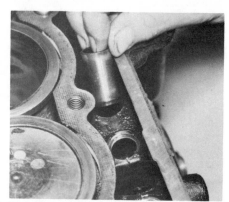

12.2 Removing a camshaft follower

12.3 Removing the camshaft

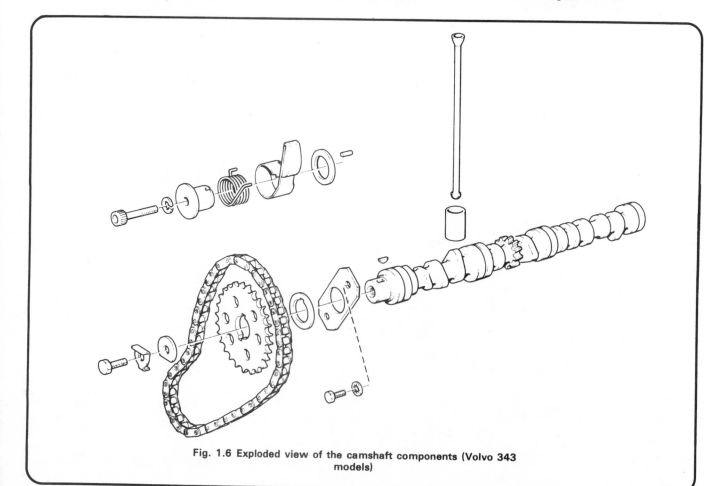

Fig. 1.6 Exploded view of the camshaft components (Volvo 343 models)

Fig. 1.7 Cylinder liner retaining clamps (arrowed)

4   Unscrew and remove the chain tensioner retaining bolts and, while holding the pad in, remove the tensioner (photo). On some early models remove the side mounted bolt and use an Allen key to retract the tensioner pad.

5   Turn the engine until the timing marks on the camshaft and crankshaft gears are facing each other and No 1 (flywheel end) and No 4 piston are at the top of their cylinders. If the cylinder head is removed the cylinder liners must be held stationary otherwise they will be displaced and the seals may subsequently leak water. Use bolts with suitable washers, screwed into the top of the block to retain the liners.

6   Bend back the locktab then unscrew the camshaft sprocket retaining bolt.

7   Withdraw the camshaft sprocket and disengage the timing chain from the crankshaft.

8   If the crankshaft gear requires removing, a suitable puller must be used and care must be taken to avoid damaging the pulley bolt threads. Extract the Woodruff key from the crankshaft once the gear is removed.

12 Camshaft and followers – removal

1   Using a length of dowel rod extract the drivegear from the distributor aperture (photo).

2   Withdraw the camshaft followers from the top of the cylinder block keeping them in order for correct refitting (photo).

3   Unscrew and remove the camshaft flange retaining bolts and carefully withdraw the camshaft, taking care not to damage the four camshaft bearings as the lobes of the cams pass through them (photo).

13 Piston/connecting rod – removal

If the engine is still in the car, carry out the following operations:

(a) Remove the cylinder head
(b) Remove the sump

1   Turn the crankshaft so that No 1 crankpin (nearest the flywheel) is at the lowest point of its travel.

2   If the big-end cap and rods are not already numbered, mark them with a centre punch on the side opposite the camshaft (right-hand side when in car). Mark both the cap and rod in relation to the bore it operates in, starting with No 1 at the flywheel end.

3   Unscrew and remove the big-end bearing cap bolts and withdraw the cap complete with bearing shells; keep the shells in their correct sequence if they are to be refitted (photo).

4   Remove the liner clamps if fitted and withdraw the pistons together with liners from the top of the block (photo).

5   Remove the pistons from the liners and mark the liners using marking tape, so they may be replaced in their original locations (photo).

14 Flywheel – removal

1   Lock the flywheel using a wide blade screwdriver on the ring gear. Alternatively, if the sump is removed, place a wooden block between the crankshaft web and the block.

2   Unscrew and remove the retaining bolts and lift the flywheel from the crankshaft. Mark the flywheel in relation to the crankshaft on models where the retaining bolts are not offset.

15 Crankshaft and main bearings – removal

1   If the main bearing caps are not already numbered, mark them with a centre punch on the side opposite the camshaft (right-hand side when in car). Mark them starting with No 1 at the flywheel end.

2   Unscrew and remove the main bearing bolts and withdraw the caps complete with bearing shells (photo). Note the location of the thrust washers either side of the centre main bearing (photo).

3   Carefully lift the crankshaft from the crankcase.

4   Extract the bearing shells from the crankcase recesses (photo). If the original shells are to be refitted, mark their locations using pieces of masking tape.

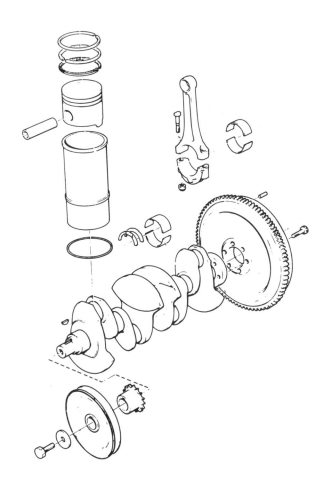

Fig. 1.8 Exploded view of the crankshaft and piston components

Fig. 1.9 Removing the camshaft flange retaining bolts

Fig. 1.10 Removing the crankshaft rear oil seal

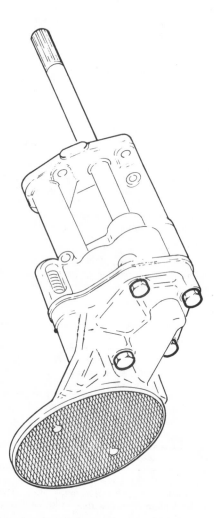

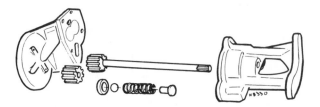

Fig. 1.12 Oil pump components

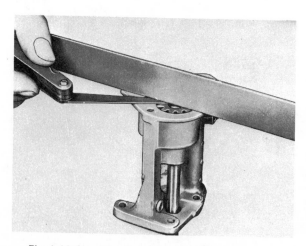

Fig. 1.13 Checking the oil pump gear end clearance

Fig. 1.11 The oil pump and strainer

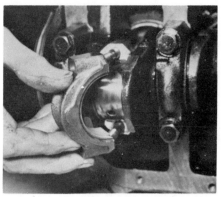
13.3 Removing a big-end bearing cap

13.4 Withdrawing a cylinder liner and piston

13.5 Removing a piston from the liner

15.2A A main bearing shell and cap

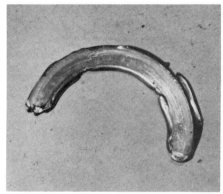
15.2B A badly worn thrust washer

15.4 Removing a main bearing shell

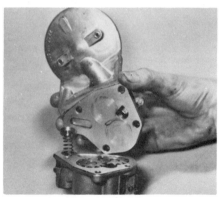
17.1A Removing the oil pump cover

17.1B Oil pressure relief valve and spring location

17.1C Relief valve spring and seat location

17.4 Checking the oil pump gear end clearance

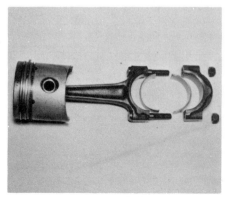
21.3A Piston and connecting rod components

21.3B Piston identification marks

16 Examination and renovation – general

With the engine now completely stripped, clean all components and examine them for wear. Each part should be checked and where necessary renewed or renovated as described in the following Sections.

17 Oil pump – examination and renovation

1   Remove the oil pump cover (four bolts) and withdraw the oil pressure relief valve ball, spring, and seat (photos).
2   Lift out the idler gear and drive-gear spindle.
3   Clean the components and examine them for wear; renew any that are worn.
4   Install the spindle and gear then check the end clearance between the gears and the pump body. If this is greater than 0·008 in (0·2 mm) the gears must be renewed. Use a straight edge and feeler gauge to make the check (see Fig. 1.13) (photo).
5   The oil pressure relief valve is non-adjustable but it is possible after high mileages for the spring to weaken (check free length in Specifications).
6   Refit the cover and tighten the retaining bolts.

18 Crankcase ventilation system – description and maintenance

1   1100 engines are fitted with a hose whereby crankcase fumes are drawn from the rocker cover into the carburettor inlet.
2   All other models are fitted with an additional hose which is connected to the inlet manifold (via a calibrated restriction) and to the rocker cover hose.
3   This connection with the inlet manifold ensures that a partial vacuum is always present in the crankcase. This prevents crankcase pressure causing oil leakage past seals.
4   Daf and Volvo 66/1300 models are equipped with an air filter in the ventilation system which limits crankcase vacuum at high engine speeds.
5   The ventilation system hoses and filter, where fitted, should be periodically removed and any sludge or congealed oil cleaned out.

19 Crankshaft and main bearings – examination and renovation

1   Remove the crankshaft rear oil seal and discard it.
2   Examine the bearing surfaces of the crankshaft for scratches or scoring and, using a micrometer check each journal and crankpin for ovality. Where this is found to be in excess of 0·001 in (0·0254 mm) the crankshaft will have to be reground and undersize bearings fitted.
3   The crankshaft can be reground to a maximum of 0·040 in (1·016 mm) undersize, but your Daf/Volvo dealer will decide how much is acceptable and supply you with the appropriate undersize main and big-end shell bearings.
4   When installed, the bearings should have a running clearance as given in Specifications, but these clearances can only be checked by using a proprietary product. However it is usually assumed that the running clearances will be correct if the reconditioning has been carried out by a reliable company.
5   If the crankshaft bearing surfaces are not worn, check the main and big-end bearing shells for wear and renew them if necessary.

20 Cylinder liners and crankcase – examination and renovation

1   Remove the pistons from the liners but keep them in strict order.
2   Examine the liners for taper, ovality, scoring and scratches. If a ridge is found at the top of the bore on the thrust side, the bores are worn. The owner will have a good indication of the bore wear prior to dismantling the engine on removing the cylinder head. Excessive oil consumption accompanied by blue smoke from the exhaust is a sure sign of worn bores and piston rings.
3   Measure the bore diameter just under the ridge with a micrometer and compare it with the diameter at the bottom of the bore which is not subject to wear. If the difference between the two measurements exceeds 0·008 in (0·2032 mm) then it will be necessary to fit special pistons and rings or obtain new piston and liner assemblies. Contrary

to popular belief the liners can be rebored if necessary and fitted with oversize pistons.
4   The liners should also be checked for cracking.
5   If the bores are only slightly worn, special oil control rings and pistons can be fitted which will restore compression and stop the engine burning oil. Several different types are available and the manufacturer's instructions concerning their fitting must be followed closely.
6   If new pistons are being fitted and the bores have not been reground, it is essential to slightly roughen the hard glaze on the sides of the bores with fine glass paper to enable the new piston rings to bed in properly.
7   Examine the crankcase for cracks and leaks, then clean the oil galleries and waterways using a piece of wire.

21 Piston/connecting rod assemblies – examination and renovation

1   Checking the big-end shell bearings is covered in Section 19.
2   If new pistons are being fitted, removal of the gudgeon pin is best left to a Daf/Volvo dealer as it is an interference fit and a press and installation tool is required to carry out the operation successfully.
3   When correctly assembled the arrow on the piston crown must face the rear (flywheel end) of the engine with the connecting rods in their normal position (photos).
4   If new piston rings are to be fitted to the original pistons, remove the old rings by expanding them and withdrawing them with a twisting motion. The use of two or three old feeler blades placed at equidistant points between the piston and ring will prevent a ring dropping into an empty groove during removal.
5   Install the new rings by reversing the removal process, but make sure that the following conditions are complied with:

   (a) The top compression ring must be stepped to avoid the wear ridge which will have formed at the top of the cylinder liner bore
   (b) The ring gaps and groove clearances are as given in Specifications
   (c) Space the piston ring gaps at equidistant points so that the gaps are not in alignment
   (d) The second compression ring is tapered and must be installed with the mark uppermost

22 Camshaft and followers – examination and renovation

1   Examine the camshaft bearing surfaces, cam lobes, and gear teeth for wear and scoring.
2   Temporarily fit the sprocket to the front of the camshaft (timing mark facing outwards) and tighten the bolt to the correct torque wrench setting.
3   Using a feeler gauge check that the end clearance is within the limits given in Specifications; if not the flange must be renewed by using a press to remove it and install the new part.
4   Removal of the camshaft bearings is best left in the hands of your Daf/Volvo agent or local engineering works.
5   Check the followers for wear and if evident renew them.

23 Timing gear and chain – examination and renovation

1   Examine the camshaft and crankshaft sprockets and renew them if their teeth are hooked in appearance.
2   Examine the chain tensioner. If the rubber pad is worn or hardened it must be renewed.
3   Examine the timing chain. If it has been in operation for a considerable time or excessive lateral movement is evident on the links, renew it.

24 Cylinder head – decarbonising, valve grinding, and renovation

1   This operation will normally only be required at comparatively high mileages due to the improvements in fuel and oil quality, and modern engine design. However, if a lack of power is noticed or pinking occurs, but the engine is otherwise in a good tuned condition, it will be

necessary to decarbonise the head and grind in the valves.

2 With the cylinder head removed, use a blunt scraper to remove all traces of carbon from the combustion spaces and ports. Use a wire brush to clean the flat surface of the head, then wash the complete head with paraffin and wipe it dry, paying particular attention to the internal cavities and holes.

3 Similarly clean the cylinder block upper face, but if the engine is still in the car be careful not to allow carbon to fall into the cylinder liner bores. Clean the tops of the pistons with them at the top of their strokes but first mask the oil and waterways to prevent contaminating them. It is a good plan to press a little grease into the gap between the pistons and liner bores to prevent carbon entering; wipe the grease and carbon away when the cleaning is finished. To prevent the build up of carbon on the piston crown it can be polished with a metal polish.

4 Check the cylinder head for distortion using a straight edge and feeler gauge and if warping in excess of 0·004 in (0·10 mm) has occurred the head will have to be resurfaced by a specialist engineering works.

5 Examine the heads of the valves for pitting and burning especially the heads of the exhaust valves. Also examine the valve seatings, and if there are only slight marks on both faces grinding the seats and valves together with coarse then fine grinding paste will be sufficient.

6 Where excessive pitting has occurred, the valves must be renewed, and the seats recut as necessary by a specialist engineering works.

7 To grind in the valves smear a trace of coarse grinding paste on the valve face and, using a suction grinding tool grind the valve head onto the valve seat using a semi-rotary action, occasionally lifting the valve from the seat. When a dull matt finish is produced on both surfaces evenly, wipe off the paste and repeat the process using fine paste. A light spring placed beneath the valve head will greatly assist this operation. When an even light matt ring is produced on the valve and seat the grinding operation is finished.

8 Clean away every trace of grinding past and if available use an air line to blow out the ports and valve guides.

9 If the valve guides are worn (indicated by a side-to-side rocking motion of the valve) oversize valve guides should be fitted by a specialist engineering works.

10 Check the free length of the valve springs, and if they are shorter than the dimension given in Specifications renew them.

11 Examine the rocker shaft and rockers for wear and renew them as necessary. Make sure that the bearing pads on the rocker arms do not show signs of deterioration.

25 Flywheel – examination and renovation

1 Examine the surface of the flywheel and if it is scored or damaged it should be renewed or refaced.

2 Using a suitable metal drift, drive the pilot bearing from the flywheel and check it for wear and roughness by spinning it. Renew it if necessary and drive the new bearing into position. **Note**: *the bearing is located by a star ring on Daf 55 models.*

3 Examine the teeth of the flywheel starter ring gear. If they are chipped or worn, the ring must be renewed. To do this split the ring with a cold chisel and remove it.

4 Heat the new ring to the temperature indicated (usually around 392°F – 200°C) in an electric oven, and then quickly fit it to the flywheel so that the chamfered side of the teeth is towards the engine side of the flywheel.

5 Allow the ring to cool naturally without quenching.

26 Engine reassembly – general

1 To ensure maximum life from a rebuilt engine, not only must everything be correctly assembled, but each component must be spotlessly clean. All the oilways must also be clean and unobstructed.

2 Spring and lockwashers must always be fitted where indicated and all bearing and working surfaces must be thoroughly lubricated during reassembly.

3 Before starting reassembly, renew any damaged bolts or studs and obtain a set of gaskets, crankshaft front and rear oil seals, and a new oil filter element.

4 Wherever possible tighten all nuts and bolts to the specified torque settings using an accurate torque wrench.

27 Crankshaft and main bearings – installation

1 Clean the backs of the bearing shells and the bearing recesses in both the crankcase and the caps.

2 The bearing shells with the oil holes are fitted in the cylinder block, and the shells without the oil holes in the bearing caps. Fit the thrust washers to the centre bearing in the crankcase, using grease to hold them in position (photo).

3 Oil the bearings liberally, then carefully lower the crankshaft into position (photo).

4 The thrust washers to the centre main bearing cap are positioned on the crankshaft using grease to hold them in place, while the bearing cap is being installed. Ensure that the thrust washers are fitted with the lubrication grooves facing the crankshaft webs.

5 Install the remaining main bearing caps matching the identification marks, and tighten the retaining bolts evenly to the specified torque (photo).

6 Turn the crankshaft and check that it rotates smoothly.

7 Check the crankshaft endfloat using a dial gauge or feeler gauge (photo); if new thrust washers have been fitted the endfloat should be

Fig. 1.14 Checking the camshaft end clearance

Fig. 1.15 Fitting the crankshaft thrust washers

27.2 Location of the centre bearing thrust washers in the crankcase

27.3 Crankshaft assembled to the crankcase

27.5 Tightening the crankshaft main bearing cap bolts

27.7 Checking the crankshaft endfloat

27.8 Installing the crankshaft rear oil seal

28.12 Tightening the big-end cap bolts

29.2 Tightening the flywheel retaining bolts

31.3 Checking the timing gear alignment

31.4 Tensioning the chain will move the timing marks slightly

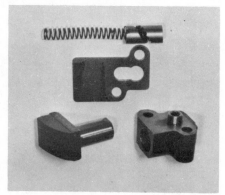
31.6A Timing chain tensioner components (Daf 66 models)

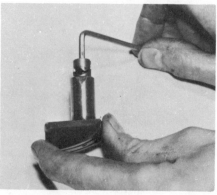
31.6B Priming the timing chain tensioner (Daf 66 models)

in accordance with Specifications; if the original washers have been refitted and the endfloat is excessive, new thrust washers must be fitted (they are obtainable in a number of oversizes).

8 Smear the rear oil seal with engine oil on its inner and outer surfaces and carefully install it over the crankshaft rear journal with the aid of a metal tube; make sure that the open end of the seal faces inwards, and that the outer face of the seal is flush with the block. If the original crankshaft is serviceable and is being refitted, drive the seal in a further 0·118 in (3·0 mm) so that it does not bear on the worn section of the journal (photo).

28 Piston/connecting rod – installation

1 The piston/connecting rod is fitted into its respective cylinder liner and the liner, complete with piston and connecting rod is installed into the cylinder block. Before the complete assemblies are installed a trial fit of the liners should be made to check the protrusion of the liners above the cylinder block upper face (except Volvo 343 models).

2 Fit a *red* gasket to the base of each liner and install them into the cylinder block, making sure that they are replaced in their original locations and that the flats are adjacent. *Note: No 1 bore is at the flywheel end of the cylinder bore.*

3 Press the liners into their seatings. Using a dial gauge or a straight edge and feeler gauge check that the protrusion of each liner above the cylinder block upper face is in accordance with Specifications. If not, remove the liner and fit alternative gaskets as necessary. Remove the liners taking care to keep the gaskets in position on their respective liners.

4 Lubricate the cylinder liner bores and the piston rings.

5 Fit a piston ring compressor to No 1 piston and with the liner inverted on the bench, install it into the liner to a position about 1·0 in (25 mm) from the top of the bore.

6 On Volvo 343 models fit the O-ring seal to the bottom of each liner.

7 Clean the big-end bearing shells and the connecting rod and big-end caps. Press the shells into the connecting rod and cap.

8 Turn the crankshaft so that No 1 crankpin (flywheel end) is at its lowest point, then insert the piston and liner assembly into the block, making sure that the liner is positioned correctly and that the arrow on the piston crown is facing the flywheel end of the engine.

9 Clamp the liner in position then lubricate the crankpin with engine oil.

10 Using the handle of a hammer, tap the piston down the liner, at the same time guide the connecting rod onto the crankpin. Make sure that the bearing shell does not become displaced.

11 Install the big-end bearing cap complete with bearing shell, making sure that the matching marks on the rod and cap are in alignment and are on the correct side of the engine. This will be automatic, provided the piston has been assembled to the connecting rod correctly and the arrows on the piston crown are pointing towards the flywheel end of the engine.

12 Screw in the big-end bolts and tighten them to the specified torque (photo).

13 Turn the crankshaft to check that the bearings are free then repeat the foregoing operations on the remaining three piston/liner assemblies.

29 Flywheel – installation

1 Clean the flywheel and crankshaft faces, then fit the flywheel and make sure that any previously made marks are aligned.

2 Smear the threads of the retaining bolts with a liquid locking agent, then tighten them to the specified torque, while restraining the flywheel with a wide blade screwdriver inserted into the teeth of the ring gear (photo).

30 Camshaft and followers – installation

1 Lubricate the camshaft bearings with engine oil and carefully insert the camshaft from the front of the cylinder block.

2 Install the flange retaining bolts and tighten them to the specified torque, then check that the camshaft rotates smoothly.

3 Lubricate the followers and insert them into the cylinder block; if the original followers are being installed make sure that they are replaced in their correct locations.

31 Timing cover, gears, and chain – installation

1 If the crankshaft sprocket has been removed, locate the Woodruff key and tap the sprocket back into position making sure that the timing mark is to the front. Turn the crankshaft until No 1 piston is at the top of its cylinder.

2 Temporarily locate the camshaft sprocket on the camshaft and turn it until the timing marks on both sprockets are facing each other, and coincide with the line joining the crankshaft and camshaft centres, then remove the sprocket.

3 Fit the timing chain to the camshaft sprocket, then offer the timing chain to the crankshaft sprocket keeping the camshaft sprocket over its location and the timing marks in alignment (photo).

4 Locate the timing chain over the crankshaft sprocket and fit the camshaft sprocket to the camshaft. Check that the timing marks are still aligned. *Note: Tensioning the chain will displace the timing marks from the centerline.*

5 Install the camshaft sprocket bolt with a new lockplate, tighten it to the specified torque, and bend the tabs over the bolt head to lock it.

6 Install the chain tensioner and tighten the retaining bolt(s). On some early models it will be necessary to use an Allen key to retract the tensioner pad before refitting; turn the key clockwise until a click is heard to release the pad, then check that the tensioner is functioning correctly by pressing the chain on the opposite side (photos). Bend over the lockplate tabs if fitted, and install the tensioner side screw.

7 If a hydraulically regulated chain tensioner is being fitted a stop pin must first be located in the cylinder block.

8 Remove the timing cover oil seal and drive in a new one using a piece of tubing as a drift. Apply engine oil to the seal lips and then install the timing cover, using a new gasket. Tighten the bolts only finger tight at this stage.

9 Install the crankshaft pulley and tighten the securing bolt to the specified torque.

10 Finally tighten the timing cover bolts to the specified torque.

32 Oil pump and sump – installation

1 Install the oil pump onto the cylinder block and tighten the retaining bolts to the specified torque; note that there is no gasket between the pump and the cylinder block.

2 Locate the rubber strips in the timing cover and rear main bearing cap grooves.

3 Grease the cork gaskets sparingly and locate them on the cylinder block making sure that the ends cover the lips of the rubber strips.

4 Apply a sealing compound to the sump flange then install it into the cylinder block and tighten the retaining bolts in diagonal sequence to the specified torque.

5 On Volvo 343 models reverse the procedure given in Section 9 if the engine is in the car.

33 Cylinder head – reassembly and installation

1 Install the valves in their original sequence or, if new ones have been purchased, to the seats to which they have been ground, after having lubricated their stems.

2 Working on the first valve fit the thrust washer to the cylinder head followed by the valve spring and retainer. Note that the spring should be fitted with the end where the coils are closest towards the cylinder head.

3 Compress the valve spring and locate the split collets in the recess in the valve stem. Note that the collets are different for the inlet and exhaust valves (photo). The latter type having two curved collars. Release the compressor then repeat the procedure on the remaining valves.

4 With all the valves installed, place the cylinder head flat on the bench and using a hammer and block of wood, tap the end of each valve stem to settle the components.

5 Oil the rocker shaft, then reassemble the springs, rocker arms and pedestals in the reverse order to removal and finally fit the circlip. Check that the bolt holes in the pedestals are aligned with the recesses

Fig. 1.16 Timing chain sprocket marks in alignment

Fig. 1.17 Releasing the timing chain tensioner (early models)

Fig. 1.18 Checking that the timing chain tensioner is functioning

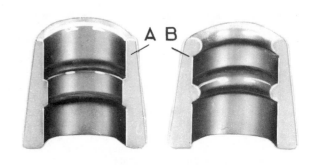

Fig. 1.19 Valve stem collets

A Inlet   *B Exhaust*

Fig. 1.20 Rocker shaft oil hole and bolt recess

Fig. 1.21 Cylinder head bolt tightening sequence

33.3 The different types of valve spring collets

33.6 Cylinder head gasket mark

33.7 Tightening the cylinder head bolts

36.10 Adjusting the valve clearances

in the rocker shaft.

6   Remove the cylinder liner clamps, if fitted, and make sure that the faces of the cylinder head and the cylinder block are perfectly clean. Lay a new gasket on the cylinder block with the words Haut-Top uppermost (photo). Do not use any kind of jointing compound.

7   Lower the cylinder head into position, insert the cylinder head bolts and tighten them to the specified torque in the sequence shown in Fig. 1.21 (photo).

8   Install the pushrods in their original locations.

9   Lower the rocker shaft assembly onto the cylinder head making sure that the adjusting ball-ends locate in the pushrods. Install the spring washers (convex side uppermost), nuts, and bolts and tighten them to the specified torque.

10   Adjust the valve clearances as described in Section 36, to the cold setting where alternative settings are given (see Specifications).

11   Using a ring spanner on the crankshaft pulley bolt, turn the crankshaft until No 1 piston (flywheel end) is at the top of its compression stroke. This position can be established by placing a finger over No 1 plug hole and rotating the crankshaft until compression can be felt; continue turning the crankshaft until the piston reaches the top of its stroke. Use a screwdriver through the plug hole to feel the movement of the piston, but be careful not to damage the piston crown or plug threads in the cylinder head.

12   Without moving the crankshaft, lower the distributor drivegear into mesh with the camshaft so that it assumes the position shown in

Fig. 1.22. The larger segment of the drivegear must face the flywheel end of the engine.

13   Install the rocker cover with a new gasket and tighten the retaining nuts.

14   If the cylinder head is being installed with the engine in the car, reverse the additional procedure given in Section 7.

34   Ancillary components – installation

1   This is a reversal of the removal sequence given in Section 6 of this Chapter, but in addition the oil filter should be renewed.

2   To fit the new oil filter element, first clean the mating surfaces of the cylinder block and oil filter, then smear a thin film of engine oil on the filter sealing ring. Screw in the filter element until it touches the block then tighten it a further one half turn by hand.

35   Engine – installation

1   This is a reversal of the removal operations described in Section 4, but the following additional points should be noted:

(a) Grease the clutch output shaft splines before engaging it with the propeller shaft

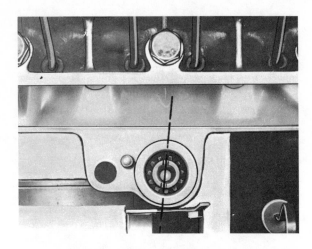

Fig. 1.22 Correct alignment of the distributor drivegear

(b) Adjust the throttle and choke cables as described in Chapter 3
(c) Vent the cooling system as described in Chapter 2
(d) Refill the engine with oil

36 Engine – adjustments after major overhaul

1   With the engine refitted, check that everything has been reconnected and that no loose rags or tools have been left within the engine compartment.

2   Turn the engine slow running screw in about half-a-turn to increase the engine idling speed (see Chapter 3). This will be necessary due to the tightness of the new engine components.

3   Pull the choke fully out and, with the selector lever in neutral (N), start the engine. This may take a little longer than usual as the fuel pump and carburettor bowl will be initially empty.

4   As soon as the engine starts, push the choke in until the engine runs at a fast tickover. Visually check the engine for leaks particularly checking the water hoses, oil filter, and fuel hose unions.

5   Run the car on the road until the engine reaches its normal operating temperature.

6   The valve clearances must now be re-adjusted by the following method.

7   Disconnect the vent hoses and throttle connections from the valve rocker cover (where fitted). Unhook the heater hose from the clips (where fitted).

8   Remove the valve cover and gasket.

9   Number the valves 1 to 8 from the front or rear of the engine then, using a ring spanner on the crankshaft pulley bolt, turn the engine in a clockwise direction until No 8 valve is fully open (ie spring compressed).

10 Insert a feeler blade of the correct thickness for an exhaust valve (see Specifications) between the end of No 1 valve stem and the rocker arm, then adjust the rocker arm ball-end (after loosening the locknut) until the feeler blade is a firm sliding fit (photo). Tighten the locknut and recheck the adjustment, then repeat the procedure on the remaining seven valves in the following sequence:

Valve open	Valve to adjust
No 8 ex	No 1 ex
No 6 in	No 3 in
No 4 ex	No 5 ex
No 7 in	No 2 in
No 1 ex	No 8 ex
No 3 in	No 6 in
No 5 ex	No 4 ex
No 2 in	No 7 in

11 Refit the valve cover and gasket when the adjustment is completed, then adjust the engine idling speed as described in Chapter 3.

12 Where new internal components have been installed, the engine speed should be restricted for the first 500 miles (800 km) and at this mileage the engine oil should be renewed, the cylinder head bolts checked for correct torque, and the valve clearances re-adjusted.

37 Fault diagnosis – engine

Symptom	Reason/s
Engine fails to start	Discharged battery Loose battery terminal Disconnected or broken ignition leads Moisture on spark plugs, distributor or leads Plugs and/or points incorrectly adjusted Dirt or water in carburettor jets Faulty fuel pump Choke inoperative Faulty starter motor Empty fuel tank
Engine idles erratically or stalls	Leaking manifold gasket or head gasket Faulty fuel pump Incorrect valve clearances Incorrect carburettor adjustment Incorrect spark plug gaps or points gap Faulty coil or condenser Incorrect ignition timing
Engine lacks power	Incorrect ignition timing Faulty coil or condenser Worn distributor Dirt or water in carburettor Incorrect spark plug gaps Incorrect carburettor adjustment Faulty fuel pump Weak valve springs Sticking valve Incorrect valve timing Incorrect valve clearances Blown cylinder head gasket Low compression Brakes binding Clutch slipping Overheating

Chapter 2 Cooling system

Contents

Specifications

System type
Daf 55, Daf 66, Volvo 66 .... Pressurised, with thermostat, water pump, and fan
Volvo 343 .... Closed system with expansion tank, thermostat, water pump and fan

Thermostat
Type .... Wax
Opening temperature:
   Daf 55 .... 83°C
   Daf 66, Volvo 66 .... 89°C
   Volvo 343 .... 86° to 89°C
Fully open temperature of thermostat .... 110°C

Radiator
Type .... Corrugated fin and tube
Pressure cap setting:
   Daf 55 .... 7 lbf/in²
   Daf 66 (up to 1972) .... 6.4 to 7.8 lbf/in²
   Daf 66 (1972 on), Volvo 66 .... 10.38 to 12.23 lbf/in²
   Volvo 343 .... 10.8 lbf/in²

Coolant capacity
Daf 55, Daf 66, Volvo 66 .... 8.5 pints (4.8 litres)
Volvo 343 (including expansion tank) .... 9.7 pints (5.5 litres)
Antifreeze coolant concentration .... $\frac{1}{3}$ Daf/Volvo antifreeze to $\frac{2}{3}$ water

Torque wrench settings

	lbf ft	Nm
Dynamo/Alternator bolt	32.5 to 36.4	45.0 to 50.0
Dynamo brace (Daf 55, Daf 66/1100)	5.1 to 8.7	7.0 to 12.0
Alternator bracket bolt	7.2 to 13.0	10.0 to 17.5
Water pump housing and cover:		
Daf 55 and Daf 66/1100	5.1 to 8.7	7.0 to 12.0
Daf 66/1300, Volvo 66, Volvo 343	5.1 to 7.2	7.0 to 10.0
Water pump pulley and fan	14.5 to 18.0	20.0 to 25.0

---

1 General description

The cooling system comprises a front mounted radiator, fan, thermostat and water pump. The system is pressurised by a valve in the radiator cap (Expansion tank cap on Volvo 343 models).

The fan and water pump are driven by a V-belt from the crankshaft pulley (this belt also drives the alternator or dynamo). The thermostat is located in the radiator top hose adjacent to the water pump. Auxiliary circuits provide hot water for the car interior heater and the heated inlet manifold.

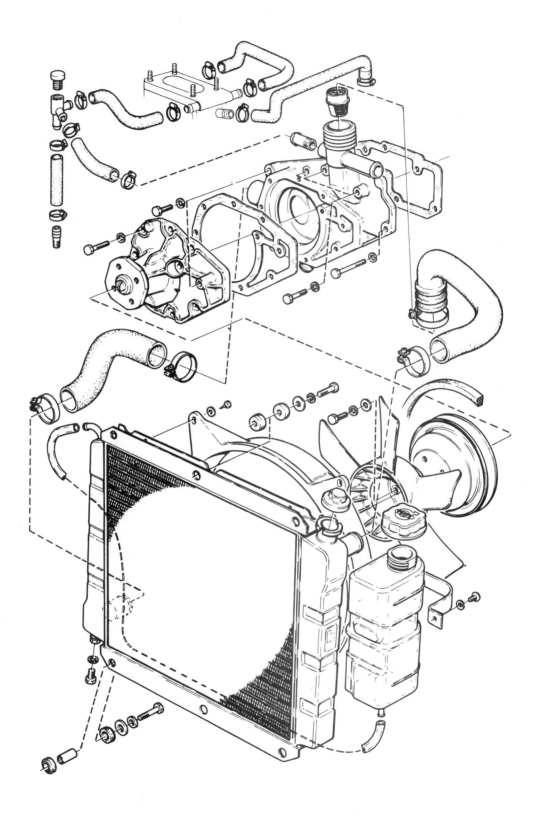

Fig. 2.1 Exploded view of the cooling system (Volvo 343 model shown)

The water pump draws cooled water from the bottom of the radiator and pumps it through the internal waterways of the cylinder head and engine block to cool the internal components of the engine. When the engine is started from cold the thermostat is shut, and the water can only circulate through the auxiliary circuits of the interior and intake heaters; this causes the engine to reach its normal working temperature in a short time. When the water reaches normal operating temperature, the thermostat opens and the water circulates through the top hose to the top of the radiator. The air flow through the radiator matrix, assisted by the action of the fan, cools the water as it passes to the bottom of the radiator. The cycle is then repeated and the engine is maintained at its most efficient operating temperature.

An electro-sensitive capsule located in the cylinder head monitors the temperature of the coolant and, according to model, operates a dash mounted temperature gauge or warning lamp.

2 Cooling system – draining

1   It is preferable to drain the cooling system when the engine has cooled. If this is not possible, place a rag over the radiator filler cap (expansion tank cap on Volvo 343 models), and turn it in an anti-clockwise direction to the first stop. Allow the pressure to escape from the system, then continue turning the cap and remove it (photo).
2   If the coolant is to be retained for further use, place suitable containers beneath the radiator and cylinder block drain plugs.
3   Unscrew and remove the drain plug from the bottom of the radiator. On Volvo 343 models it will be necessary to disconnect the bottom hose and remove the plug from the top of the radiator.
4   Unscrew and remove the cylinder block drain plug located on the right-hand side of the engine near the starter motor. Additionally on Volvo models unscrew and remove the second drain plug located beneath the water pump on the front of the cylinder block (photos).
5   Move the heater controls to Hot.

3 Cooling system – flushing

1   If the coolant appears to be rusty or dark in colour, the radiator and engine waterways may have become restricted with scale or sediment. In these circumstances it is advisable to flush the system with celan water.
2   Move the heater controls inside the car to Hot and, on Volvo 343 models, unscrew and remove the plug from the left-hand side of the radiator.
3   Insert a hosepipe into the radiator aperture and allow water to flow through the system until all the sediment had disappeared.
4   In severe cases of contamination the system should be reverse flushed. To do this, first remove the radiator as described in Section 6, invert it and insert the hosepipe into the bottom outlet. Similarly, reverse flush the engine by removing the thermostat and inserting the hosepipe into the bottom radiator hose.
5   Chemical cleaners should only be used as a last resort, and the regular renewal of the antifreeze mixture should obviate the need for flushing or other cleaning treatment.

4 Cooling system – filling

1   Refit and tighten all the design plugs and make sure that the heater controls are in the Hot position.
2   Loosen all the cooling system vent screws to ensure any air is expelled. All models are provided with a heater vent screw located on the front of the bulkhead (photo). Daf 55 models also have a vent screw located in the inlet manifold hose at the rear of the engine; Daf/Volvo 66 models have the vent screw located adjacent to the carburettor.
3   Pour the coolant (of the specified mixture – see next Section) into the radiator filler neck until it is about 1 in (25.4 mm) below the base of the filler neck.
4   Tighten the carburettor/inlet manifold vent screw when no more air bubbles emerge.

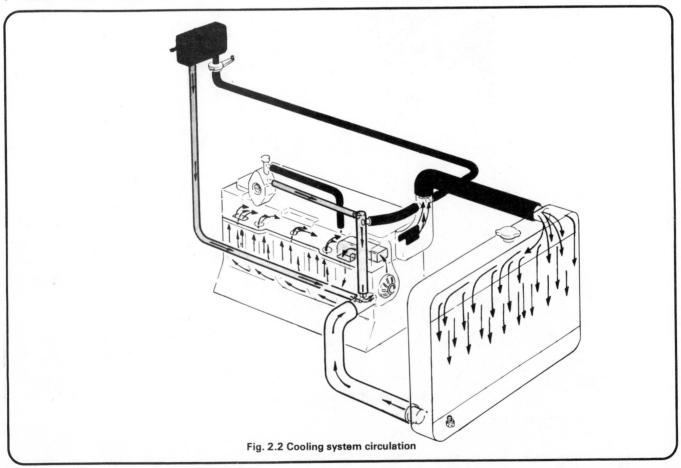

Fig. 2.2 Cooling system circulation

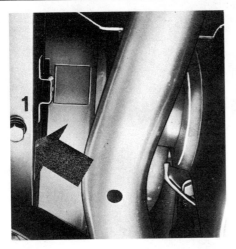

Fig. 2.3 Drain plug location

1 Radiator   2 Cylinder block

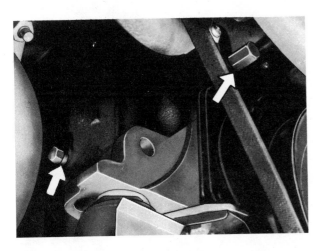

Fig. 2.4 Cylinder block drain plug location in Volvo 343 models

Fig. 2.5 Bleeding the cooling system showing the heater and manifold vent screws

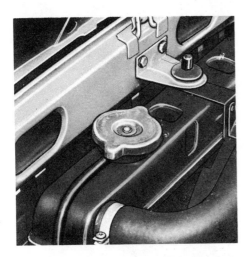

Fig. 2.6 Upper radiator mounting bracket location (Volvo 66 models)

Fig. 2.7 Location of the thermostat

2.1 Removing the radiator filler cap

2.4A Radiator drain plug location

2.4B Cylinder block drain plug locations

4.2 Heater vent screw location (Daf 66 models)

6.7 Radiator top mounting (Daf 66 models)

6.8 Removing the radiator (Daf 66 models)

7.4 Thermostat location

8.4 Removing the fan

8.5 Water pump hose connections

8.7 Water pump unit

10.2 Removing the water temperature sender unit

5 On Volvo 343 models continue to pour coolant into the radiator and expansion tank until the radiator is full and the expansion tank is half-full. Refit and tighten the radiator plug.
6 The next operation requires the use of approx 3 feet (1 metre) of hose having an inside diameter of 0.2 in (5 mm).
7 Connect the hose to the heater vent screw, and place the other end in the radiator filler neck or expansion tank.
8 Start the engine and, with the gear selector lever in neutral, run the engine for three minutes at a speed slightly faster than idling.
9 Close the heater vent screw and stop the engine.
10 On Volvo 343 models, top-up the expansion tank to the maximum mark. On all other models top-up the radiator until there is approximately 0.75 in (20.0 mm) of coolant above the radiator core.
11 Screw on the pressure cap.

5 Coolant mixture – renewal

1 The coolant should be renewed every two years in order to retain the antifreeze and corrosion inhibitor properties at a satisfactory level.
2 Before adding fresh mixture, check all hose connections and preferably check the tightness of the cylinder head bolts (see Chapter 1).
3 Mix the correct quantity of coolant in a separate container then fill the cooling system as described in Section 4.

6 Radiator – removal, inspection, cleaning, and refitting

1 Drain the cooling system as described in Section 2.
2 Disconnect the battery negative terminal.
3 Remove the spare wheel from the engine compartment.
4 Disconnect the upper and lower radiator hoses from the radiator.
5 Working beneath the front of the car, unscrew and remove the two lower radiator mounting nuts (or bolts – Volvo 343 models).
6 Detach the fan cowl from the radiator and lower it onto the fan blades away from the radiator. On Daf 66 models the cowl is welded to the radiator and removal is therefore impossible.
7 Unscrew and remove the two screws retaining the top of the radiator and withdraw the mounting bracket (photo).
8 Lift the radiator (and expansion tank – Volvo 343) up from the engine compartment, being careful not to damage the matrix on the fan blades (photo). Do not allow any coolant to drop onto the bodywork as the paintwork may be damaged.
9 Radiator repair is best entrusted to a specialist but minor leaks may be repaired with a proprietary product.
10 Clean the radiator matrix. Remove any flies or leaves with a soft brush or with a hose.
11 Flush the radiator as described in Section 3. Examine the hoses and clips for deterioration renewing them as necessary.
12 Refitting is a reversal of removal, but the following additional points should be noted:

    (a) Tighten all hoses making sure that the clips are positioned correctly
    (b) Check the pressure cap sealing washer, and if the cap is thought to be faulty, have it tested at a garage

7 Thermostat – removal, testing, and refitting

1 A faulty thermostat can cause overheating or slow engine warm-up, and can also affect the performance of the heater.
2 Drain off enough coolant to bring the level below the top of the water pump.
3 Loosen the two clips securing the top water hose to the radiator and water pump, and remove the hose.
4 Loosen the clip retaining the thermostat in the hose and remove it (photo).
5 To test whether the unit is serviceable, suspend the thermostat by a piece of string in a pan of water and heat it up. Use a thermometer to check the opening temperature which should be in accordance with the information given in Specifications.
6 Remove the thermostat from the water and allow it to cool; when completely cooled the valve must be firmly shut.
7 Refitting is a reversal of removal but make sure that the clip is fitted over the thermostat to prevent it from moving. Refill the cooling system as described in Section 4.

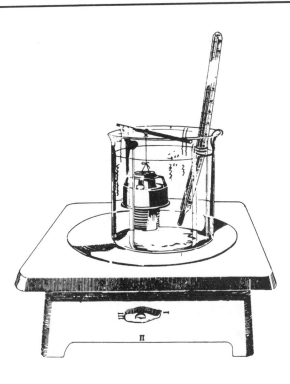

Fig. 2.8 Testing the thermostat opening temperature

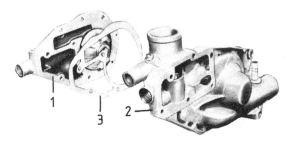

Fig. 2.9 Exploded view of the water pump

1 Cover   2 Housing   3 Gasket

Fig. 2.10 Removing the fan and pulley

Fig. 2.11 The water pump cover retaining bolts (arrowed)

Fig. 2.12 The water pump retaining bolts (arrowed)

Fig. 2.13 Drivebelt adjustment procedure (models with dynamo)

Fig. 2.14 Checking the drivebelt tension (models with alternator)

8   Water pump – removal and refitting

1   Disconnect the battery negative terminal, and drain the cooling system.

2   Remove the radiator as described in Section 6.

3   Loosen the alternator retaining and adjusting bolts and push the alternator towards the engine; the drivebelt can now be removed from the water pump pulley.

4   Unscrew and remove the fan retaining bolts and withdraw the fan and pulley from the water pump flange (photo). Note the location of the spacer ring on Volvo 343 models.

5   Loosen the clips and remove the hoses from the water pump (photo).

6   If it is only required to renew the water pump cover, unscrew and remove the cover retaining bolts evenly in diagonal sequence and carefully pull the cover assembly away from the base housing.

7   If the complete water pump is being removed, unscrew and remove the bolts shown in Fig. 2.12 and lift the unit away from the cylinder head (photo).

8   Remove all traces of gasket from the water pump and/or cylinder head, being careful not to damage the contact surfaces.

9   Refitting is a reversal of removal but the following points should be noted:

(a)   *Always fit new gaskets*

(b)   *Tighten all nuts and bolts to the correct torque wrench settings and in diagonal sequence where possible*

(c)   *Where hose clips requiring a special tool are fitted, replace them with the screw type*

(d)   *Adjust the drivebelt tension as described in Section 9*

(e)   *Run the engine and check for leaks when completed*

9   Fan/Alternator drivebelt – renewal and adjustment

1   To renew the drivebelt, first loosen the dynamo/alternator retaining and adjusting bolts, move the unit towards the engine and remove the belt from the crankshaft, dynamo/alternator, and fan pulleys, finally lifting it over the fan blades.

2   Installation is a reversal of removal but the tension should be adjusted as follows.

Note: *incorrect drivebelt tension can cause premature wear of the generator and water pump bearings or insufficient charging and cooling.*

3   The correct tension is measured by depressing the upper (alternator) or side (dynamo) run of the drivebelt with firm thumb pressure at a midway point; the belt should move between 0.039 and 0.059 in (10 and 15 mm).

4   To adjust the tension, first loosen the generator retaining and adjusting bolts. Move the unit in or out as necessary to achieve the correct tension, then tighten the bolts. Do not use levers on the alternator or damage may occur.

5   Recheck the tension after tightening the mounting bolts.

10 Water temperature sender unit – removal and refitting

1   With the exception of Daf 55 models, the sender unit is located at the rear of the cylinder head. On Daf 55 models the unit is located on the front left-hand side of the cylinder head.

2   To remove the unit, disconnect the electrical supply lead from the terminal and unscrew it. There is no need to drain the cooling system provided the new unit is fitted immediately (photo).

3   Refitting is a reversal of removal, but if coolant has been lost during the operation, the system must be topped-up referring to Section 4 as necessary.

11 Fault diagnosis – cooling system

Symptom	Reason/s
Overheating	Low coolant level
	Faulty pressure cap
	Faulty thermostat
	Loose fan belt
	Clogged radiator matrix
	Incorrect engine timing
	Clogged cooling system
	Blown cylinder head gasket
Cool running or slow warm up	Faulty or incorrect thermostat
Coolant loss	Faulty pressure cap
	Cracked hose
	Blown cylinder head gasket
	Worn water pump

Chapter 3 Carburation, fuel and exhaust systems

Contents

Specifications

Fuel tank
Capacity:
    Daf 55 models .... 8.36 galls (38.0 litres)
    Daf 66 and Volvo 66 models .... 9.38 galls (42.0 litres)
    Volvo 343 models .... 9.89 galls (45.0 litres)

Fuel pump
Type .... Mechanical
Pressure (at 725 rpm) .... 2.84 to 2.56 psi

Carburettor
Type:
    Daf 55, Daf 66 and Volvo 66 models .... Solex 32 EHSA (REN 400, 486) or 32 EHSA–2 (REN 515, 537, 559, 577, 584, 596); side-draught
    Volvo 343 models .... Weber 32 DIR 57; side-draught
Identification number
    Daf 55 standard models:
        Up to chassis No 21369 .... REN 400
        Chassis No 21370 to 30478 .... REN 486
        Chassis No 30479 on .... REN 515
    Daf 55 Marathon models:
        Up to chassis No 729011 .... REN 537
        Chassis No 729012 on .... REN 559
    Daf 66 and Volvo 66 models with 1100 engine .... REN 577
    Daf 66 Marathon .... REN 584
    Daf 66 and Volvo 66 models with 1300 engine .... REN 596
    Volvo 343 models .... 32 DIR 57–8400

Carburettor settings

REN 400:
Main jet	127.5
Pilot jet	50
Air correction jet	180–B8
Idling air jets	90 and 100
Throttle opening for accelerator pump setting	0.16 in (4.0 mm)

REN 486:
As for REN 400 except for
Main jet	130

REN 515:
Main jet	115
Pilot jet	50
Air correction jet	175 T1
Idling air jets	125 and 100
Throttle opening for accelerator pump setting	0.16 in (4.0 mm)

REN 537:
Main jet	117.5
Pilot jet	50
Air correction jet	175 T1
Idling air jets	115 and 100
Throttle opening for accelerator pump setting	0.08 in (2.0 mm)

REN 559:
As for REN 537 except for
Pilot jet	45 (+ 3/-4)
Throttle opening for accelerator pump setting	0.4 in (10.0 mm)

REN 577:
Main jet	112.5
Pilot jet	50 (+ 3/-4)
Air correction jet	175
Idling air jets	135 and 130
Throttle opening for accelerator pump setting	0.4 in (10.0 mm)

REN 584:
Main jet	117.5
Pilot jet	41 to 48
Air correction jet	175
Idling air jets	175
Throttle opening for accelerator pump setting	0.2 in (5.0 mm)

REN 596:
Main jet	112.5
Pilot jet	40 ± 3
Air correction jet	145 ± 5
Throttle opening for accelerator pump setting	0.4 in (10.0 mm)

32 DIR 57–8400:	First stage	Second stage
Main jet	127	120
Air correction jet	180	135
Pilot jet	47	60
Correction jet	115	70
Exhaust gas emission at idling speed (CO %)	2.5 ± 0.5	

Torque wrench settings

	lbf ft	Nm
Fuel pump	11 to 14	15 to 20
Inlet and exhaust manifold	11 to 14	15 to 20
Carburettor	11 to 14	15 to 20
Exhaust mounting	13 to 14	18 to 20

1 General description

The fuel system comprises a rear mounted fuel tank, a camshaft operated fuel pump, and a carburettor.

The air cleaner incorporates a disposable paper element, and an air flap which can be positioned in a summer or winter position, in order to collect cool air or warm air preheated by the exhaust manifold. On 1978 Volvo 343 models the air flap is thermostatically controlled.

2 Air filter – removal and refitting

1 A paper element type filter is fitted to the air cleaner and should be renewed every 10 000 miles (20 000 km) on Daf 55, Daf 66, and Volvo 66 models. On Volvo 343 models it should be renewed every 25 000 miles (40 000 km). Earlier renewal may be required if the car is operated in very dusty conditions.
2 To remove the air filter element, first remove the spare wheel on all except Volvo 343 models.

3 On Daf 55, Daf 66, and Volvo 66 models unscrew and remove the wingnut from the rear of the air cleaner assembly, and pull the front cover away; the element can now be withdrawn (photos).
4 On Volvo 343 models remove the filler cap then withdraw the windscreen washer reservoir. Check the setting of the air cleaner (summer or winter) then detach the hoses from the rear of the air cleaner at the same time noting their locations. Disconnect the bellows, then unscrew and remove the mounting bolts and lift the air cleaner from the car. Unscrew the wingnut and remove the end cover, O-ring, and air filter element.
5 Refitting is a reversal of removal; make sure that the O-ring is seated correctly on Volvo 343 models.

3 Air cleaner (1978 Volvo 343 models) – description and testing

1 The air cleaner fitted to late Volvo 343 models includes a thermostatically controlled air flap, instead of the earlier type air flap which

2.3A Air cleaner assembly (Daf 66 models)

2.3B Removing the air filter (Daf 66 models)

4.5 Removing the fuel pump filter (Daf 66 models)

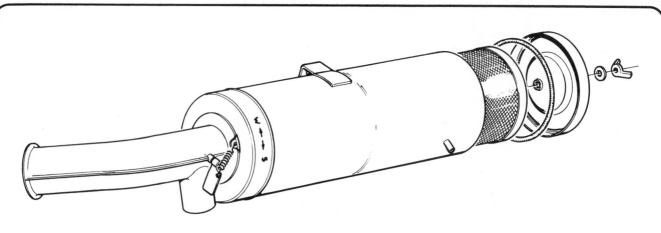

Fig. 3.1 Air cleaner and filter (pre 1978 Volvo 343 models)

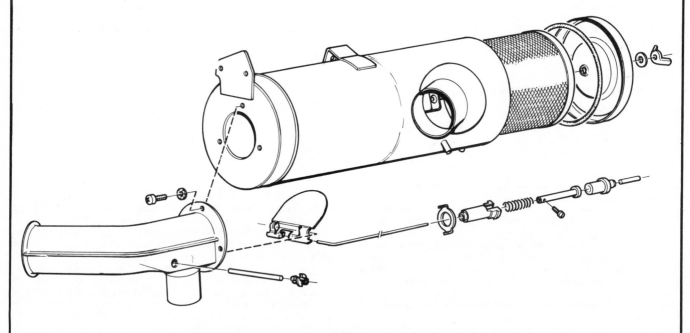

Fig. 3.2 Air cleaner, filter, and thermostatic valve (1978 Volvo 343 models)

Fig. 3.3 Air cleaner mounting bolt locations (Volvo 343 models)

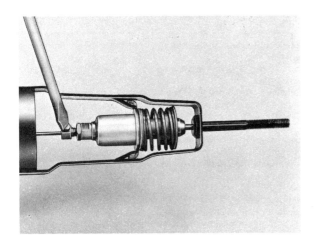

Fig. 3.4 Thermostatic valve adjustment screw (1978 Volvo 343 models)

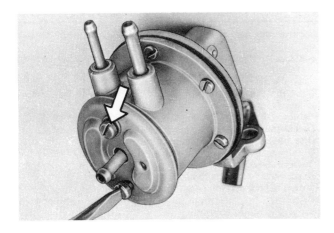

Fig. 3.5 Removing the fuel pump cover (Volvo 343 models)

is manually set to the summer or winter position.

2   Cold air is drawn into the air cleaner at engine compartment temperature while hot air is drawn through a hose from the area of the exhaust manifold.

3   The thermostatic valve is located at the air filter end of the air cleaner and is activated by the temperature of the air entering the carburettor. When the temperature of the air is below 15°C the cold air supply is closed, and when the temperature is above 25°C the hot air supply is closed. The air flap is automatically regulated between these two limits, and the air entering the engine is therefore maintained at a suitable temperature.

4   To test the thermostatic valve, first remove the air filter as described in Section 2.

5   Check the position of the air flap after removing the assembly from the air cleaner.

6   Using a thermometer and air heater such as a hair dryer, heat the air around the thermostat; when the temperature reaches 25°C the air flap should close the hot air supply completely. Cool the air and check that the cold air supply is closed at 15°C.

7   If adjustment is required, loosen the locking screw and reposition the air flap as necessary.

8   If the thermostat is proved faulty, remove it together with the spring and spacers, and renew it.

9   Reassembly of the air cleaner is a reversal of dismantling.

4   Fuel pump – description, testing, and cleaning

1   The fuel pump is located on the right-hand side of the engine, forward of the distributor, and is operated by a rocker arm which is in contact with an eccentric on the camshaft.

2   The fuel pump fitted to all Daf 66 and Volvo 66 models is of a sealed construction, and, apart from cleaning the filter at the recommended intervals, no dismantling is possible. Should the unit develop a fault, it must be renewed complete. The fuel pump fitted to all other models may be dismantled as described in Sections 6 and 7.

3   To test the operation of the pump, disconnect the fuel pipe from the carburettor. Disconnect the coil HT lead then spin the engine on the starter and observe whether well defined spurts of fuel are ejected from the open end of the pipe. If not, the pump is faulty.

4   To clean the filter, first disconnect the fuel supply pipe to the pump and plug it to prevent loss of fuel.

5   On Daf 55 models unscrew the hexagonal cap and extract the filter screen; on Daf 66 and Volvo 66 models unscrew the pump cover centre screw and lift away the cover, sealing ring, and gauze filter (photo); on Volvo 343 models disconnect the outlet pipe, unscrew the two retaining screws and lift away the cover, gasket, gauze filter, and spring.

6   Brush any dirt or sediment from the filter and pump interior, then reassemble the components in the reverse order to dismantling, but make sure that the retaining screw(s) are not overtightened.

5   Fuel pump – removal and refitting

1   Open the bonnet and remove the spare wheel.

2   Clean the fuel pump and the surrounding area of the engine.

3   Disconnect the inlet and outlet pipes from the pump and plug the

4   Unscrew and remove the retaining nuts and bolts as applicable and lift the fuel pump from the engine (photo).

5   Remove the gasket(s) and clean the contact surfaces of the pump and engine. Where an insulating flange is fitted, clean all traces of gasket from both sides.

6   Refitting is a reversal of removal, but apply grease to the rocker arm before installing the pump. Where an insulating flange is fitted, fit one gasket either side, but if it is found that the operating pressure after refitting is too high, a further one or more gaskets may be fitted to reduce the pressure. The pressure gauge should be inserted into the pump outlet pipe with a T-connector when checking the pressure, and reference should be made to Specifications for the correct pressure.

6   Fuel pump (Daf 55 models) – dismantling, inspection, and reassembly

1   First clean the pump exterior thoroughly and mark the edges of the

5.4 Removing the fuel pump (Daf 66 models)

two halves of the body.

2   Remove the filter as described in Section 4.

3   Remove the eight screws and washers holding the two halves of the pump together and the top half may then be lifted off.

4   The diaphragm and pushrod should be removed next but you will have to remove the pump lever and its spindle to release it. This is done by releasing one of the spindle circlips. This can prove to be very fiddly but with patience and a strong blunt penknife blade the circlip can be 'peeled' off. Push the spindle through and pull out the lever. Retrieve the lever spring. Lift out the diaphragm and its rod carefully. This spindle is usually known as the rocker arm pivot pin.

5   If there are signs of wear in the rocker arm pivot pin, rocker arn and link bushes then they should be renewed.

6   The valve assemblies should only be removed from the upper body if renewal is necessary. They are staked into the body and are destroyed when levered out.

7   Examine the diaphragm for signs of cracking or perforation and renew if necessary.

8   Overhaul kits are available for all pumps and are supplied with a new diaphragm, valves and sealing rings.

9   When fitting new valve assemblies to the body, first fit the seating washers and then place the valves, making sure that they are the correct way up according to inlet and outlet. The body will have to be restaked at six places round the edge so that the assemblies are firmly held in their positions. If this is not done properly and leakage occurs between the valve assembly and the seating ring the pump will not operate efficiently.

10 To replace the diaphragm and lever arm it will be necessary to place the diaphragm spring in the body of the pump. Then the diaphragm and its rod. Press the diaphragm spring down and fit the spring, push in the lever (the right way up) and connect over the top of the machined stop of the rod. Push in the rocker arm pivot pin and push through the lever. Replace the circlip on the pivot pin. Always use a new circlip.

11 Fit the upper half of the pump body and line up the mating marks. In order to assemble the two halves and the diaphragm properly push the rocker arm upwards so that the diaphragm is drawn level. Then place the eight screws in position lightly. It is best if the base of the pump is held in a vice whilst the rocker arm is pushed right up to bring the diaphragm to the bottom of its stroke. A short piece of tube over the rocker arm will provide easy leverage. In this position the screws should be tightened evenly and alternately.

12 Refit the filter and retaining screw.

13 When the pump is reassembled the suction and delivery pressure can be felt at the inlet and outlet ports when the rocker arm is operated. Be careful not to block the inlet port completely when testing suction. If the rocker arm were to be operated strongly and the inlet side was blocked the diaphragm could be damaged.

7 Fuel pump (Volvo 343 models) – dismantling, inspection, and reassembly

1   Clean the pump exterior and mark the upper and lower halves of the pump in relation to each other.

2   Remove the filter as described in Section 4.

3   Unscrew the retaining screws and lift the upper half away.

4   Press the diaphragm into the lower half and disconnect it from the rocker arm, then lift it out and remove the spring, washer, and seal.

5   Using a screwdriver, prise the return spring from the rocker arm.

6   Drive the pivot pin through the lower half and rocker arm using a suitable soft metal drift.

7   Withdraw the rocker arm and thoroughly clean all components with paraffin, then dry them with a lint-free cloth.

8   Examine all the components and check them for wear, damage, and deterioration. In particular check the diaphragm for cracks and fractures and renew it if necessary.

9   Reassembly is a reversal of dismantling, but the following additional points should be noted:

(a)   Lock the rocker arm pivot pin in position by staking it each side of the lower half with a centre punch

(b)   Tighten the retaining screws evenly in diagonal sequence

(c)   Test the operation of the pump by referring to Section 6 of paragraph 13

8 Fuel tank (Daf 55, Daf 66, and Volvo 66 models) – removal, servicing, and refitting

1   Jack up the rear of the car and support it adequately on axlestands.

2   Remove the filler cap and syphon out any fuel left in the tank with a suitable hose.

3   Detach the exhaust pipe from the two rear suspension rubbers, then detach the fuel outlet hose and plug it.

4   Unscrew and remove the two retaining bolts and detach the mounting straps at the rear of the car.

5   Lower the tank slightly, then push it forwards until the filler neck has disengaged the rear panel.

6   Disconnect the leads from the fuel level transmitter unit, noting their location.

7   Lower the fuel tank and remove it from under the car.

8   Remove the four mounting rubbers.

9   A leak in the fuel tank should be repaired by specialists or alternatively a new tank fitted; never be tempted to solder or weld a leaking fuel tank.

10 If the tank is contaminated with sediment or water, it can be swilled out using several changes of fuel, but if any vigorous shaking is required to dislodge accumulations of dirt or rust, the tank transmitter unit should first be removed as described in Section 10.

11 Refitting is a reversal of removal.

9 Fuel tank (Volve 343 models) – removal, servicing, and refitting

1   Jack up the rear of the car and support it adequately on axlestands.

2   Remove the filler cap and syphon out any fuel left in the tank with a suitable hose.

3   Open the tailgate and remove the parcel shelf.

4   Push the rear seat forwards and remove the right-hand side central panel.

5   Remove the tail light interior cover on the right-hand side.

6   Detach the right-hand side hinge from the rear seat backrest.

7   Disconnect the battery negative terminal.

8   Disconnect the leads from the luggage compartment interior light.

9   Remove the right-hand side rear panel.

10 Disconnect the fuel tank vent hose at the tank end.

11 Move the floor mat to one side and remove the transmitter cover.

12 Disconnect the leads from the transmitter unit, then detach the fuel supply and return hoses.

13 Disconnect the fuel filler hose at the tank end.

14 Unscrew and remove the mounting bolts and lower the fuel tank from the car.

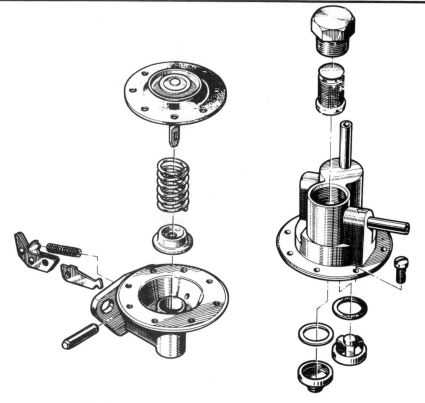

Fig. 3.6 Exploded view of the fuel pump (Daf 55 models)

Fig. 3.7 Fuel pump filter and spring (Volvo 343 models)

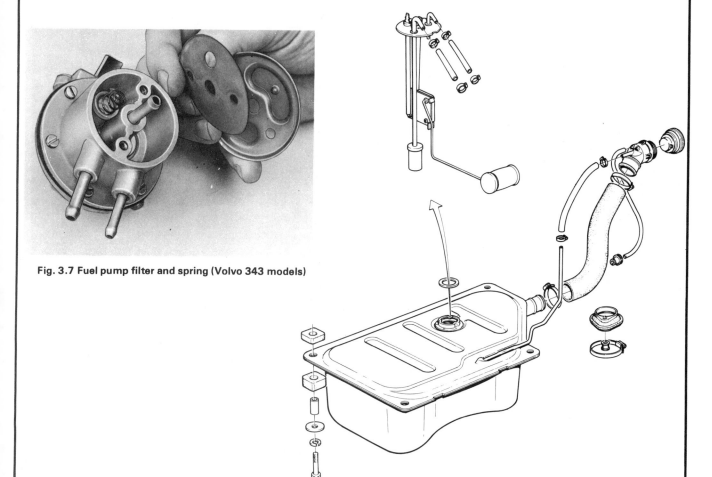

Fig. 3.8 Fuel tank components (Volvo 343 models)

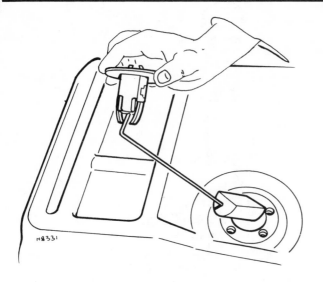

Fig. 3.10 Removing the fuel tank transmitter retaining ring (Volvo 343 models)

Fig. 3.9 Removing the fuel tank transmitter unit (Daf 55 models)

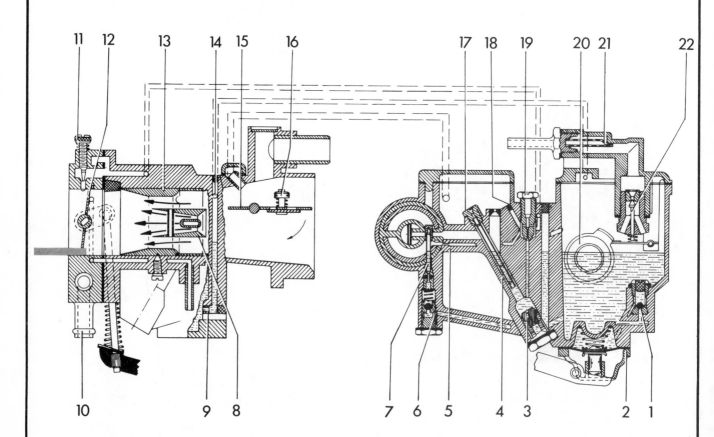

Fig. 3.11 Cross section view of the Solex carburettor

1	Pump valve	7	Injector	13	Choke tube	18	Calibrated bore
2	Diaphragm	8	Sprayer with nozzle	14	Econostat	19	Pilot jet
3	Main jet	9	Econostat jet	15	Choke valve	20	Float
4	Emulsion tube	10	Coolant inlet	16	Air valve	21	Filter
5	Calibrated bore	11	Volume control screw	17	Correction jet	22	Needle valve
6	Pump valve housing	12	Throttle valve				

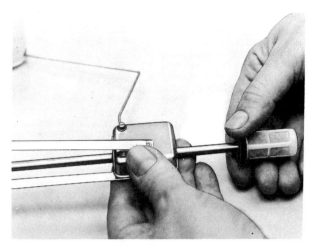

Fig. 3.12 Removing the filter from the tank transmitter unit (Volvo 343 models)

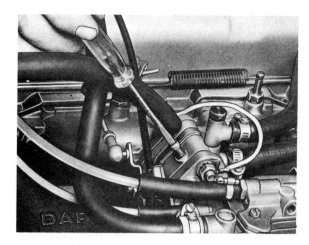

Fig. 3.13 Adjusting the volume control screw (Solex carburettors)

15 Remove the rubber mountings from the tank.
16 For servicing the fuel tank refer to Section 8 paragraphs 9 and 10.
17 Refitting is a reversal of removal.

10 Fuel tank transmitter unit – removal and refitting

1 On Daf 55, Daf 66, and Volvo 66 models the fuel tank must first be removed by referring the Section 8.
2 On Volvo 343 models, open the tailgate and move the mat to one side, then remove the transmitter cover and disconnect the two leads from the terminals. Detach the fuel supply and return hoses.
3 On some early models the transmitter unit is attached to the fuel tank with screws, but later models are fitted with a clamp which must be turned to release the unit. With the type fitted to Volvo 66 models, the use of two screwdrivers inserted in opposite recesses and then crossed will release the unit.
4 Remove the gasket or seal as applicable and clean the faces of the transmitter and fuel tank. On Volvo 343 models check the condition of the fuel filter on the outlet pipe and the condition of the plastic float; if either of these items is unserviceable it may be renewed separate to the transmitter unit.
5 Refitting is a reversal of removal, but always fit a new gasket or rubber seal, and make sure that the lugs on the unit locate in the fuel tank recess on Volvo 343 models.

11 Carburettor (Daf 55, Daf 66, and Volvo 66 models) – general description

The carburettor is a Solex 32 EHSA side draught type with fixed jets and manually operated choke valve. The throttle valve is housed in a detachable flange which is heated by water from the cooling system. The throttle valve is cable operated on Daf 55 and Daf 66 models but a control linkage is fitted to Volvo 66 models.
When idling, the pilot jet supplies fuel to the engine and air is supplied through two internal calibrated bores. At increased engine speed fuel is supplied through the main jet and mixes with the airflow in the choke tube. At wide throttle openings air is introduced into the emulsion tube via the air correction jet and is mixed with the fuel internally to prevent the mixture becoming too rich. The carburettor is also fitted with an Econostat system whereby additional fuel is supplied to the choke tube dependent on the air velocity and depression in the choke tube, thus allowing a leaner overall setting to be achieved. A diaphragm type accelerator pump applies extra fuel when the throttle is opened.

12 Carburettor (Daf 55, Daf 66, and Volvo 66 models) – idling speed adjustment

1 Run the engine until it reaches the normal operating temperature

with the choke fully returned.
2 Connect a tachometer to the engine and adjust the throttle stop screw until the engine speed is between 700 and 750 rpm.
3 Unscrew the volume control screw several turns then slowly screw it in again until the engine runs evenly.
4 Adjust the throttle stop screw again if necessary as described in paragraph 2.
5 With the engine idling, operate the low ratio hold switch; the speed of the engine should not decrease by more than 50 rpm. If it does the vacuum control micro-switch (when fitted) should be adjusted as described in Chapter 6.

13 Carburettor (Daf 55, Daf 66, and Volvo 66 models) – removal and refitting

1 Open the bonnet and remove the spare wheel.
2 Disconnect the throttle control, choke cable, heater hoses, crankcase breather hose, and vacuum hose.
3 Disconnect the fuel line from the carburettor and plug it to prevent the ingress of foreign matter (photo).
4 Loosen the clip and detach the air cleaner bellows.
5 Disconnect the leads from the micro-switch.
6 Drain the cooling system as described in Chapter 2, then remove the coolant hoses from the carburettor.
7 Unscrew the retaining nuts, remove the earth lead, and withdraw the carburettor (photo).
8 Remove the flange gaskets.
9 Refitting is a reversal of removal, but always fit a new flange gasket on both sides of the heat shield. The throttle cable or rod should be adjusted so that there is a little free play with the throttle in the closed position. Also, with the accelerator pedal fully depressed the throttle lever on the carburettor should be fully open. The choke cable must be adjusted so that when fully released the stop ball engages the hole in the lever. Fill the cooling system referring to Chapter 2.

14 Carburettor (Daf 55, Daf 66, and Volvo 66 models) – dismantling and reassembly

1 Clean the exterior of the carburettor before dismantling.
2 If the throttle spindle is worn excessively, both the spindle and throttle body will need renewing, in which case it may be more economical to obtain a new or reconditioned carburettor (photo).
3 Unscrew and remove the float chamber retaining screws and withdraw the cover and gasket together with the float and needle valve.
4 Unscrew and remove the jets from the carburettor noting their locations. Note: *On 32 EHSA-2 the air correction jet and emulsion tube connot be removed.*
5 Unscrew the accelerator pump retaining screws and remove the cover and diaphragm, noting that the large spring diameter is located

against the pump body.

6   Clean all components and renew any that are worn. Obtain new gaskets, diaphragm etc in the form of a repair kit.

7   Check the float for leakage by shaking it vigorously and listening for any fuel which may have entered it. Renew it if it is faulty.

8   Do not attempt to remove the emulsion tube on Daf 55 models after Chassis No 30479 (32 EHSA - 2 carburettor). If it has been loosened remove the main jet and carefully press the emulsion tube out. Apply a liquid locking agent to the head of the emulsion tube and press it back into position making sure that the slot is at right angles with the choke tube centre line.

9   Start reassembly by fitting the accelerator spring, diaphragm, and cover; tighten the screws in diagonal sequence.

10 Refit the throttle housing with a new gasket, but make sure that it is the correct way round otherwise it will restrict the passage to the volume control screw.

11 Tighten the jets into their locations.

12 Install the pump discharge nozzle making sure that it faces the choke tube.

13 Fit a new gasket to the float chamber cover and then check that the distance from the centre of the float to the gasket with the needle valve closed is 1.28 in (32.5 mm); adjust if necessary.

14 Locate the cover over the float chamber and tighten the retaining screws evenly.

15 Check the stroke of the accelerator pump by first opening the throttle valve and inserting a drill of the diameter given in Specifications between the choke wall and the butterfly valve.

16 With the valve closed onto the drill check that the adjusting nut is just in contact with the pump operating lever; if not, fully unscrew the nut then screw it in until it just touches the lever, then lock the nut.

15 Carburettor (Volvo 343 models) – general description

The carburettor is a Weber 32 DIR 57 twin choke down-draught type with fixed metering jets and a manually operated choke. A hot spot is fitted to the bottom of the carburettor and is heated by the engine cooling system. Its function is to heat the air entering the

engine and it is separated from the carburettor and manifold by insulating flanges.

When the engine is idling, fuel flows from the primary well, through the pilot jet to the idling control screw. Air is supplied through the air jet, and the electrically controlled pilot jet stops the supply of fuel into the idling circuit when it is de-energised; this prevents any tendency for the engine to run-on. At increased engine speed the by-pass bores of the idling circuit are opened and the primary venturi provides increased amounts of fuel and air through the primary venturi.

After the primary throttle valve has opened a predetermined amount, further movement of the accelerator pedal will operate the secondary throttle valve and both venturis will then supply fuel and air mixture to the engine. A diaphragm type accelerator pump is fitted to the carburettor and supplies extra fuel to both venturis when the throttle is opened.

The carburettor is also equipped with a pneumatic chock control which automatically opens the choke valves as soon as the engine starts. The unit is of diaphragm type and is operated by the depression within the carburettor on the engine side of the throttle valves.

16 Carburettor (Volvo 343 models) – idling speed adjustment

1   Note that in order to adjust the carburettor correctly the ignition timing should be correct and the air filter should be on the correct setting (manual operation) or functioning correctly (automatic thermostatic operation).

2   Connect a tachometer to the engine.

3   With the engine cold, pull the choke control fully out and start the engine; the engine speed should be between 1800 and 2000 rpm. If the engine speed is incorrect the carburettor will have to be removed and adjusted as described in Section 18.

4   Run the engine until it reaches normal operating temperature, then check the engine idling speed which should be between 700 and 750 rpm. Adjust the throttle valve adjusting screw if necessary.

17 Carburettor (Volvo 343 models) – removal and refitting

1   Open the bonnet and remove the air cleaner assembly as

13.3 Fuel line to carburettor connection (Daf 66 models)

13.7A Carburettor earth lead location

13.7B Removing the carburettor (Daf 66 models)

14.2 Carburettor throttle housing (Daf 66 models)

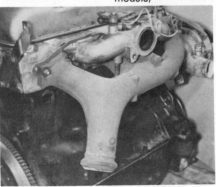

19.6 Inlet and exhaust manifolds (Daf 66 models)

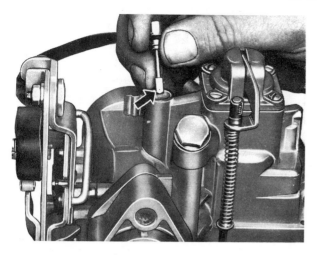

Fig. 3.14 Correct fitting of the pump discharge nozzle (Solex carburettors)

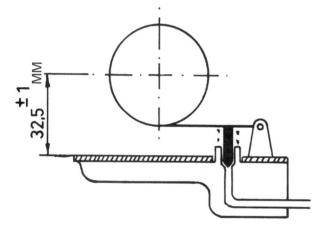

Fig. 3.15 Float setting dimension (Solex carburettors)

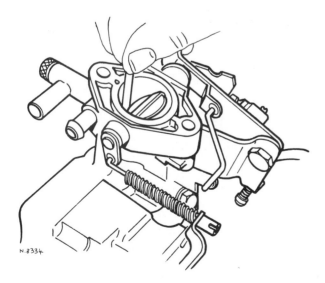

Fig. 3.16 Checking the accelerator pump stroke (Solex carburettors)

described in Section 2.

2   Disconnect the crankcase breather hose and detach the air supply pipe from the carburettor.

3   Pull the throttle control rod from the carburettor, then detach the fuel supply and vent hoses.

4   Pull the vacuum advance hose from the carburettor, then detach the fuel supply and vent hoses.

5   Disconnect the lead to the electrically controlled pilot jet.

6   On early models unscrew the two retaining screws and remove the vacuum control micro-switch.

7   Drain the cooling system as described in Chapter 2, then detach the two hoses from the carburettor hot spot.

8   Unscrew and remove the four carburettor retaining nuts evenly and withdraw the carburettor from the manifold.

9   Lift the insulating flange from the manifold and clean the mating faces of the carburettor and manifold.

10   Refitting is a reversal of removal, but the following additional points should be noted:

(a)   Always fit a new gasket on both sides of the insulating flange

(b)   Adjust the throttle rod so that there is a little free play with the throttle in the closed position. Check that with the accelerator pedal fully depressed, the throttle lever on the carburettor is fully open

(c)   Adjust the choke cable so that the operating lever is in the fully released position with the control knob pushed fully in Check that the choke valve plates are in the closed position with the control knob pulled fully out

(d)   After fitting the micro-switch adjust it as described in Chapter 6

(e)   Fill the cooling system referring to Chapter 2 as necessary

(f)   Make sure that the rubber seal is correctly located to the air supply pipe

18 Carburettor (Volvo 343 models) – dismantling and reassembly

1   Clean the exterior of the carburettor before dismantling.

2   From the bottom of the carburettor, unscrew the retaining screws and remove the hot spot and insulating flange.

3   Clean away any remains of gasket from the insulating flange, hot spot, and carburettor faces. **Note:** *the second stage throttle valve screw must not be adjusted as it is set during manufacture.*

4   Unscrew the hexagon bolt at the fuel inlet and remove the gauze filter.

5   Prise the spring clips from the choke control rods on either side of the carburettor and disconnect them from the levers.

6   Unscrew the upper cover retaining screws and lift the cover from the main body of the carburettor together with the float.

7   Extract the pivot pin and withdraw the float and needle valve, then unhook the needle valve from the float.

8   Remove the gasket from the upper cover.

9   Extract the spring clips and remove both choke control rods and washers from the cover noting their locations.

10   Unscrew the retaining screws evenly and remove the accelerator pump cover, diaphragm, and spring.

11   Slacken the Allen screw, then remove the electrically controlled pilot jet.

12   Unscrew and remove the second pilot jets, both air correction jets, the two main jets, the pump injector, and emulsion tubes.

13   Unscrew and remove the volume control screw and seal.

14   Unscrew the choke control diaphragm unit retaining screws, remove the circlip and washer, and withdraw the diaphragm unit from the main body.

15   Dismantle the choke control diaphragm unit by removing the three screws and withdrawing the diaphragm, and spring. Mark the two halves of the unit to ensure correct reassembly.

16   Slide both venturis from the choke tubes but be very careful to mark them in relation to their correct locations.

17   Clean all components and renew any that are worn. Obtain new gaskets, diaphragms etc in the form of a repair kit.

18   Check the float for leakage by shaking it vigorously and listening for any fuel which may have entered it. Renew it if it is faulty.

19   Start reassembly by installing the two main jets in the bottom of the float chamber.

20   Fit the two emulsion tubes and correction jets.

21   Fit the pump injector with seals and tighten the assembly into the

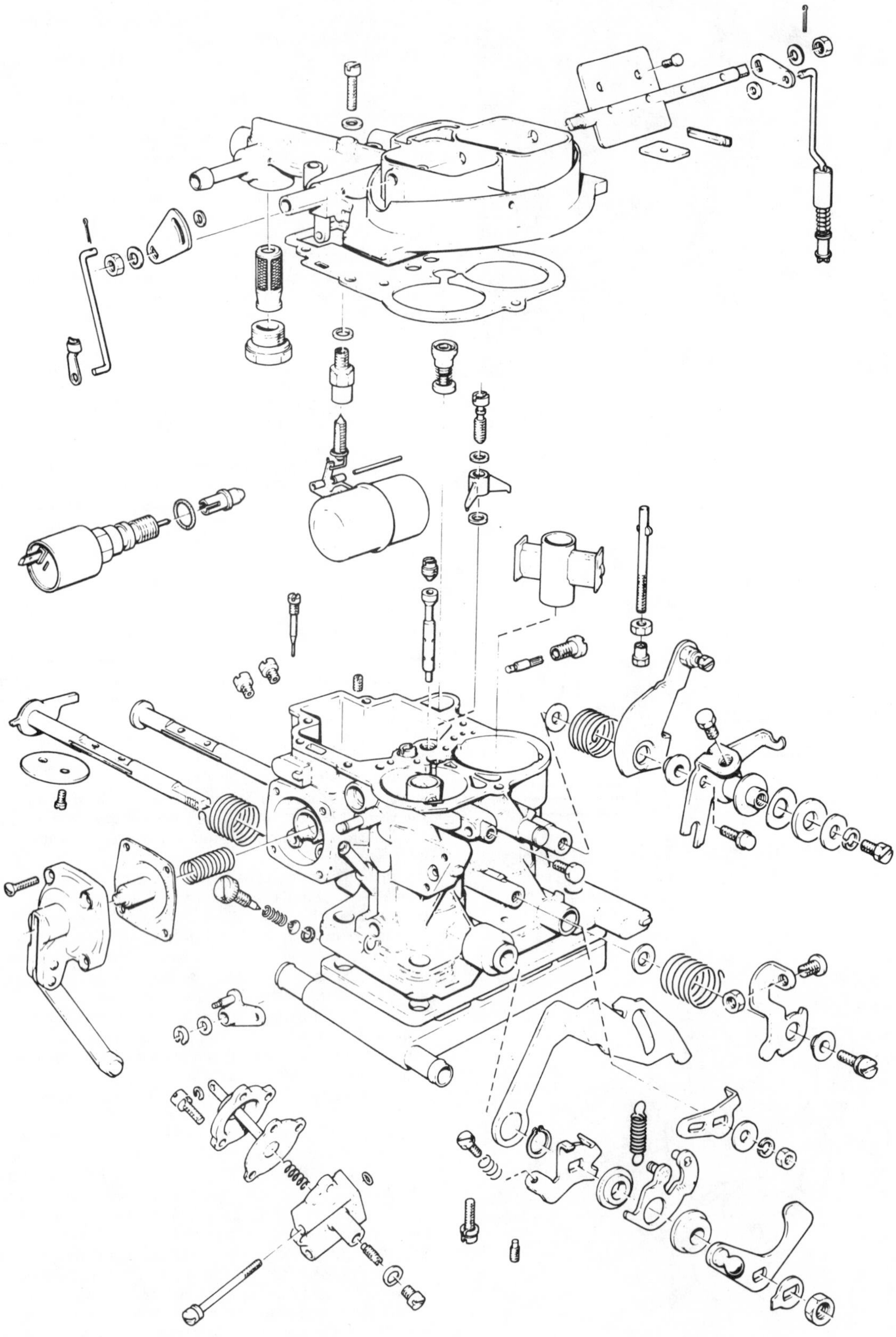

Fig. 3.17 Exploded view of the Weber carburettor

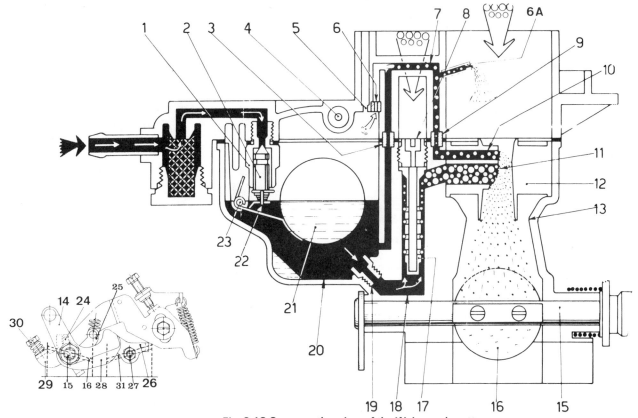

Fig. 3.18 Cross section view of the Weber carburettor

1	Needle valve housing	8	Air correction jet	16	Throttle valve	24	Engaging lug
2	Needle valve	9	Calibrated jet	17	Emulsion tube	25	Lug
3	Calibrated jet	10	Auxiliary fuel supply	18	Mixing chamber	26	Lever
4	Vent	11	Main fuel supply	19	Main jet	27	Pivot
5	Vent passage	12	Venturi	20	Float chamber	28	Lever
6	Calibrated jet	13	Body	21	Float	29	Lever
6A	Calibrated jet	14	Throttle operating lever	22	Float arm	30	Volume control screw
7	Venturi passage	15	Throttle valve spindle	23	Float pivot		

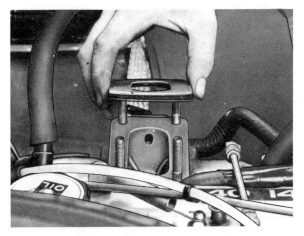

Fig. 3.19 Removing the carburettor insulating flange (Volvo 343 models)

Fig. 3.20 Removing the inlet filter (Volvo 343 models)

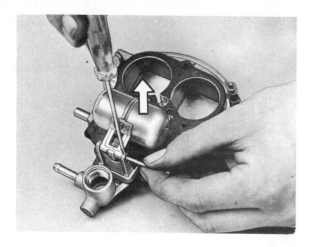

Fig. 3.21 Extracting the float pivot pin (Volvo 343 models)

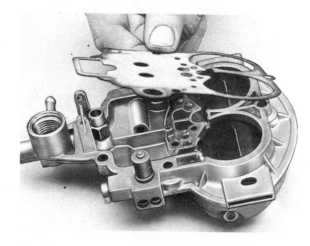

Fig. 3.22 Removing the carburettor cover gasket (Volvo 343 models)

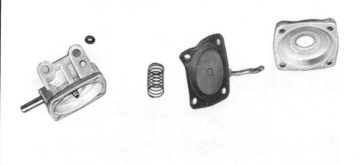

Fig. 3.23 Accelerator pump components (Volvo 343 models)

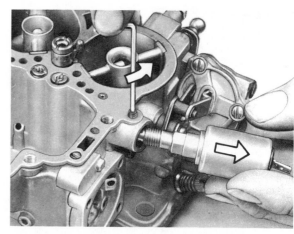

Fig. 3.24 Removing the electric pilot jet (Volvo 343 models)

Fig. 3.25 Removing the air correction jets and emulsion tubes (Volvo 343 models)

Fig. 3.26 Removing the main jets (Volvo 343 models)

carburettor main body.

22 Install the venturis into the choke tubes making sure that they are each located in the correct stage.

23 Assemble the choke control diaphragm unit and tighten the three screws, then fit it to the carburettor main body.

24 Install the second pilot jets.

25 Screw the electrically controlled pilot jet into the main body and lock it in position by tightening the Allen screw.

26 Fit the spring and seal onto the volume control screw then screw it into the side of the main body.

27 Assemble the accelerator pump with a new diaphragm and gasket, then tighten the retaining screws evenly in diagonal sequence.

28 Locate a new gasket on the upper cover then install the needle valve and float. When the pivot pin is correctly located, use a pair of pliers to close the split pillar and lock the pin.

29 Invert the upper cover and measure the distance between the gasket and the float; this should be 0.28 in (7.0 mm). Adjust the float arm if necessary.

30 Tighten the filter into the upper cover.

31 Lower the upper cover onto the main body and tighten the retaining screws evenly in diagonal sequence.

32 Connect the two choke control rods and secure with the spring clips.

33 Locate the hot spot insulating flange with a new gasket on each side, then install the hot spot and tighten the retaining screws to the carburettor.

34 With the carburettor assembled, use a suitable size drill to check that the clearance between the choke valves and choke wall when the choke is operated is between 0.14 and 0.18 in (3.5 and 4.5 mm); if not, bend the choke control rod as necessary.

35 Check the pneumatic choke control by operating the choke until the valve plates are about to move, then fully press in the vacuum chamber rod; the clearance as checked in paragraph 34 should now be between 0.16 and 0.20 in (4.0 and 5.0 mm). If not remove the pneumatic control screw plug and turn the adjusting screw as necessary.

36 Fully operate the choke and check that the first stage throttle valve is open by 0.035 in (0.9 mm) measured with a suitable drill: if not, adjust the screw on the control rod.

37 Check that the vent valve closes as soon as the throttle lever is operated; if not, adjust the operating rod as necessary.

---

19 Inlet and exhaust manifold (Daf 55, Daf 66, and Volvo 66 models) – removal and refitting

1 Disconnect the battery negative terminal.

2 Remove the carburettor as described in Section 13.

3 Detach the vacuum hose from the inlet manifold.

4 Extract the spring clip and remove the intermediate throttle arm from the inlet manifold.

5 Unscrew the exhaust pipe to manifold retaining nuts, then loosen

Fig. 3.27 Choke control diaphragm unit components (Volvo 343 models)

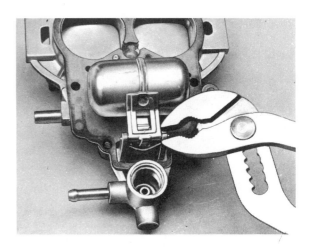

Fig. 3.28 Retaining the float pivot pin (Volvo 343 models)

Fig. 3.29 Manifold retaining nut locations (except Volvo 343 models)

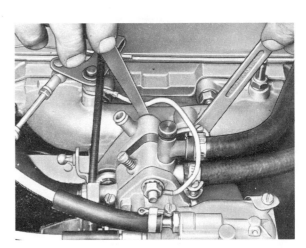

Fig. 3.30 Checking the flange clearance (except Volvo 343 models)

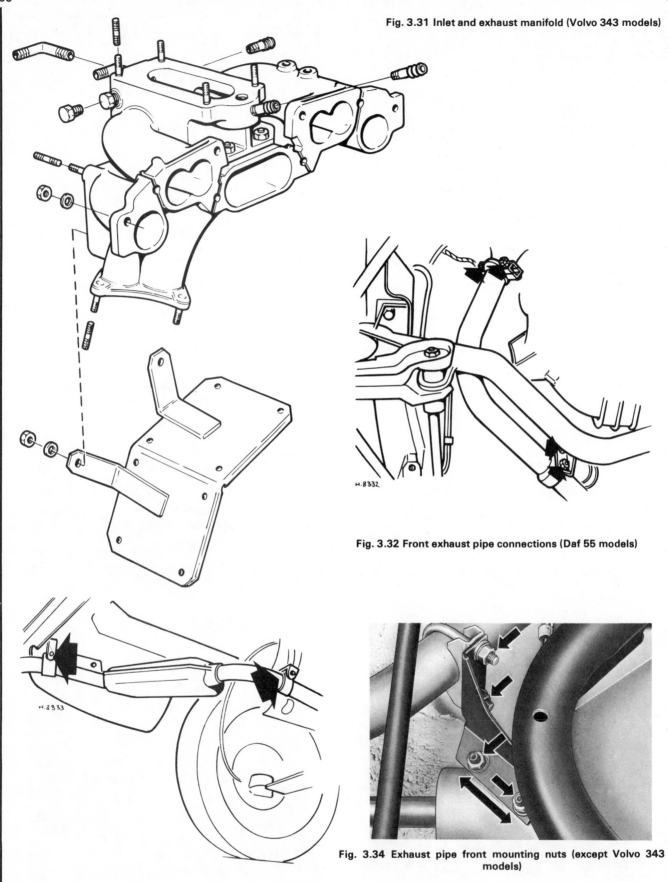

Fig. 3.31 Inlet and exhaust manifold (Volvo 343 models)

Fig. 3.32 Front exhaust pipe connections (Daf 55 models)

Fig. 3.34 Exhaust pipe front mounting nuts (except Volvo 343 models)

Fig. 3.33 Rear exhaust pipe mountings (Daf 55 models)

21.3A Exhaust system to manifold clamp (Daf 66 models)

21.3B Exhaust clutch housing mounting (Daf 66 models)

21.4 Exhaust system mounting rubbers (Daf 66 models)

21.5A Exhaust system section joint

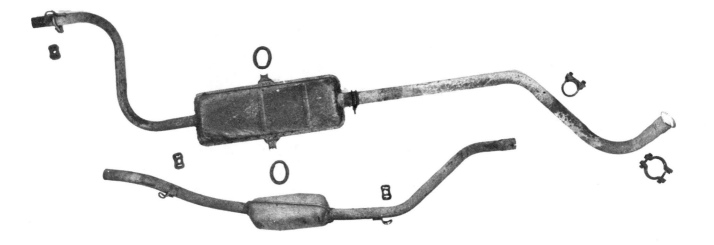

21.5B Exhaust system components (Daf 66 models)

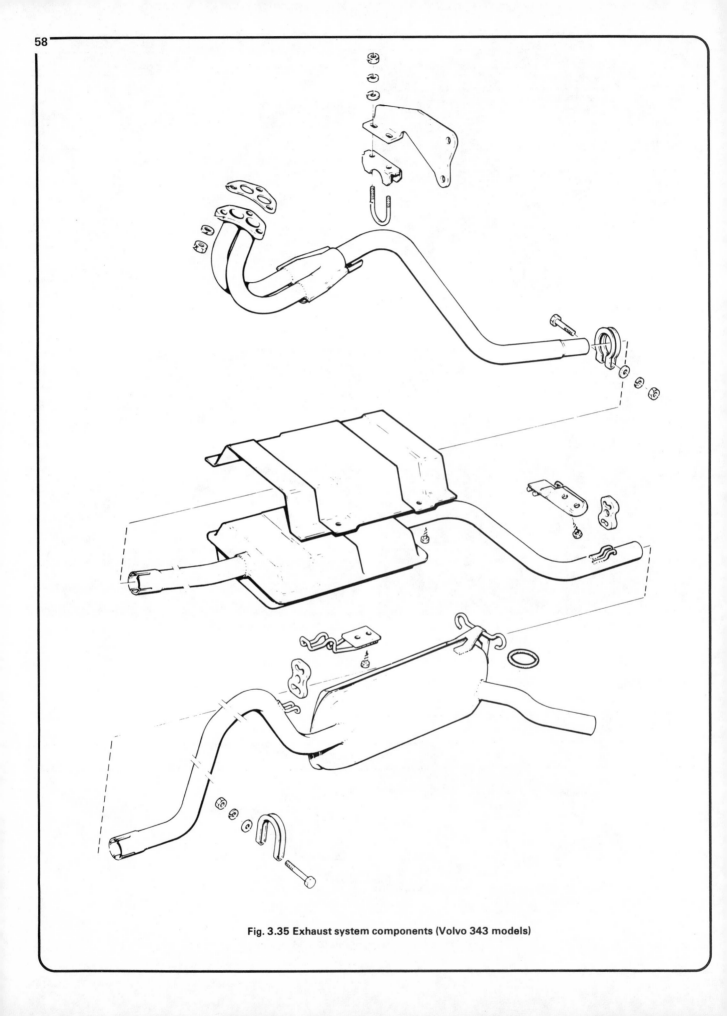

Fig. 3.35 Exhaust system components (Volvo 343 models)

the mounting bolts at the clutch housing and pull the exhaust pipe from the exhaust manifold.

6 Unscrew and remove the manifold retaining nuts and washers, withdraw the heatshield, and lift the manifold assembly from the engine (photo).

7 Do not separate the two manifolds, if one is defective both must be renewed.

8 Thoroughly clean the cylinder head and manifold faces and examine the manifolds for damage and deterioration.

9 Refitting is a reversal of removal, but the following additional points should be noted:

  (a) Always fit a new gasket
  (b) Fit the exhaust pipe to the manifold before tightening the clutch housing mounting
  (c) Tighten all nuts to the correct specified torque wrench settings; when tightening the carburettor mounting nuts the distance from the hot spot flange to the manifold must not be less than 0.028 in (0.7 to 0.8 mm)
  (d) Adjust the carburettor as described in Section 12
  (e) Adjust the vacuum control micro-switch as described in Chapter 6

20 Inlet and exhaust manifold (Volvo 343 models) – removal and refitting

1 Disconnect the battery negative terminal.

2 Detach the filler cap then remove the windscreen washer reservoir.

3 Remove the carburettor as described in Section 17.

4 Detach the vacuum hoses from the inlet manifold.

5 Detach the heating and crankcase ventilation hoses.

6 Remove the engine guard plates.

7 Unscrew the exhaust pipe-to-manifold vents, detach the mounting at the starter motor and pull the exhaust pipe from the manifold.

8 Unscrew and remove the manifold retaining nuts and washers, withdraw the heatshield, and lift the manifold assembly from the engine.

9 Thoroughly clean the cylinder head and manifold faces and examine the manifolds for damage and deterioration.

10 Refitting is a reversal of removal but the following additional points should be noted:

  (a) Always fit a new gasket
  (b) Tighten all nuts to the correct specified torque wrench setting but make sure that the components are tightened in the following sequence: manifold to cylinder head, exhaust pipe to manifold, exhaust mounting to clutch housing
  (c) Adjust the carburettor as described in Section 16

  (d) Adjust the vacuum control micro-switch when fitted, as described in Chapter 6

21 Exhaust system (Daf 55, Daf 66, and Volvo 66 models) – removal and refitting

1 Jack up the front and rear of the car and support it adequately on the axle-stands.

2 If the retaining nuts are rusted, the application of penetrating oil will assist in subsequent operations.

3 Unscrew and remove the exhaust pipe to manifold retaining nuts and the clutch housing mounting nuts; on 100 engine models remove the mounting clamp (photos).

4 Disconnect the exhaust system suspension rubbers or mountings and withdraw the complete system forwards (photo).

5 Loosen the clamps and remove the front and rear sections as necessary (photo); if the joints are rusted together a little heat from a blowlamp will free them.

6 Refitting is a reversal of removal but loosen the clutch housing mounting bracket and delay tightening the nuts until the system has been secured to the exhaust manifold. Make sure that at no point is the exhaust pipe closer than 0.78 in (20 mm) to the transmission guard panel(s).

22 Exhaust system (Volvo 343 models) – removal and refitting

1 Jack up the front and rear of the car and support it adequately on axle-stands.

2 If the retaining nuts are rusted, apply penetrating oil to them to facilitate removal.

3 Loosen the rear-to-control section clamps, detach the rear section mounting rubbers and withdraw the rear section from the centre section.

4 Loosen the control-to-foremost section clamps, detach the control section mounting rubbers and withdraw the control section from the foremost section.

5 Detach the right-hand engine guard plate and unscrew the exhaust pipe-to-manifold retaining nuts.

6 Remove the mounting clamp at the starter motor and withdraw the front exhaust section.

7 Refitting is a reversal of removal but the following additional points should be noted:

  (a) When renewing the front section always fit a new gasket
  (b) Secure the front section to the manifold before tightening the mounting clamp

3 Fault diagnosis – fuel and exhaust systems

Symptom	Reason/s
Excessive fuel consumption	Air filter choked
	Leak in fuel tank, carburettor, or fuel lines
	Incorrect fuel level in float chamber
	Mixture too rich
	Faulty accelerator pump or out of adjustment
	Incorrect valve clearances (See Chapter 1)
	Brake binding (see Chapter 7)
	Tyres under-inflated
Insufficient fuel delivery or weak mixture	Float chamber needle valve stuck
	Faulty fuel pump
	Leak in fuel system
	Leaking manifold gasket or flange gasket
	Incorrect carburettor adjustment
	Faulty accelerator pump or out of adjustment

Chapter 4 Ignition system

Contents

Specifications

System type .... 12 volt battery and coil

Distributor

Make .... Ducellier
Type:
    Daf 55 (Standard) .... 4144 B
    Daf 55 (Marathon) and Daf 66/1100 .... 4168 A (can be replaced by type 4458 A)
    Daf 66/1300 .... 4502 A (can be replaced by type 6623 A)
    Volvo 66/1100 .... 4458 A
    Volvo 66/1300 .... 6623 A
    Volvo 343 6623
Contact breaker gap .... 0.016 to 0.020 in (0.4 to 0.5 mm)
Dwell angle:
    Daf 55, Daf 66 and Volvo 66 .... $55° \pm 2.75°$
    Volvo 343 .... $57° \pm 2.7°$
Direction of rotation (from above) .... Clockwise
Firing order .... 1–3–4–2 (No 1 cylinder furthest from radiator)
Ignition timing:
    1100 cc engines .... $0° \pm 1°$
    1300 cc engines .... $6° \pm 1°$ BTDC
    1400 cc engines .... $3° \pm 1°$ BTDC

Spark plugs

Type:
    Daf 55 .... Champion L87Y, AC44F or equivalent
    Daf 66 (up to 1972) .... Champion L87Y, AC43F or equivalent
    Daf 66 (1972 on) and Volvo 66 .... Eyquem 7055, AC42FS, Champion L92Y, Bosch W175T 35, or equivalent
    Volvo 343 .... Bosch W175T 35, Champion L87Y, AC42 FS, or equivalent
Gap .... 0.024 to 0.028 in (0.6 to 0.7 mm)

Torque wrench settings

	lbf ft	Nm
Spark plugs	10.85 to 14.47	15.0 to 20.0

---

1 General description

The ignition system is conventional and comprises a 12 volt battery, coil, distributor, and spark plugs. The distributor is driven by a skew gear on the camshaft.

Correct running of the engine depends on a spark occurring at the spark plugs at exactly the right moment in relation to engine speed and load.

The ignition system is divided into two circuits, the low tension (LT) circuit, and the high tension (HT) circuit.

Fig. 4.1 Adjusting the contact breaker points – adjustment screw arrowed

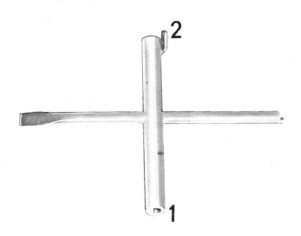

Fig. 4.2 Distributor adjustment tool

1 Vacuum cam fine adjustment
2 Vacuum cam toothed segment adjustment

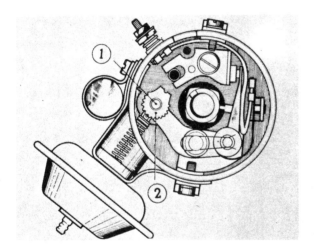

Fig. 4.3 Vacuum advance adjustment tool engagement point

1 Cam   2 Serrated segment

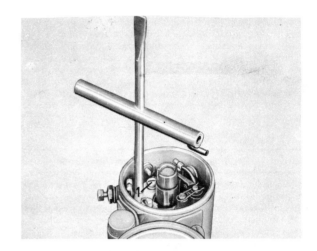

Fig. 4.4 Adjusting the contact point gap with the special tool

1 Locking screw

Fig. 4.5 Removing the contact breaker arm and lead

Fig. 4.6 Timing mark location on Daf 55 models

The low tension (sometimes known as the primary) circuit consists of the battery, lead to the ignition switch, lead from the ignition switch to the low tension or primary coil windings (terminal +), and the lead from the low tension coil windings (terminal -) to the contact breaker points and condenser in the distributor.

The high tension (or secondary) circuit consists of the high tension or secondary coil windings, the HT lead from the centre of the coil to the centre terminal of the distributor cap, the rotor arm, spark plug leads and spark plugs.

The system functions in the following manner. Low tension voltage in the coil produces an electromagnetic field around the secondary windings. When the contact breaker points separate, the collapse of the magnetic field induces a much higher voltage in the secondary windings which is fed via the distributor cap and carbon brush to the rotor arm. The rotor arm turns at half engine speed and releases the HT current to each of the four segments in the distributor cap as required. The current finally reaches the spark plug electrodes and the spark is produced.

The ignition advance is controlled both mechanically and by a vacuum operated system. The mechanical mechanism comprises weights which move out from the distributor shaft under centrifugal force as the engine speed rises, and the distributor cam is thus rotated and the spark advanced. The weights are held in position by the light springs, and it is the tension of these springs which control the amount of advance.

The vacuum control consists of a diaphragm, one side of which is connected via a small pipe to the carburettor and the other side to the contact breaker plate. Depression in the inlet manifold and carburettor (which varies with engine speed and throttle opening) causes the diaphragm to move, thus advancing or retarding the spark. A fine degree of control is achieved by a spring in the vacuum assembly.

The contact points are of the self-cleaning type where the action of the vacuum advance moves the points in relation to each other, thus ensuring that the electrical contact occurs over a wide area of the contact points.

2   Contact breaker points – adjustment and lubrication

1   To check the contact breaker gap, first remove the distributor cap by unclipping the two springs.
2   Pull off the rotor arm and remove the plastic dust shield, if fitted.
3   Turn the crankshaft pulley bolt with a spanner, until the heel of the movable contact breaker is on the high point of the cam.
4   Insert a feeler gauge between the two contact breaker points (photo) and check that the gap is as given in Specifications. If adjustment is required, loosen the baseplate securing screw and move the contact breaker point until the correct feelergauge blade is a sliding fit between the points. Tighten the screw and recheck the adjustment. If available, use the special adjustment tool (see Fig. 4.2) obtainable from motor accessory shops.
5   Periodically, inject two or three drops of engine oil through the hole in the distributor baseplate to lubricate the advance mechanism.
6   Lubricate the cam with a thin film of lithium based grease and apply one or two drops of engine oil to the felt pad at the top of the distributor shaft.
7   Refit the dust shield, rotor and distributor cap.
8   Where a dwell meter is available, check the contact points gap and dwell angle in accordance with Specifications and make any final adjustments as previously described.

3   Contact breaker points – renovation or renewal

1   Remove the distributor cap, rotor and dust shield (if fitted), and prise the contact breaker points apart. If they are discoloured or pitted, remove them as follows.
2   Slide the spring clip off the moving contact pivot post and carefully lift the contact breaker arm and spring from the baseplate (photo).
3   Disconnect the ignition low tension lead from the distributor then unscrew the inner terminal nut until the contact breaker lead can be released from the inner terminal.
4   Unscrew and remove the fixed contact retaining screw and lift the screw and contact point from the baseplate.
5   Do not disturb the vacuum advance serrated cam setting as this

requires special equipment to adjust correctly.
6   Where only small pips or craters appear on the contact point surfaces, these may be removed by using an oilstone, but care should be taken to retain the original contour of the points. If the contact points are badly worn, they must be renewed.
7   Refitting is a reversal of removal but the following additional points should be noted:

  (a) Thoroughly clean the contact points
  (b) Lubricate the moving contact pivot post with a little engine oil
  (c) Clean the baseplate with a fuel moistened cloth to prevent the points being contaminated
  (d) Adjust the points gap as described in Section 2

4   Condenser – testing, removal and refitting

1   The condenser acts as a buffer by absorbing the surges of current caused by the opening and closing of the contact points; it thus reduced arcing, subsequent pitting and wear of the contact point surfaces.
2   Failure of the condenser will automatically affect the complete ignition circuit as the points will be prevented from functioning correctly.
3   One simple way to test the condenser is to switch on the ignition with the contact points closed, then separate them with a screwdriver blade. If this action is accompanied by a blue flash, a faulty condenser is indicated. Difficult starting, misfiring and discoloured points are other indications of a faulty condenser.
4   To remove the condenser, unscrew and remove the nut and detach the ignition lead from the distributor terminal, then unscrew and remove the inner nut and disconnect the condenser lead.
5   Unscrew and remove the single retaining screw and washers and withdraw the condenser.
6   Refitting is a reversal of removal.

5   Distributor – removal and refitting

1   Before removing the distributor it is helpful to mark the distributor housing position relative to the engine block; use a centre punch or touch-up paint.
2   Turn the engine until the timing marks (see Section 6) are aligned, with No 1 (furthest from radiator) piston at the top of its compression stroke.
3   Disconnect the HT leads from the spark plugs and from the centre terminal of the coil, then remove the distributor cap and note that the rotor is pointing towards the No 1 HT segment of the cap.
4   Disconnect the LT ignition lead from the distributor terminal.
5   Unscrew and remove the vertical bolt and withdraw the distributor clamp plate; the distributor can now be lifted from its recess (photos).
6   Refitting is a reversal of removal but the following additional points should be noted:

  (a) When inserting the distributor it will be necessary to turn the shaft a little in order to bring the drive lugs into alignment with the drivegear
  (b) Adjust the ignition timing as described in Section 6
  (c) Any difficulty encountered in refitting the distributor correctly or timing the ignition, may be due to incorrect installation of the drivegear (see Chapter 1)

6   Ignition timing – adjustment

One of two methods may be used to check the ignition timing, with a test bulb or with a stroboscope. Of these two methods the stroboscope is the more accurate.

Test bulb

1   Connect a 12 volt test lamp and leads between a good earth and the distributor LT terminal.
2   Rotate the crankshaft with a spanner on the pulley bolt in the normal direction of rotation, until No 1 piston (furthest from radiator) starts its compression stroke; this can be ascertained by removing No 1 spark plug and feeling the compression being generated with the finger.

3 Disconnect the HT lead from the coil.

4 Continue turning the crankshaft until the correct timing marks are in alignment. On Daf 55 models the 0° pointer on the timing cover must be in alignment with the notch in the crankshaft pulley. On all other models, the timing marks are on the flywheel periphery, and should be aligned with the cutaway on the clutch housing at the rear of the engine (photo). Refer to Specifications for the correct timing applicable to each model.

5 Loosen the distributor clamp and switch on the ignition.

6 If the test lamp is on, turn the distributor slightly clockwise until it goes out.

7 Turn the distributor anti-clockwise until the test lamp just lights up then tighten the clamp.

8 Test the setting by turning the engine one complete turn and observing when the lamp glows.

9 Switch off the ignition, remove the test lamp, and refit the HT lead to the coil.

Stroboscope (timing lamp)

10 Disconnect the vacuum pipe from the distributor and plug its end with a pencil or similar object.

11 To make subsequent operations easier, it is advisable to mark the timing marks with chalk or white paint.

12 Connect the timing light in accordance with the manufacturer's instructions (usually interposed between the end of No 1 spark plug HT lead and No 1 spark plug terminal).

13 Start the engine and make sure that the idling speed is below 800 rpm.

14 Point the timing light at the timing marks, and they will appear to be stationary. The correct marks should be in alignment, but if this is not the case, loosen the distributor clamp and turn it one way or the other until the setting is correct. Tighten the clamp and check the adjustment again.

15 With the timing light still connected, a check can be made on the operation of the advance mechanism by momentarily increasing the engine speed. The crankshaft pulley or flywheel mark will advance in relation to the fixed point if the mechanism is working correctly.

16 A similar check can be made on the vacuum advance by refitting the vacuum pipe and observing the additional advance.

17 When completed, remove the timing light and ensure that the spark plug and vacuum pipe connections are secure.

7 Distributor – dismantling and reassembly

1 The distributor is designed to operate without the need for major dismantling, and when wear does eventually take place at a high mileage it is recommended that a new or reconditioned unit is obtained. However, for those who wish to dismantle and repair a faulty or worn distributor, the following points are given as a guide.

2 Check that spare parts are available before starting work.

3 Note the position of the serrated cam in relation to the vacuum diaphragm spring connection as this affects the vacuum advance characteristics. If necessary, the distributor should be taken to a suitable equipped garage or auto electrician to have the setting checked.

4 The mainshaft can be removed after driving out the drive dog retaining pin.

5 Where possible mark items in relation to each other to ensure correct reassembly, in particular the drive dog and mainshaft.

8 Coil – description

The coil is bolted to the left-hand side of the cylinder block below the distributor (photo). Accurate testing of the coil requires specialised equipment and is therefore best left to an auto electrician. Alternatively, if it is thought to be faulty, a new coil should be fitted and a comparison made with the original unit.

Besides periodically cleaning the coil there is little that can be done in the way of maintenance. Make sure the low tension (LT) leads are connected to their correct terminals; failure to do this can result in a 60% loss of efficiency. The LT wire from the distributor must be connected to the negative (-) terminal on the coil, the positive (+) terminal being connected to the ignition switch lead.

2.4 Checking the contact breaker points gap

3.2 Contact breaker point components

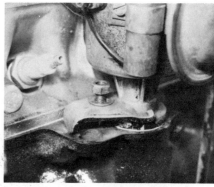
5.5A Distributor clamp location

5.5B Removing the distributor

6.4 Flywheel timing mark location (Daf 66 model shown)

8.1 Location of the coil

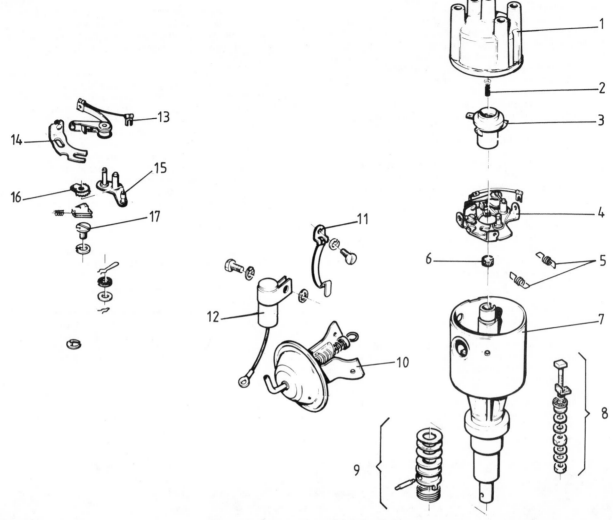

Fig. 4.7 Exploded view of the distributor

1	Cap
2	Carbon brush
3	Rotor arm
4	Baseplate
5	Advance weight return springs
6	Lubrication felt
7	Housing
8	Terminal bolt
9	Drive dog
10	Vacuum diaphragm assembly
11	Cap retaining clip
12	Condenser
13	Contact breaker arm and lead
14	Fixed contact
15	Vacuum advance arm
16	Vacuum adjustment serrated cam
17	Fixed contact retaining screw

Fig. 4.8 Flywheel timing marks visible through the clutch housing aperture (except Daf 55 models)

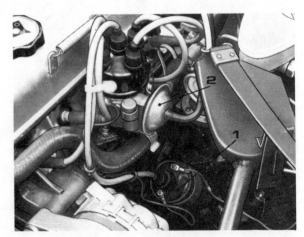

Fig. 4.9 Location of coil 1 and distributor 2

Measuring plug gap. A feeler gauge of the correct size (see ignition system specifications) should have a slight 'drag' when slid between the electrodes. Adjust gap if necessary

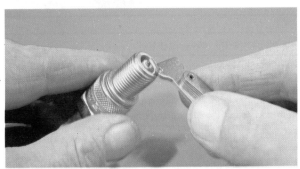

Adjusting plug gap. The plug gap is adjusted by bending the earth electrode inwards, or outwards, as necessary until the correct clearance is obtained. Note the use of the correct tool

Normal. Grey-brown deposits, lightly coated core nose. Gap increasing by around 0.001 in (0.025 mm) per 1000 miles (1600 km). Plugs ideally suited to engine, and engine in good condition

Carbon fouling. Dry, black, sooty deposits. Will cause weak spark and eventually misfire. Fault: over-rich fuel mixture. Check: carburettor mixture settings, float level and jet sizes; choke operation and cleanliness of air filter. Plugs can be re-used after cleaning

Oil fouling. Wet, oily deposits. Will cause weak spark and eventually misfire. Fault: worn bores/piston rings or valve guides; sometimes occurs (temporarily) during running-in period. Plugs can be re-used after thorough cleaning

Overheating. Electrodes have glazed appearance, core nose very white – few deposits. Fault: plug overheating. Check: plug value, ignition timing, fuel octane rating (too low) and fuel mixture (too weak). Discard plugs and cure fault immediately

Electrode damage. Electrodes burned away; core nose has burned, glazed appearance. Fault: pre-ignition. Check: as for 'Overheating' but may be more severe. Discard plugs and remedy fault before piston or valve damage occurs

Split core nose (may appear initially as a crack). Damage is self-evident, but cracks will only show after cleaning. Fault: pre-ignition or wrong gap-setting technique. Check: ignition timing, cooling system, fuel octane rating (too low) and fuel mixture (too weak). Discard plugs, rectify fault immediately

9 Spark plugs and HT leads – general

1   Correct functioning of the spark plugs is vital for peak engine performance and efficiency, and therefore only the recommended type (see Specifications) should be fitted.

2   At intervals of 3000 miles (5000 km) remove the spark plugs, clean them and adjust the electrode gaps to the dimensions given in Specifications. Cleaning can be carried out with a wire brush but it is preferable to take them to a service station and have them sand blasted.

3   The spark plug gap is of prime importance as, if incorrect, the combustion of the fuel/air mixture within the engine will be seriously impaired. The gap should be measured with a feeler gauge and if adjustment is necessary, the outer electrode must be bent accordingly. Never bend the centre electrode otherwise damage will occur and the plug insulation will break down.

4   At intervals of 6000 miles (10 000 km) the spark plugs should be renewed. Always check the gap of new plugs before fitting them.

5   The condition and appearance of the spark plugs will tell much about the condition and tune of the engine (Fig. 4.10).

6   If the insulator nose is white in colour with no deposits, a weak mixture is indicated or alternatively the plug is too hot (a hot plug transfers heat away from the electrode slowly – a cold plug transfers it away quickly).

7   Black soot deposits on the insulator nose indicate a rich mixture and, if oil is also present, the engine is likely to be well worn.

8   Light tan to greyish brown deposits on the insulator nose indicate that the mixture is correct and the engine is in good condition.

9   If the plug has a faulty internal seal (a relatively unusual occurance), the white portion of the insulator may exhibit long brown tapering stains. If this is the case, the plug must be renewed, as gas is escaping from the combustion chamber.

10 As the cylinder head is made of aluminium alloy, care must be taken when installing the spark plugs to prevent damage to the threads in the cylinder head. It is recommended that a little engine oil or graphite grease is applied to the threads and that the spark plugs are screwed in as far as possible with the fingers. Finally tighten the spark plugs to the correct torque wrench setting.

11 Wipe the HT leads occasionally with a rag and always connect them in the correct order.

12 The interior of the distributor cap should be periodically wiped clean and the carbon brush checked for freedom of movement; it should return to its original position after being depressed into the cap against the spring. At the same time check that the HT leads are fully entered into the distributor cap terminals.

10 Ignition system – fault finding

By far the majority of breakdown and running troubles are caused

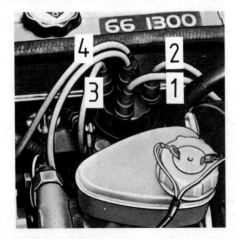

Fig. 4.10 Correct location of the spark plug leads (No 1 furthest from radiator)

by faults in the ignition system either in the low tension or high tension circuits.

There are two main symptoms indicating ignition faults. Either the engine will not start or fire, or the engine is difficult to start and misfires. If it is a regular misfire, ie; the engine is running on only four or five cylinders, the fault is almost sure to be in the secondary or high tension circuit. If the misfiring is intermittent, the fault could be in either the high or low tension circuits. If the car stops suddenly, or will not start at all, it is likely that the fault is in the low tension circuit. Loss of power and overheating, apart from faulty carburation settings, are normally due to faults in the distributor or to incorrect ignition timing.

11 Fault diagnosis – engine fails to start

1   If the engine fails to start and the car was running normally when it was last used, first check that there is fuel in the petrol tank. If the engine turns over normally on the starter motor and the battery is evidently well charged, then the fault may be in either the high or low tension circuits. First check the HT circuit. If the battery is known to be fully charged, the ignition light comes on and the starter motor fails to turn the engine check the tightness of the leads on the battery terminals and also the secureness of the earth lead to its connection to the body. It is quite common for the leads to have worked loose, even if they look and feel secure. If one of the battery terminal posts gets very hot when trying to work the starter motor this is a sure indication of a faulty connection to that terminal.

2   One of the commonest reasons for bad starting is wet or damp spark plug leads and distributor. Remove the distributor cap. If condensation is visible internally dry the cap with a rag and also wipe over the leads. Refit the cap.

3   If the engine still fails to start, check that the current is reaching the plugs, by disconnecting each plug lead in turn at the spark plug end, holding the end of the cable about $\frac{3}{16}$ inch (5 mm) away from the cylinder block. Spin the engine on the starter motor.

4   Sparking between the end of the cable and the block should be fairly strong with a strong regular blue spark. (Hold the lead with rubber to avoid electric shocks). If current is reaching the plugs then remove them and clean and regap them to 0.025 inch (0.60 mm). The engine should now start.

5   If there is no spark at the plug leads take off the HT lead from the centre of the distributor cap and hold it to the block as before. Spin the engine on the starter once more. A rapid succession of blue sparks between the end of the lead and the block indicate that the coil is in order and that the distributor cap is cracked, the rotor arm faulty, or the carbon brush in the top of the distributor cap is not making good contact with the spring on the rotor arm. Possibly, the points are in bad condition. Renew them as described in this Chapter, Sections 2 and 3.

6   If there are no sparks from the end of the lead from the coil check the connections at the coil end of the lead. If it is in order start checking the low tension circuit.

7   Use a 12v voltmeter or a 12v bulb and two lengths of wire. With the ignition switched on and the points open, test between the low tension wire to the coil (it is marked SW or +) and earth. No reading indicates a break in the supply from the ignition switch. Check the connections at the switch to see if any are loose. Refit them and the engine should run. A reading shows a faulty coil or condenser, or broken lead between the coil and the distributor.

8   Take the condenser wire off the points assembly and with the points open test between the moving point and earth. If there is now a reading then the fault is in the condenser. Fit a new one as described in this Chapter, Section 4, and the fault is cleared.

9   With no reading from the moving point to earth, take a reading between earth and the CB or negative (-) terminal of the coil. A reading here shows a broken wire which will need to be renewed between the coil and distributor. No reading confirms that the coil has failed and must be renewed, after which the engine will run once more. Remember to refit the condenser wire to the points assembly. For these tests it is sufficient to separate the points with a piece of dry paper while testing with the points open.

12 Fault diagnosis – engine misfires

1   If the engine misfires regularly run it at a fast idling speed. Pull off each of the plug caps in turn and listen to the note of the engine. Hold

the plug cap in a dry cloth or with a rubber glove as additional protection against a shock from the HT supply.

2   No difference in engine running will be noticed when the lead from the defective circuit is removed. Removing the lead from one of the good cylinders will accentuate the misfire.

3   Remove the plug lead from the end of the defective plug and hold it about $\frac{3}{16}$ inch (5 mm) away from the block. Re-start the engine. If the sparking is fairly strong and regular the fault must lie in the spark plug.

4   The plug may be loose, the insulation may be cracked, or the points may have burnt away giving too wide a gap for the spark to jump. Worse still, one of the points may have broken off.

5   If there is no spark at the end of the plug lead, or if it is weak and intermittent, check the ignition lead from the distributor to the plug. If the insulation is cracked or perished, renew the lead. Check the connections at the distributor cap.

6   If there is still no spark, examine the distributor cap carefully for tracking. This can be recognised by a very thin black line running between two or more electrodes, or between an electrode and some other part of the distributor. These lines are paths which now conduct electricity across the cap thus letting it run to earth. The only answer is a new distributor cap.

7   Apart from the ignition timing being incorrect, other causes of misfiring have already been dealt with under the section dealing with the failure of the engine to start. To recap – these are that:

(a) *The coil may be faulty giving an intermittent misfire*

(b) *There may be a damaged wire or loose connection in the low tension circuit*

(c) *The condenser may be short circuiting*

(d) *There may be a mechanical fault in the distributor (broken driving spindle or contact breaker spring)*

8   If the ignition timing is too far retarded, it should be noted that the engine will tend to overheat, and there will be quite a noticeable drop in power. If the engine is overheating and the power is down, and the ignition timing is correct, then the carburettor should be checked, as it is likely that this is where the fault lies.

Chapter 5 Clutch

Contents

Specifications

Clutch type
Daf 55 .... Centrifugal, drum and shoe segment
Daf 66, Volvo 66, Volvo 343 .... Centrifugal, disc, and roller pressure plate

Clutch engagement speeds
Daf 55:
    Primary .... 800 to 1000 rpm
    Secondary .... 2250 to 2400 rpm
Daf 66, Volvo 66, Volvo 343:
    Starts to engage .... 1050 to 1200 rpm
    Fully engaged .... 2300 to 2500 rpm
Clutch release speed (declutching mechanism) .... 2000 rpm

Clutch plate diameter
Daf 66, Volvo 66 .... 6.3 in (160 mm)
Volvo 343 .... 7.1 in (181.5 mm)

Clutch return springs extended length
All models except Daf 55 .... 2.1 in (53.0 mm)

Pivot pin protrusion
Daf 55 models:
    Light metal segments .... 1.01 to 1.02 in (25.75 to 25.95 mm)
    Heavy steel segments .... 0.96 to 0.97 in (24.4 to 24.6 mm)

Clutch shaft spline lubricant .... Molykote BR2 – 8 or equivalent

Torque wrench settings

	lbf ft	Nm
Clutch cover bolts	13 to 16	18 to 22
Clutch housing bolts	32	45
Bearing housing bolts (Volvo 343 models only) ...	17 to 17.5	23 to 24

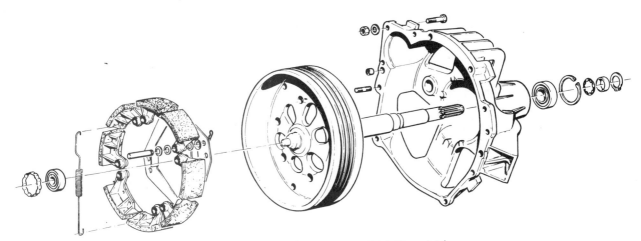

Fig. 5.1 Centrifugal clutch components (Daf 55 models)

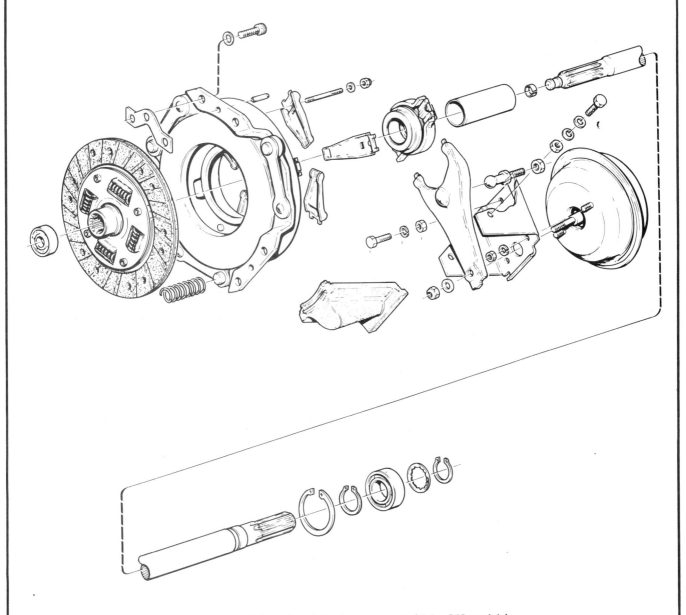

Fig. 5.2 Centrifugal clutch components (Volvo 343 models)

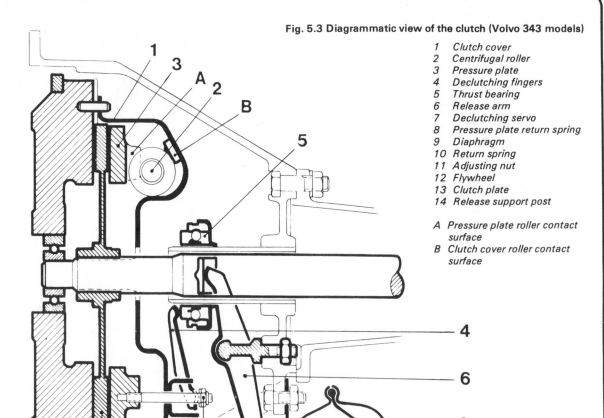

Fig. 5.3 Diagrammatic view of the clutch (Volvo 343 models)

1 Clutch cover
2 Centrifugal roller
3 Pressure plate
4 Declutching fingers
5 Thrust bearing
6 Release arm
7 Declutching servo
8 Pressure plate return spring
9 Diaphragm
10 Return spring
11 Adjusting nut
12 Flywheel
13 Clutch plate
14 Release support post

A Pressure plate roller contact surface
B Clutch cover roller contact surface

X = 7 MM

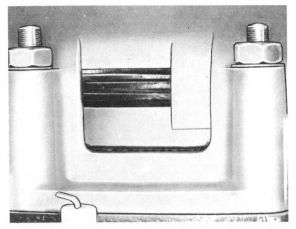

Fig. 5.4 Clutch lining inspection hole (Daf 66 models)

Fig. 5.5 Clutch inspection hole (Volvo models)

Fig. 5.6 Removing the clutch housing (Daf 55 models)

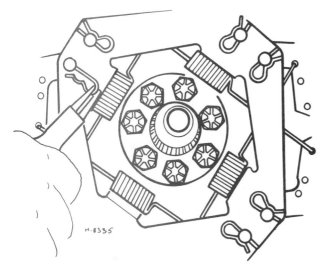

Fig. 5.7 Removing the spring clips retaining the clutch shoe plate

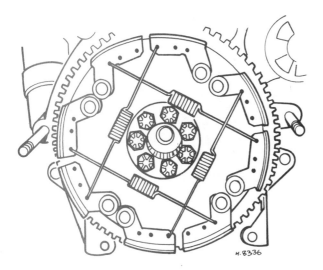

Fig. 5.8 Correct fitted position of the heavy steel segment clutch shoes (Daf 55 models)

1   General description

A centrifugal clutch is fitted to all models and engagement occurs at a predetermined engine speed. Daf 55 models are fitted with a shoe and drum centrifugal clutch. These are four primary and four secondary clutch shoes which are pivoted in the engine flywheel and operate against spring tension. A controlled engagement of the clutch is made by the primary shoes contacting the drum before the secondary shoes. Daf 66, Volvo 66 and Volvo 343 models are fitted with a centrifugal clutch closely resembling the normal manual type of clutch. A clutch disc is sandwiched between the flywheel and clutch cover pressure plate, and three metal rollers act as centrifugal weights to force the pressure plate against the clutch disc.

All Volvo models are equipped with a declutching servo mechanism, which effectively raises the engagement speed of the clutch to allow the transmission selector lever to be moved to position R or D when the engine is turning at a speed higher than the normal clutch engagement speed. The servo is operated electrically by a release valve connected to the engine inlet manifold vacuum, or by a switch located in the selector lever handgrip.

2   Clutch – maintenance

1   Due to the construction of the clutch fitted to the Daf 55 models, it is impossible to check the condition of the shoe linings without dismantling.

2   An inspection hole is provided at the top of the clutch housing on Daf 66 models and the thickness of the clutch disc linings should be checked (see Specifications) every 6000 miles (10 000 km).

3   On Volvo models an inspection hole is provided at the bottom of the clutch housing. Every 6000 miles (10 000 km) the thickness of the clutch disc linings should be checked (see Specifications). The clutch plate clearance should be checked at the same time, and adjustment made to the shims as necessary (see Section 7). The clutch servo adjustment should also be checked and reset as necessary.

3   Clutch (Daf 55 models) – removal and refitting

1   Remove the engine as described in Chapter 1 and place it on a firm workbench.

2   Unscrew and remove the clutch housing retaining nuts and bolts.

3   Withdraw the clutch housing together with the clutch shaft, clutch drum, and clutch pilot bearing; if the housing assembly will not release, it will be necessary to obtain a slide hammer and adaptor (Daf tool No 3-99-535640).

4   Extract the spring clips retaining the plate to the clutch shoe pivots, and withdraw the plate.

5   Note the fitted position of the clutch shoes then remove them together with the wave washers and unhook the return springs. Mark those items to facilitate their correct refitting.

6   Examine the clutch shoes for excessive wear of the linings and pivot holes, and renew them all if any are unserviceable. If the pivot pins are worn, the flywheel must be removed (see Chapter 1) and new pins fitted; this work is best entrusted to your local Daf/Volvo garage.

7   The shoe washers should be examined and if possible compared with new ones. Renew all the washers if any are unserviceable.

8   Refitting the clutch is a reversal of the removal procedure but the following additional points should be noted:

(a)   *If the pivot pins have been renewed, check that their protrusion from the face of the flywheel is in accordance with the dimension given in Specifications*

(b)   *When fitting new inner shoe washers, the convex sides should face the flywheel; if the original washers are refitted, they must have their concave sides facing the flywheel*

(c)   *Make sure that the thin wave washers are fitted on the outside of the shoes*

(d)   *Apply a little brake shoe grease to the pivot pins*

(e)   *Always fit new return springs*

(f)   *Where double wave washers are fitted, make sure that they are installed as shown in Fig. 5.11*

(g)   *Ensure that new shoes are of the identical type and weight as those removed. Two types are manufactured but are not interchangeable with each other*

Fig. 5.9 Correct fitted position of the light metal segment clutch shoes (Daf 55 models), showing the position of the flywheel collar (arrowed)

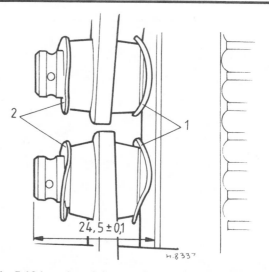

Fig. 5.10 Location of shoe washers on early Daf 55 models

1 Thick formed washer   2 Thin wave washer

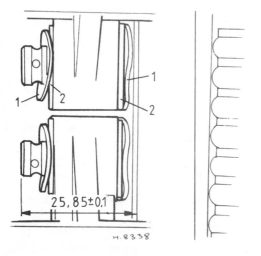

Fig. 5.11 Location of the shoe washers on late Daf 55 models

1 Thin wave washers   2 Thick plain washers

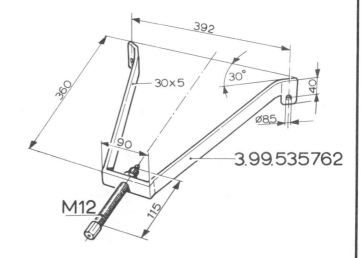

Fig. 5.12 Clutch housing puller dimensions (mm)

Fig. 5.13 Using a slide hammer to remove the clutch (Daf 66 models)

Fig. 5.14 Tightening the clutch cover bolts (Daf 66 models)

4 Clutch housing assembly (Daf 55 models) – dismantling and reassembly

1 Remove the clutch housing assembly as described in Section 3 of this Chapter.
2 With the clutch shaft splines uppermost, support the housing on suitable wooden blocks, then using a mallet and a further block of wood, drive the shaft and drum down through the bearing. On some models it will be necessary to remove a circlip, bush, and washer from the clutch shaft before it can be removed.
3 Extract the circlip from the housing and carefully drive at the bearing with a suitable metal punch.
4 Examine the clutch drum and bearing for excessive wear and renew each component as necessary.
5 Reassembly of the clutch housing assembly is a reversal of the removal procedure, but the following additional points should be noted:

   (a) If the clutch shaft pilot bearing was removed with the assembly, it must be reinstalled into the flywheel together with the corrugated star ring where fitted
   (b) Where a bearing lockring support is fitted, use a length of tubing of 1.0 in (25 mm) internal diameter to drive the toothed lockring into position, the teeth facing to the rear

5 Clutch (Daf 66 models) – removal and refitting

1 Remove the engine as described in Chapter 1 and place it on a firm workbench.
2 Extract the circlip from the splined end of the clutch shaft and withdraw the bush.
3 Unscrew and remove the clutch housing retaining nuts and bolts, and remove the front cover (photo).
4 Withdraw the clutch housing from the rear of the engine; if it will not release, it will be necessary to use a puller obtained from a tool agent or made up in accordance with Fig. 5.12. Remove the rear engine mountings first, and then bolt the puller into position and carefully withdraw the housing (photo).
5 If the clutch housing assembly was removed complete, use an Allen key to unscrew and remove the clutch cover retaining bolts, then lift the cover and clutch plate from the flywheel. If the clutch shaft is still in position, unscrew and remove the clutch cover bolts with the Allen key and use a slide hammer and adaptor (Daf tool No 3-99-535640) to remove the shaft, cover, and clutch plate from the flywheel (photo).
6 Where the clutch shaft pilot bearing is still attached to the shaft, use a soft head mallet to remove it.
7 Clean the surfaces of the flywheel and pressure plate with a petrol soaked rag, and examine them for excessive scoring. Light scoring is acceptable, but if it is very deep, the pressure plate unit must be renewed, and the flywheel re-machined within limits by a competent engineering firm.
8 Renew the clutch plate if the linings are worn to a thickness of 0.04 in (1 mm), or if the plate shows signs of general wear or distortion.

9 Refitting the clutch is a reversal of the removal procedure but the following additional points should be noted:

   (a) Install the pilot bearing into the flywheel if it has come out. Use a suitable tube (on the outer race only) to press it in until its outer race is flush with the flywheel. Clean the bearing inner bore and apply a thin film of Loctite 241
   (b) It is not necessary to centralise the clutch plate as the pressure plate is not in contact with it
   (c) Tighten the clutch cover bolts in diagonal sequence to the correct torque wrench setting given in Specifications
   (d) Apply a small amount of grease (see Specifications) to the splines on the clutch shaft to ensure free movement of the clutch plate
   (e) Install the clutch shaft to the housing before refitting the assembly to the engine, refer to Section 4 as necessary

6 Clutch housing assembly (Daf 66 models) – dismantling and reassembly

1 With the exception of the inner splines on the clutch shaft, the housing assembly is identical to that fitted to the Daf 55 and the procedure is therefore similar to the instructions given in Section 4.

7 Clutch (Volvo 66 models) – removal and refitting

1 Remove the engine as described in Chapter 1 and place it on a firm workbench.
2 Remove the starter motor (see Chapter 8).
3 Detach the clutch housing guard plate, then unscrew and remove the housing retaining nuts and bolts and withdraw the housing from the rear of the engine. If the housing will not release, or if the pilot bearing comes away from the flywheel, it will be necessary to use a puller obtained from a tool agent or constructed in accordance with Fig. 5.12. The pilot bearing is fitted with a corrugated star ring on some models to prevent it coming out.
4 When using the puller, the circlip must first be extracted from the rear of the housing, and the rear engine mountings removed to enable the puller to be bolted into position.
5 Early models may be fitted with a clutch cover similar to Daf 66 models and in this case reference should be made to Section 5 for details of the removal procedure, otherwise continue as follows.
6 Obtain special tool No 5945 (267345) from a tool agent or local Volvo garage and fit it to the rear of the engine. Alternatively have an assistant restrain the flywheel with a wide blade screwdriver inserted into the starter ring gears.
7 Using an Alley key, unscrew and remove the clutch cover retaining bolts and withdraw the assembly together with the clutch plate. At the same time, note the location and amount of shims fitted beneath the cover, also the three return springs.
8 Using a petrol soaked rag, clean the surfaces of the flywheel and pressure plate and examine them for excessive scoring; on the pressure place scoring is acceptable, but if very deep, the pressure plate unit must be renewed. If the flywheel is deeply scored, it may be

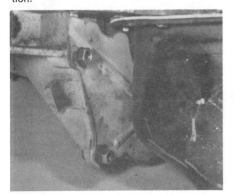

5.3 Removing the clutch housing front cover

5.4 The clutch cover assembled to the flywheel (Daf 66 models)

5.5 Clutch components (Daf 66 models)

re-machined within limits by a competent engineering firm.
9   Renew the clutch plate if the linings are worn to a thickness of less than 0.04 in (1 mm) or if the plate shows signs of general wear and distortion.
10 If the release levers are in need of adjustment (noticeable by a difference in height in their retracted position), they must be adjusted by a Volvo garage or clutch specialist using a special rig.
11 Refitting the clutch is a reversal of the removal procedure but the following additional points should be noted:

    (a) Refit the pilot bearing to the flywheel as necessary
    (b) The clutch plate must be fitted with the extended side towards the clutch cover
    (c) It is not necessary to centralise the clutch plate as the pressure plate is not in contact with it
    (d) Make sure that the 2.7 mm thick shims are fitted beneath the cover when the bolts are fitted, and then tighten the bolts to the correct torque setting, in diagonal sequence (see Specifications). Using a feeler gauge, check that the clearance between the flywheel and the clutch plate is within the limits given in Specifications. Make the check at three points and if incorrect, remove the adjacent shims and substitute two more shims (of identical thickness to each other) accordingly
    (e) Apply a small amount of grease (see Specifications) to the splines on the clutch shaft to ensure free movement of the clutch plate
    (f) Where necessary, install the clutch shaft to the housing before refitting the assembly to the engine; refer to Section 4 for this procedure
    (g) Adjust the clutch servo as described in Section 11

8   Clutch housing bearing (Volvo 66 models) – removal and refitting

1   Remove the clutch housing as described in Section 7.
2   Withdraw the thrust washer from the end of the clutch shaft, then extract the inner and outer bearing retaining circlips.
3   Using a gas (butane) blow torch, heat the housing around the bearing and withdraw the shaft and bearing from the housing; have an assistant tap the clutch end of the shaft during this operation.
4   Mount the shaft and bearing in a soft jawed vice and drive the shaft through the bearing.
5   Refitting the bearing is a reversal of the removal procedure, and it will be necessary to heat the housing when installing the bearing. Lightly lubricate the splines of the clutch shaft with grease before refitting the assembly.

9   Clutch thrust bearing (Volvo 66 models) – removal and refitting

1   Remove the clutch housing as described in Section 7.
2   Prise the spring clip from the hinge pin and disconnect the fork from it.
3   Withdraw the release fork from the guide and prise the hinge springs from the bearing. The thrust bearing can now be removed from the fork.
4   Refitting the thrust bearing is a reversal of the removal procedure but make sure that the servo cable is correctly located over the roller and adjust the servo diaphragm as described in Section 11.

10 Declutching servo (Volvo 66 models) – removal and refitting

1   Disconnect the vacuum hose from the front of the servo unit after detaching the left-hand guard panel from the engine.
2   Push the clutch release arm forward as far as possible, and plug the servo with a rubber seal; this will assist subsequent operations.
3   Unscrew the domed nut and disconnect the release cable from the servo operating rod.
4   Unscrew and remove the servo retaining nuts and remove it from the mounting bracket.
5   Remove the rubber seal from the servo.
6   Refitting is a reversal of removal but it will be necessary to adjust the release cable as described in Section 11. To assist fitting the cable,

Fig. 5.15 Removing the clutch cover shims (Volvo models)

Fig. 5.16 Checking the clutch plate clearance with a feeler gauge (Volvo models)

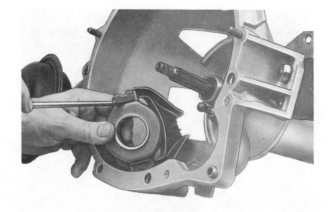

Fig. 5.17 Removing the thrust bearing (Volvo 66 models)

Fig. 5.18 Using vernier calipers to adjust the clutch servo diaphragm

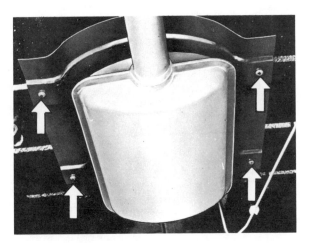

Fig. 5.19 Exhaust silencer heat shield retaining screws

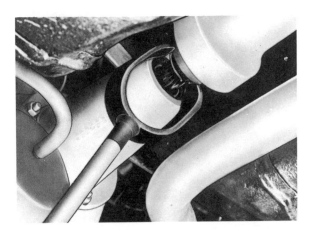

Fig. 5.20 Removing the propeller shaft with the special tool

pull the operating rod out from the servo as far as possible and insert a rubber seal.

11 Servo release cable (Volvo 66 models) – removal, refitting, and adjustment

1   Push the clutch release arm forward as far as possible and plug the servo with a rubber seal.
2   Unscrew and remove the domed nut, thus disconnecting the cable from the servo.
3   Unscrew the adjustment nut and detach the cable from the release arm.
4   Refitting the cable is a reversal of removal but make sure that it locates over the roller correctly; it will also be necessary to adjust the cable as described in the following paragraphs.
5   With the rubber seal removed from the servo, loosen the cable adjustment until there is free play, indicating that the internal diaphragm is touching the cover.
6   Using a length of dowel rod or preferably vernier calipers, measure the distance from the diaphragm to the top of the entry tube.
7   Progressively tighten the cable adjustment until this dimension has been increased by 0.28 in (7 mm) then reconnect the vacuum hose. The cable is now adjusted and the clutch should engage at the engine speeds given in Specifications.

12 Clutch servo release valve (Volvo 66 models) – removal and refitting

1   The release valve is located on the right-hand side inner wing panel and controls the vacuum for the servo unit.
2   Disconnect both vacuum hoses from the unit, noting their location.
3   Mark the two electrical leads to ensure that they are refitted in the correct position, then disconnect them from the unit.
4   Unscrew and remove the release valve retaining bolts and rubber connections and withdraw the unit.
5   Remove the attachment rubbers.
6   Refitting is a reversal of removal.

13 Clutch (Volvo 343 models) – removal and refitting

1   Jack up the front of the car and place it on axle-stands.
2   Unscrew and remove the nuts and washers, and remove the front exhaust clamp from the exhaust pipe.
3   Remove the starter motor (see Chapter 8).
4   Unscrew and remove the screws retaining the exhaust heat shield from above the exhaust silencer.
5   Push the propeller shaft to the rear as far as it will go and detach it from the clutch shaft. A special tool (No 5948) is made by the manufacturers but careful use of tyre levers is a satisfactory alternative.
6   Slide the propeller shaft forwards, disengage it from the transmission and lower it from the car.
7   Unscrew and remove the retaining nuts and bolts and withdraw the engine guard plate and the guard plate from the front of the clutch housing.
8   Pull the hose from the clutch servo unit.
9   Using a trolley jack and a block of wood, support the engine beneath the sump.
10   Unscrew and remove the nuts and bolts retaining both rear engine mountings, and remove them from the clutch housing and support bracket.
11   Unscrew and remove the bolts retaining the clutch housing and withdraw it from the rear of the engine.
12   The remaining procedure is identical to that for the Volvo 66 models and reference should therefore be made to Section 7, paragraphs 6 to 11 inclusive.

14 Clutch shaft and bearing (Volvo 343 models) – removal and refitting

1   Remove the clutch housing as described in Section 13.
2   Unscrew and remove the three nuts and washers, and separate

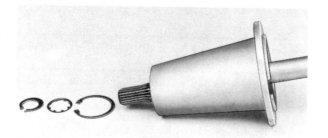

Fig. 5.21 Two circlips and lockring removed from the clutch shaft
(Volvo 343 models)

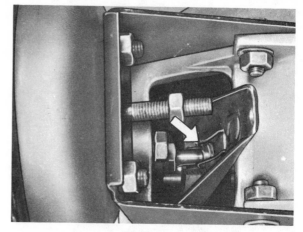

Fig. 5.22 Location of the clutch release arm retaining spring clip

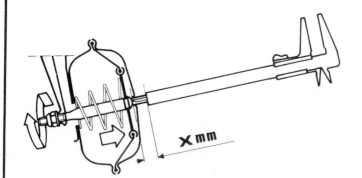

Fig. 5.24 Clutch thrust bearing removal (arrowed)

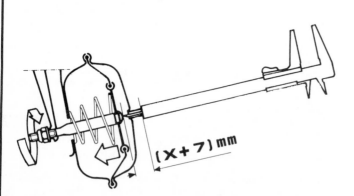

Fig. 5.23 Adjustment procedure for the clutch servo (Volvo
models)

Fig. 5.25 Location of thrust bearing retaining clips

the bearing housing and clutch shaft from the clutch housing.
3   Using circlip pliers, extract the two circlips and the lockring from the rear of the clutch shaft.
4   Heat the bearing housing with a gas Butane blowtorch then support the housing and drive out the shaft and bearing using a soft head mallet.
5   Mount the shaft and bearing in a vice and drive the shaft through the bearing; alternatively, use a suitable puller to remove the bearing.
6   Refitting is a reversal of removal, but the following additional points should be noted:

(a)   When refitting the bearing to the shaft apply a small amount of Loctite 241 to the inner diameter
(b)   Heat the housing when installing the shaft and bearing
(c)   Tighten all nuts and bolts to the correct torque wrench settings (see Specifications)
(d)   Adjust the clutch servo as described in Section 16

15   Clutch thrust bearing (Volvo 343 models) – removal and refitting

1   Remove the clutch housing as described in Section 13.
2   Prise the plastic cover from the clutch housing.
3   Unscrew and remove the clutch servo adjusting nut and detach the release arm.
4   Prise the spring clip from the hinge pin and disconnect the fork from it.
5   Withdraw the release fork from the guide and slide the bearing from the fork.
6   Refitting is a reversal of the removal but the following additional

points should be noted:

(a)   Make sure that the bearing and fork retaining spring clips are correctly located
(b)   Adjust the clutch servo as described in Section 16

16   Declutching servo (Volvo 343 models) – removal, refitting, and adjustment

1   Disconnect the vacuum hose from the front of the servo unit after detaching the left-hand guard panel from the engine.
2   Prise the plastic cover from the clutch housing.
3   Unscrew and remove the adjusting nut from the operating rod and detach the release arm.
4   Unscrew and remove the servo retaining nuts and withdraw it from the mounting bracket.
5   Refitting is a reversal of removal but before fitting the plastic cover and vacuum hose, the operating rod must be adjusted.
6   Loosen the adjusting nut until there is free play, indicating that the internal diaphragm is touching the cover.
7   Using a length of dowel rod or preferably vernier calipers, measure the distance from the diaphragm to the outer edge of the entry tube.
8   Screw the locknut up the operating rod to allow subsequent adjustment, then progressively tighten the adjusting nut until the dimension obtained in paragraph 7 has been increased by 0.28 in (7 mm).
9   Tighten the locknut and refit the plastic cover, vacuum hose, and engine guard plate.
10 With the clutch servo adjusted correctly, the clutch should engage in accordance with the engine speeds given in Specifications.

17   Fault diagnosis – clutch

Symptom	Reason/s
Judder when taking up drive	Loose engine mountings Worn friction surfaces or contaminated with oil Clutch shaft splines worn (except Daf 55 models) Worn pilot bearing in flywheel Clutch return springs weak (Daf 55 models) Clutch out of adjustment (except Daf 55 models)
Clutch fails to disengage	Seized pilot bearing in flywheel Seized clutch plate on clutch shaft (except Daf 55 models) Engine idling speed too high Clutch out of adjustment (except Daf 55 models)
Clutch fails to fully engage	Seized shoe segments (Daf 55 models) Worn shoe segments (Daf 55 models) Worn or oil contaminated clutch plate (except Daf 55 models) Faulty or seized clutch servo unit (except Daf 55 models)
Clutch servo inoperative	Broken release cable (where fitted) Internal diaphragm broken or leaking
Noise from clutch	Worn linings or internal components Worn thrust bearing (Volvo models only) Worn pilot bearing in flywheel

Chapter 6 Transmission and final drive

Contents

Specifications

Transmission type . . . . Automatic – continuously variable with two drivebelts, vacuum control system and centrifugal weights

Propeller shaft . . . . Aluminium tube with rubber coupling inserts

Primary variomatic transmission unit
Gear reduction ratio . . . . 1.53 : 1
Fluid for sliding discs . . . . ATF type A/A
Gear case oil . . . . Hypoid SAE 80 W

Secondary variomatic transmission unit
Gear reduction ratio:
    Daf 55 models pre chassis No 561257 . . . . 3.875 : 1
    Daf 55 models post chassis No 561257 . . . . 3.857 : 1
    Daf 66, Volvo 66 and Volvo 343 models . . . . 4.51 : 1
Fluid for sliding discs . . . . ATF type A/A
Gear case oil . . . . Hypoid SAE 80 W
Total transmission reduction ratio range . . . . 14.2 : 1 maximum, 3.8 : 1 minimum

Torque wrench settings

	lbf ft	Nm
Primary unit sealing sleeve nut (Daf 55 models)	65 to 72	90 to 100
Primary unit pinion shaft nut	29 to 43	40 to 60
Primary unit drain and level plugs	30	42
Axle tube retaining nut (Daf 55 models)	29 to 32	40 to 44
Secondary unit drain and level plugs	30	42
Secondary unit pinion shaft (Daf 55 models) pre chassis No 716706:		
$\frac{1}{2}$ in UNF	64 to 72	88 to 99
$\frac{9}{16}$ in UNF	85 to 94	117 to 130
Secondary unit pinion shaft (Daf 55 models) chassis No 716706 on	110 to 123	152 to 170
Secondary unit reduction case half (Daf 55 models)	12	16
Primary unit sealing sleeve nut (Daf 66 models)	100 to 115	138 to 159
Driveshaft bolts	23 to 26	32 to 36

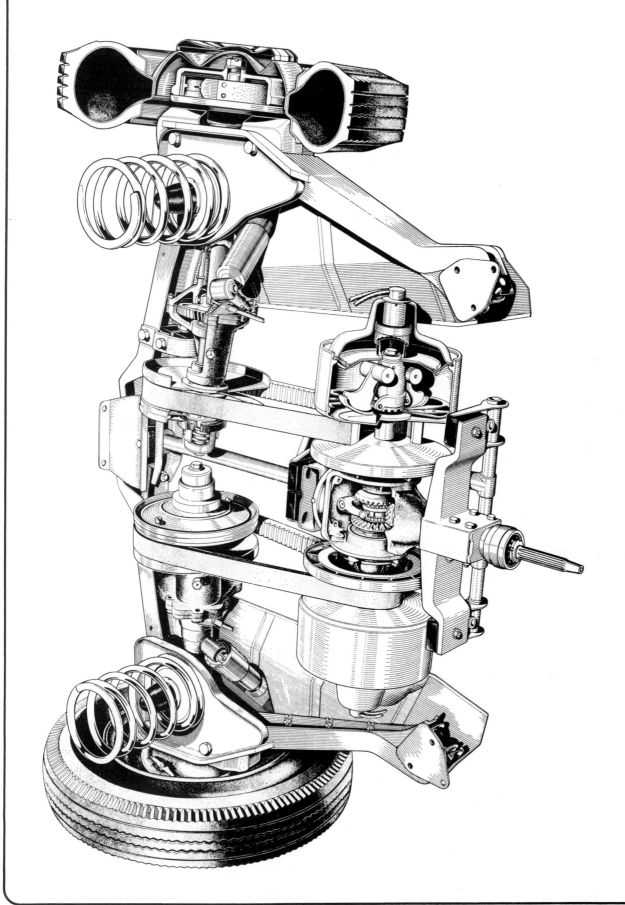

Fig. 6.1 Cutaway view of the Daf 55 model variomatic transmission

Secondary unit mounting nuts (Daf 66 and Volvo 66 models)	36 to 40	50 to 55
Primary unit sealing sleeve nut (Volvo 66 and Volvo 343 models) . . .	80 to 90	110 to 125
Secondary unit fixed disc nut	130 to 144	180 to 200
Secondary unit flange bolt	16 to 19	23 to 26
Secondary unit case half (Daf 66, Volvo 66 and Volvo 343 models) . .	13	18
Secondary unit rear cover	10 to 12	14 to 16
Primary unit retaining nuts	18 to 20	24 to 27
Secondary unit mounting nuts (Volvo 343 models)	18 to 20	24 to 27

1 General description

The transmission is of the automatic continously variable type. The drive is taken from the propeller shaft to the two primary pulleys, via two drivebelts to the two secondary pulleys, then through separate axle reduction gear-cases on Daf 55 models, or through a single reduction gear and differential unit on all other models, to the rear wheels (photos).

No differential unit is fitted to the Daf 55 models as both drivebelts operate independently, any difference in speed on cornering being taken up by the drivebelts.

The reduction ratio produced by a drivebelt running between two pulleys depends on the ratio of the pulley diameters. Changing the pulleys diameter changes the reduction ratio and this is the basic principle employed in the variomatic continuously variable transmission (VT). The CVT consists of two separate units connected by drivebelts. The primary unit comprises an input pinion shaft which is in constant mesh with two bevel gears. Forward or reverse gear is provided by engaging a sliding collar in either one of these bevel gears and as the collar is splined to the cross-shaft, the drive is transmitted to the primary pulleys at either side of the transmission, and so to the secondary pulleys.

On Daf 55 models the secondary pulleys are mounted on the individual axleshafts which incorporate reduction gears and form the secondary units. On all other models the secondary pulleys drive a chassis mounted secondary unit containing a spur gear reduction train, a differential and driveshaft flanges.

On the primary pulleys the inner discs are fixed and the outer ones may be moved in and out to vary the effective diameter of the pulley. On the secondary pulleys the outer discs are fixed and the inner ones can move outwards against the tension of an internal spring. As the primary pulley expands the drivebelt is pulled deeper into the secondary pulley against the spring loading; as the primary pulley contracts the belt relaxes its tension and the spring pushes the discs together and the effective diameter of the pulley increases.

The expansion and contraction of the primary pulley which results in the variations in the gear ratio is caused by:

(1) Centrifugal weights operating inside the disc which push the sliding discs towards the fixed inner discs as the engine speed increases

(2) Vacuum to the inner chambers which counteracts the action of the centrifugal weights

(3) Vacuum to the outer chambers which augments the action of the centrifugal weights to provide an overdrive effect

A vacuum valve, operated electrically by a throttle controlled micro-switch controls the application of the vacuum from the engine inlet manifold to the primary sliding disc chambers, so that when acceleration is required the action of the centrifugal weights is counteracted and the transmission reduction is increased to provide good acceleration (photo). When the throttle is at a cruising position, vacuum is channeled to the outer chambers which assist the centrifugal weights and provide an overdrive condition.

In addition to the characteristics already described, road conditions will automatically alter the position of the drivebelts. Increased resistance when ascending a hill will tension the drivebelts causing them to run deeper in the primary pulleys, thus providing greater overall reduction. On the overrun the converse will apply. A *low ratio hold* is provided whereby vacuum is continuously channeled to the inner sliding disc chambers.

The transmission is cooled by an air flow system through grilles at the front of the car (photo); the guard panels also serve to direct the air over the transmission. Because of this, the transmission should never be operated for long periods with the car stationary.

When the brakes are applied, the stoplight circuit activates the vacuum control valve to supply vacuum to the primary sliding disc inner chambers. At the same time the outer chambers are connected to atmospheric pressure. This action causes the sliding discs to move outwards quickly, and the transmission is therefore changed immediately to a low ratio ready for starting off again.

On all models the selector lever is provided with reverse (R), neutral (N), and drive (D) positions. On late Volvo 66 and all Volvo 343 models, the lever also has a park (P) position. With the lever in position P the reverse drive gear in the primary transmission is engaged and the forward gear is also mechanically locked. Starting the engine is only

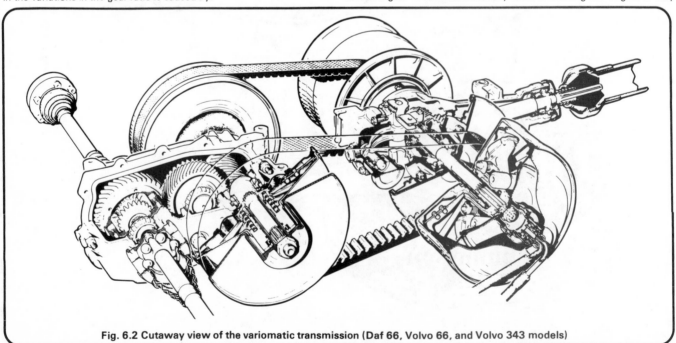

Fig. 6.2 Cutaway view of the variomatic transmission (Daf 66, Volvo 66, and Volvo 343 models)

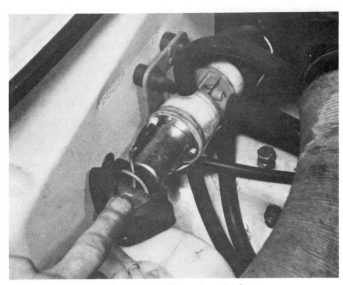

1.8 Vacuum control valve location (Daf 66 models)

1.11 Transmission cooling duct grille

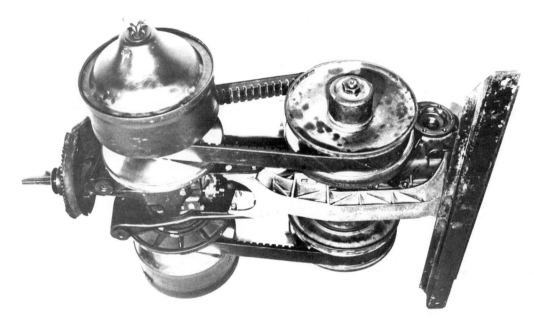

1.1A Transmission unit (Daf 66 models)

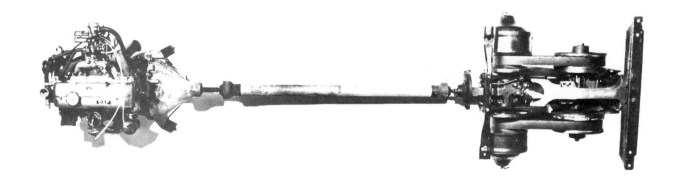

1.1B Engine and transmission unit (Daf 66 models)

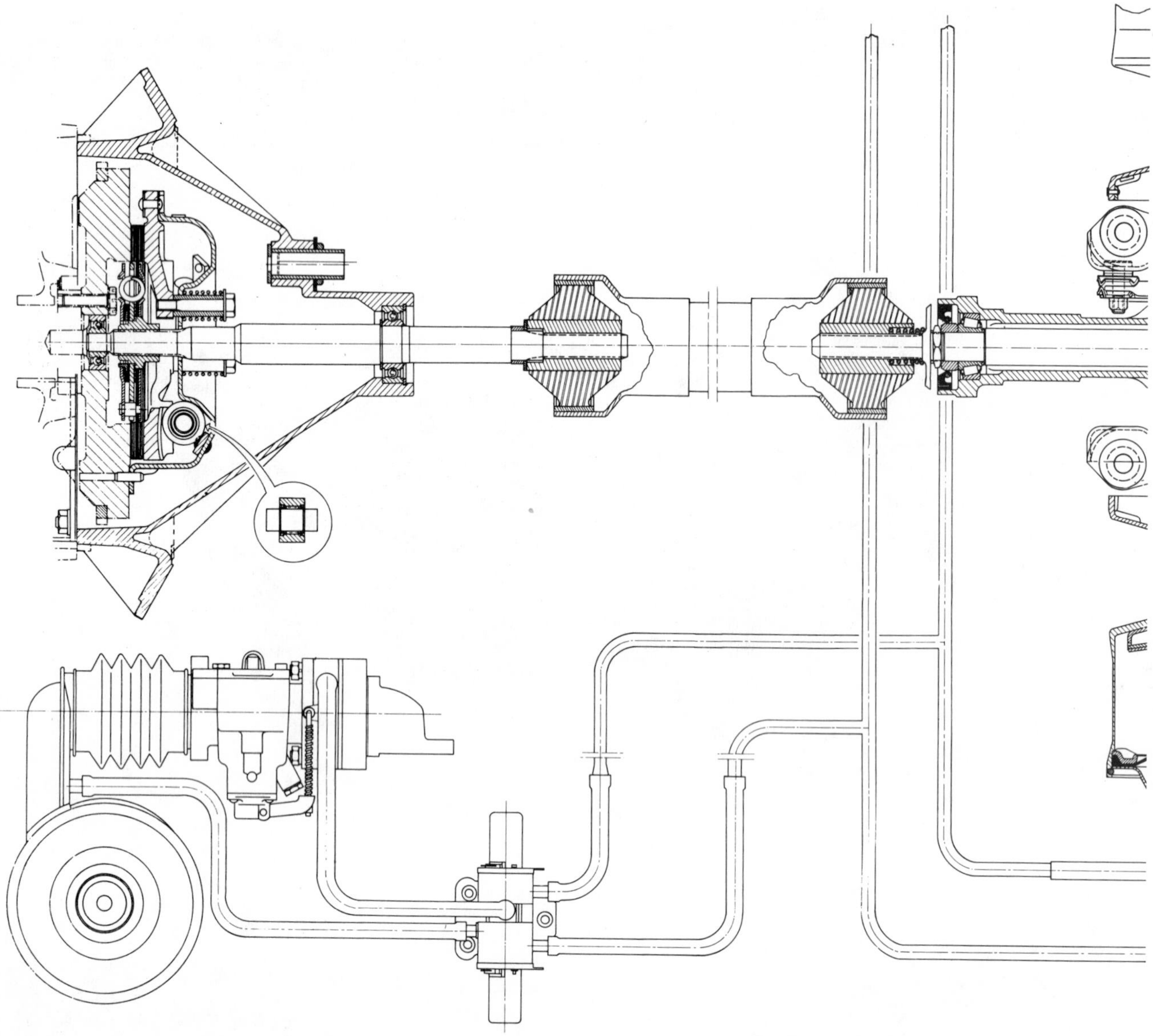

Fig. 6.3 Diagrammatic view of the variomatic transmission (Daf 66 models)

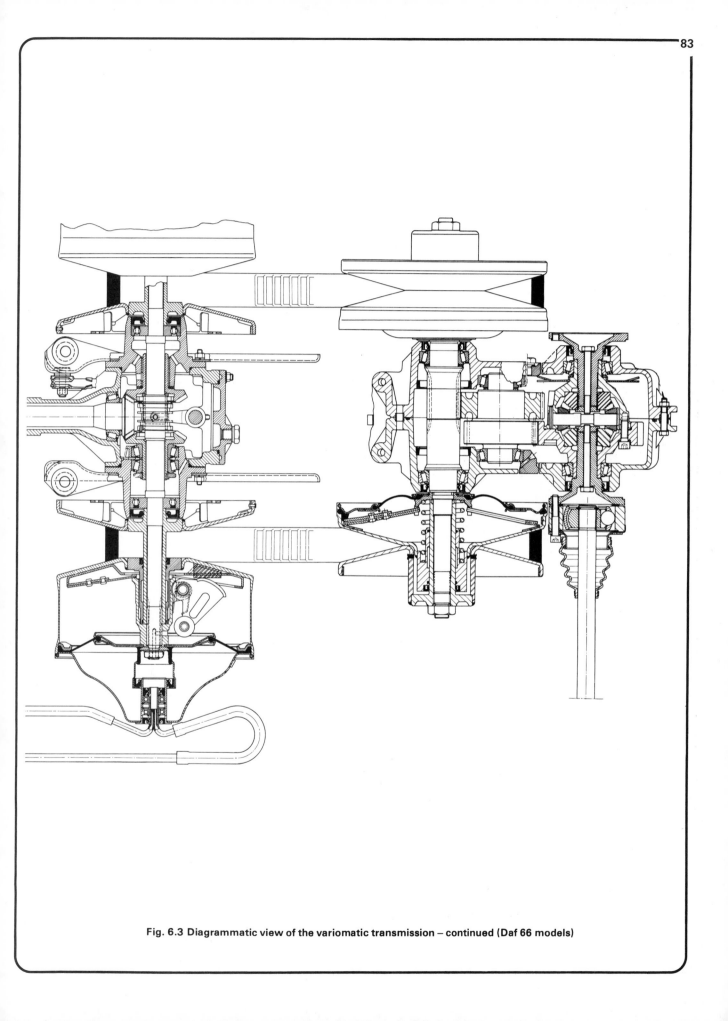

Fig. 6.3 Diagrammatic view of the variomatic transmission – continued (Daf 66 models)

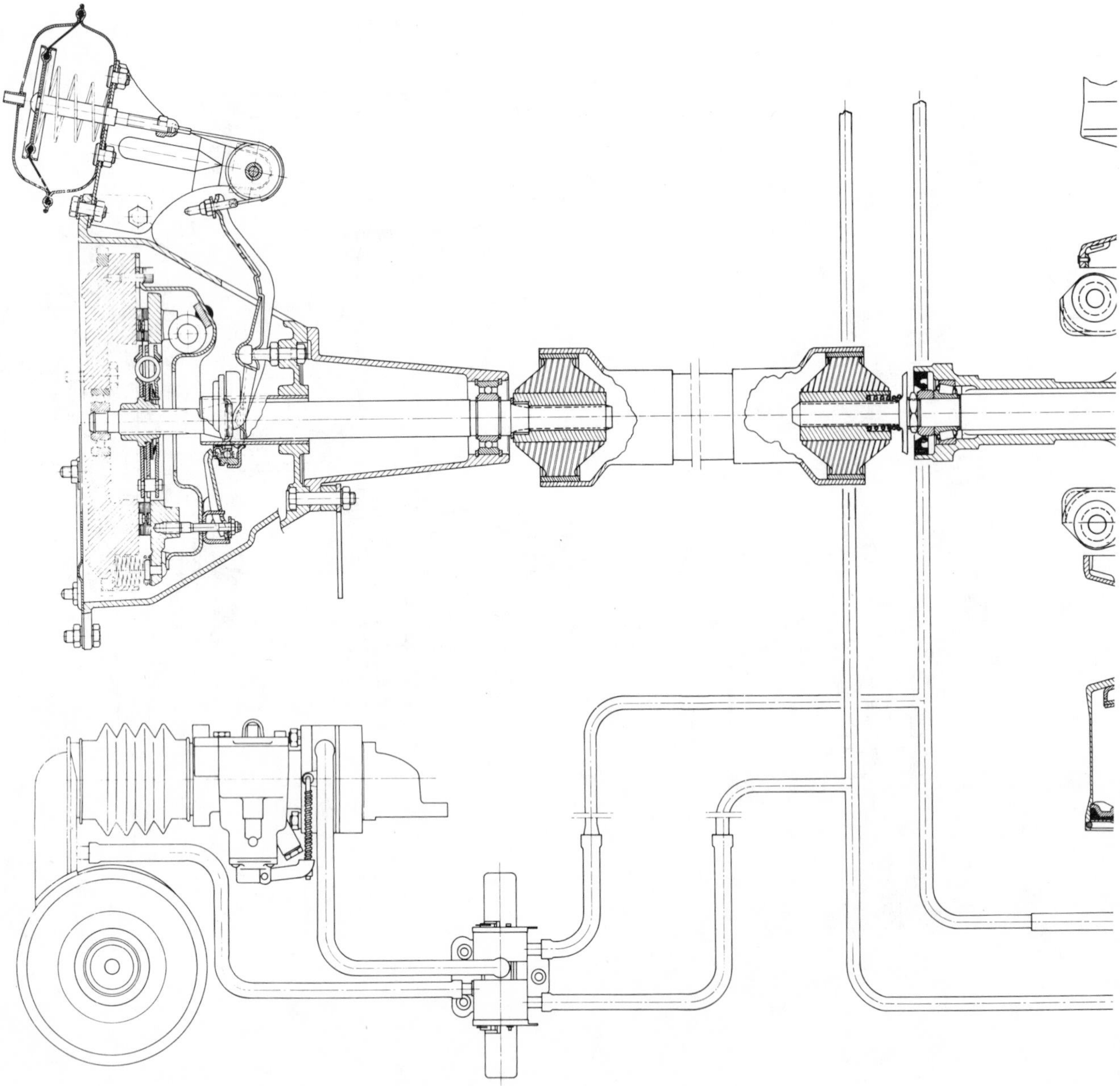

Fig. 6.4 Diagrammatic view of the variomatic transmission (Volvo 66 models)

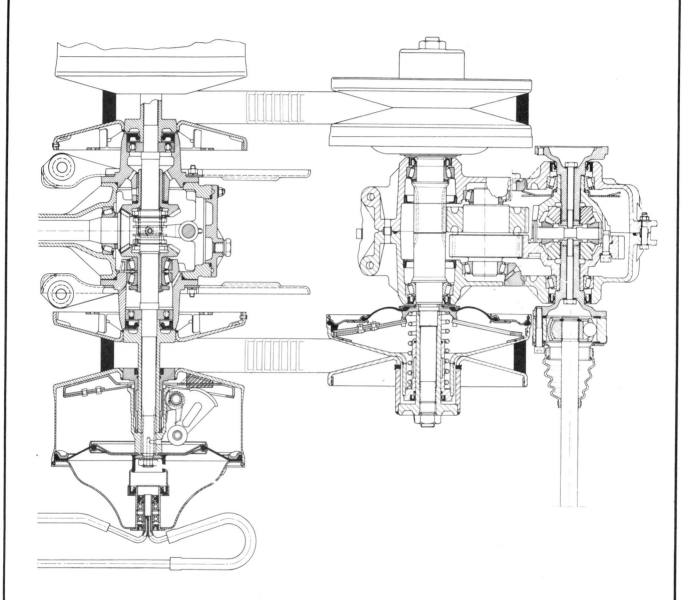

Fig. 6.4 Diagrammatic view of the variomatic transmission – continued (Volvo 66 models)

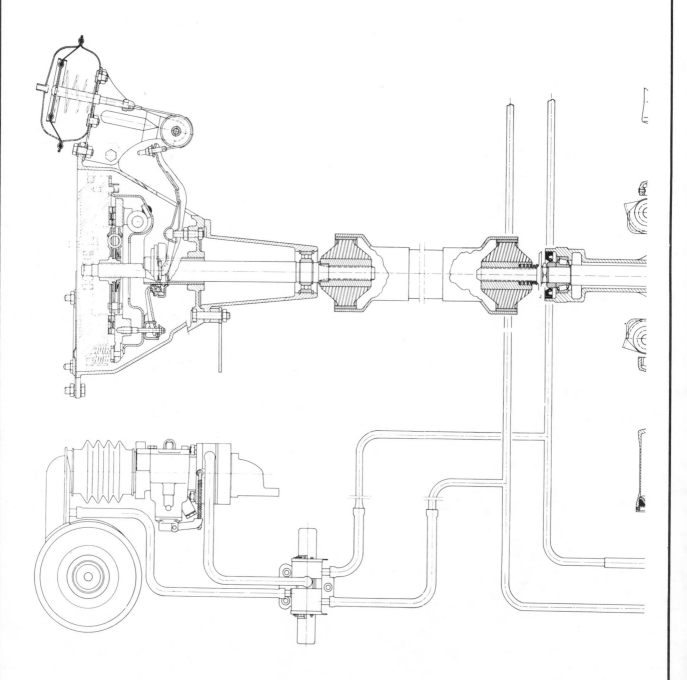

Fig. 6.5 Diagrammatic view of the variomatic transmission (Volvo 66 and Volvo 343 models with park selector position)

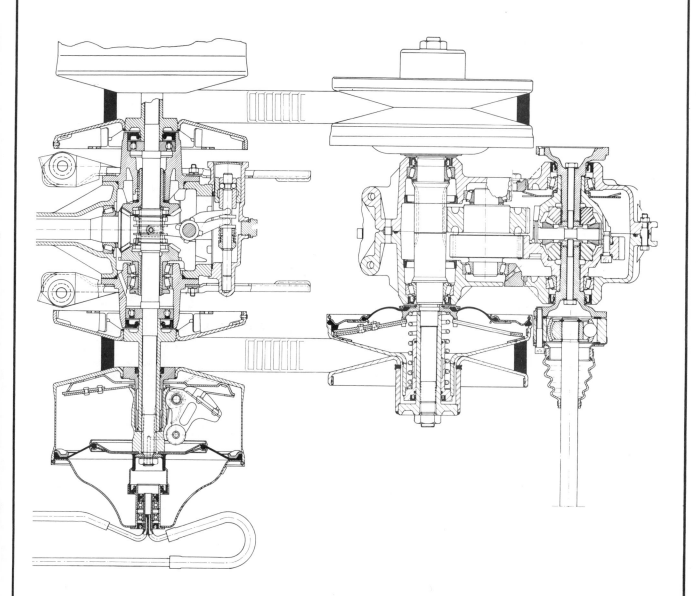

Fig. 6.5 Diagrammatic view of the variomatic transmission – continued (Volvo 66 and Volvo 343 models with park selector position)

possible with the selector lever in position P or N.

1978 Volvo 343 models are equipped with an electronic vacuum control unit instead of the throttle operated micro-switch. The unit is linked to engine speed by a tachometric relay and to the braking system by a switch on the master cylinder; the unit operates at an engine speed of between 1700 and 1800 rpm.

2   Transmission drivebelts – removal, refitting and adjustment

1   Place the car over an inspection pit, or alternatively jack up the rear and support it adequately on axle-stands.
2   Unscrew and remove the retaining screws and lower the guard panel(s) from the car.
3   Carefully pull the vacuum hoses from both sides of the primary transmission unit (photo); the hoses are of different diameters and it is therefore not possible to refit them incorrectly.
4   On Daf 55 models prise the plastic caps from the crossmember beneath the primary transmission unit then loosen the four primary unit mounting nuts.
5   On all except Daf 55 models, loosen the four secondary unit mounting nuts, and adjustment bracket nuts (photo).
6   On all models loosen the locknut and fully unscrew the drivebelt adjustment bolt or nut as applicable until all tension is removed from the drivebelts.
7   On Daf 55 models, slide the primary unit to the rear as far as possible; on all other models slide the secondary unit forwards as far as possible.
8   To simplify the next operation it is advisable to obtain a special clamping tool from a tool agent, or to construct a similar tool.
9   Clamp the drivebelt so that the secondary pulley halves are forced apart then insert a 1 in (25 mm) spacer between the halves to keep them apart. If a tool is not available, pull the lower section of the drivebelt downwards so that the secondary pulley halves move apart.
10 Pull the drivebelts on both sides into the primary (front) pulley halves.
11 On all but Daf 55 models, loosen the secondary unit mounting nuts sufficiently to allow clearance between the rear pulleys and underbody for the removal of the drivebelts.
12 Remove the drivebelts from the rear pulleys, then from the front pulleys.
13 Examine the drivebelts for deterioration, cracks and loss of toothed segments and if evident, renew both drivebelts. Renewal of one drivebelt is not possible because of the difference in length between new and worn belts.
14 Clean the pulley surfaces with a cloth moistened with methylated spirit.
15 Refitting is a reversal of removal but care must be taken to avoid contaminating the pulley surfaces with oil or foreign matter, and the drivebelts must be tensioned as follows (photo).
16 Turn either the rear wheels or transmission pulleys until the drivebelts have settled at the top of the secondary pulleys.
17 Turn the adjustment bolt or nut (as applicable) until the drivebelts are tensioned, and the gap between the inner and outer rear pulleys on both sides is between 0.08 and 0.12 in (2 and 3 mm) for Daf 55 models and 0.06 and 0.08 in (1.5 and 2.0 mm) on all other models (photo). Measure the gap at the centre of the discs with a feeler gauge or length of metal of suitable thickness (photo).
18 The transmission pulleys should be turned several times and the final adjustment checked after the retaining nuts and adjustment locknut have been tightened.
19 The difference between left and right-hand pulley gaps should not exceed 0.04 in (1.0 mm), but if it does, the belts should be changed side-to-side and the adjustment made again. The belts must be renewed if correct adjustment cannot be obtained.
20 After fitting new drivebelts the adjustment should be checked again after 3300 miles (5000 km) have been completed.

3   Primary variomatic transmission unit – removal and refitting

1   Jack up the rear of the car and support it adequately on axle-stands. Allow plenty of room for manoeuvring the transmission unit from under the car; the use of a ramp or pit is preferable.
2   Disconnect the exhaust pipes from the engine and its mountings and remove it from the car (all models except the Volvo 343, on which

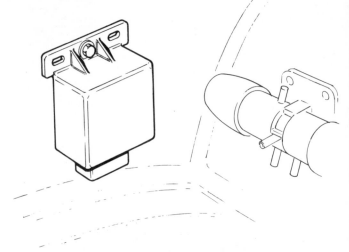

Fig. 6.6 Electronic vacuum control unit fitted to 1978 models

Fig. 6.7 Primary transmission retaining nut locations (1 to 4) and drivebelt tension bolt (5) (Daf 55 models)

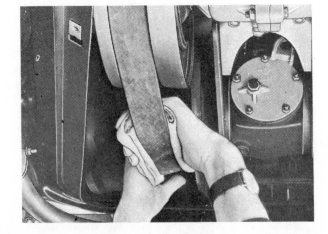

Fig. 6.8 Releasing the transmission drivebelt tension without the aid of the special clamp

2.3 Primary transmission vacuum hoses (note different diameters)

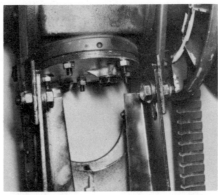

2.5 Transmission inter support frame (Daf 66 models)

2.15 Refitting a drivebelt (transmission removed)

2.17A Drivebelt adjusting bolt (Daf 66 models)

2.17B Checking the drivebelt tension adjustment (Daf 66 models)

3.10 Reversing light switch location (Daf 66 models)

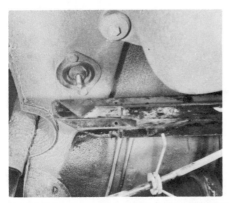

3.12A Primary transmission mounting (Daf 66 models)

3.12B Transmission intermediate bracket (Daf 66 models)

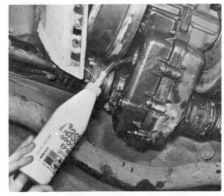

4.6 Refilling the transmission secondary unit with oil (Daf 66 models)

5.5 Halfshafts disconnected from the transmission (Daf 66 models)

5.6A Halfshaft tied with wire when removing secondary transmission unit (Daf 66 models)

5.6B Secondary transmission unit drive flange (Daf 66 models)

Fig. 6.9 Checking the secondary transmission disc gap on Daf 66, Volvo 66, and Volvo 343 models

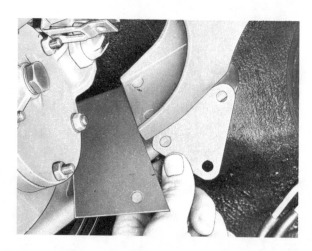

Fig. 6.10 Guard panel retaining bolt locations on Daf 55 models

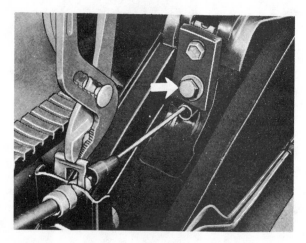

Fig. 6.11 Removing the handbrake clamp and bracket on Daf 55 models

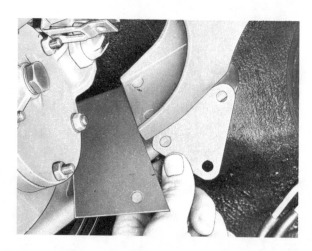

Fig. 6.12 Installing a transmission intermediate bracket spacer

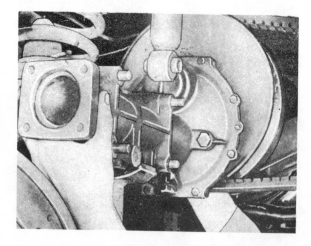

Fig. 6.13 Removing the axle tube on Daf 55 models

Fig. 6.14 Location of the drain plug (1) and filler plug (2) on the secondary transmission unit (Daf 55 models)

it is only necessary to unhook the front mounting rubber).

3   Unscrew the retaining screws and remove the exhaust pipe heat shield where this is fitted.

4   Remove the guard panel(s) from the transmission unit.

5   On Daf 66 and Volvo 66 models, place a length of wood over the rear springs and beneath the secondary unit to support it in subsequent operations.

6   Remove the drivebelts as described in Section 2.

7   On Daf 55 models unscrew and remove the retaining bolts and remove the front guard panel crossmember, then disconnect the handbrake cable at the compensator. Extract the handbrake cable clamp and remove the cable from the bracket.

8   On Daf 66 and Volvo 66 models, disconnect the handbrake cable at the compensator.

9   On all models, support the primary transmission unit with a trolley jack.

10   Disconnect the selector linkage by removing the clevis (photo) pin; also disconnect the reversing light switch wires (if fitted).

11   On Volvo 343 models unscrew and remove the retaining bolts and adjusting locknut, and withdraw the adjustment bracket from the primary and secondary units.

12   Unscrew and remove the primary transmission unit retaining nuts; on Daf 55 models there are only four, which are clearly visible from beneath the unit, on all other models the forward crossmember must be detached from the underbody (photo). Additionally on Daf 66 and Volvo 66 models the intermediate angled bracket must also be removed (photo).

13   Lower the primary transmission unit a little, then move it rearwards away from the propeller shaft and fully lower it to the ground. Make sure that the propeller shaft remains engaged in the clutch output shaft and be careful not to damage the splines.

14   Refitting is a reversal of removal but the following additional points should be noted:

   (a) *Grease the pinion shaft splines sparingly before inserting it into the propeller shaft*
   (b) *Where spacers are fitted to the intermediate angled bracket, make sure that these are refitted in equal numbers to each side. Where only one spacer is fitted it should be located on the left-hand side*
   (c) *Adjust the drivebelt tension as described in Section 2*

4   Secondary variomatic transmission unit (Daf 55 models) – removal and refitting

1   Separate secondary units are fitted to each rear wheel and each unit is attached to the lower suspension arm. This Section describes the procedure for one unit; the procedure is identical on both sides of the car.

2   Remove the rear hub bearing and seal as described in Chapter 9, Section 22.

3   Unscrew and remove the shock absorber lower retaining nut, then drive the bolt from the secondary reduction gear unit case, and push the shock absorber to one side.

4   Support the secondary unit with a trolley jack.

5   Unscrew and remove the four retaining nuts, then lift the unit

forwards off the mounting bolts and detach it from the drivebelt.

6   Refitting is a reversal of removal, but the following additional points should be noted:

   (a) *Thoroughly clean the drive pulley surfaces with methylated spirit*
   (b) *Renew self locking nuts and tighten them to the specified torque wrench settings*
   (c) *Refill the secondary gear case to the bottom of the filler plug aperture with the correct grade of oil; the filler plug is located above the drain plug (photo)*
   (d) *Adjust the drivebelt tension as described in Section 2*

5   Secondary variomatic transmission unit (Daf 66, Volvo 66 and Volvo 343 models) – removal and refitting

1   Jack up the rear of the car and support it adequately on axle-stands. Allow plenty of room for manoeuvring the transmission unit from under the car; the use of a ramp or pit is preferable.

2   On all but Volvo 343 models, disconnect the exhaust pipe from the engine and mountings, and remove it from the car.

3   Unscrew and remove the retaining bolts and withdraw the transmission guard panel(s).

4   Remove the drain plug and drain the oil into a suitable container.

5   Mark the driveshaft inner couplings in relation to the transmission drive flanges, then unscrew and remove the retaining bolts and plates. An Allen key will be required to do this (photo).

6   Detach the driveshafts from the transmission unit and tie them to the handbrake cables (photo). At the same time remove the flange gaskets (photo).

7   Remove both drivebelts as described in Section 2.

8   Support the secondary transmission unit with a trolley jack, then unscrew and remove the retaining nuts, and pull the intermediate brackets from the front bolts.

9   Lower the transmission unit to the ground; the help of an assistant is desirable in order to prevent the unit slipping from the trolley jack.

10   Extract the rubber bushes from the transmission case mounting holes and renew them if they show signs of deterioration.

11   Refitting is a reversal of removal, but the following additional points should be noted:

   (a) *Fit new gaskets to the driveshaft flanges*
   (b) *Renew all self locking nuts and tighten all nuts and bolts to the correct specified torque wrench settings*
   (c) *Thoroughly clean the drive pulley surfaces with methylated spirit*
   (d) *Refill the secondary transmission to the bottom of the filler plug aperture with the correct grade of oil; the filler plug is located forward of the drain plug*
   (e) *Adjust the drivebelt tension as described in Section 2*
   (f) *Make sure thatthe driveshaft is clean and free of any foreign matter which could contaminate the drive pulleys*

6   Primary and secondary variomatic transmission units (Daf 66, Volvo 66 and Volvo 343 models) – removal and refitting

1   If repairs are required on both the primary and secondary

6.2 Primary transmission unit front cross-member (Daf 66 models)

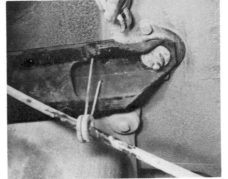

6.3 Rear handbrake cable mounting (Daf 66 models)

6.7 Front transmission mounting (Daf 66 models)

Fig. 6.15 The transmission guard panel (Volvo 343 models)

Fig. 6.16 Removing the halfshaft flange bolts

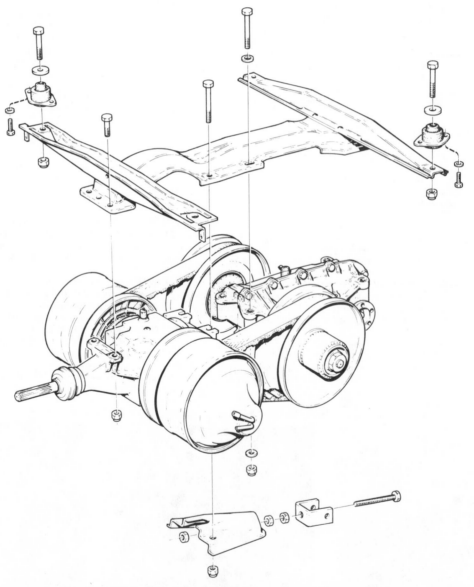

Fig. 6.17 The secondary transmission mounting frame components (Volvo 343 models)

7.2 Transmission drain plug (primary)

7.5 Removing the primary transmission outer cover lockring (Daf 66 models)

7.6 Removing the primary transmission outer cover

7.12 Primary transmission centrifugal weight location

7.15 Primary transmission with discs removed

7.17 Primary transmission pinion shaft dust cover

7.18 Primary transmission pinion shaft collar

7.28 Installing the primary transmission fixed disc

7.30 Location of air hole in primary transmission cross-shaft

7.43 Stake the primary transmission pinion shaft retaining nut

7.45 Primary transmission rear cover sealing ring

7.46 Refilling the primary transmission with oil

Fig. 6.18 Secondary transmission retaining nuts (except Daf 55 models)

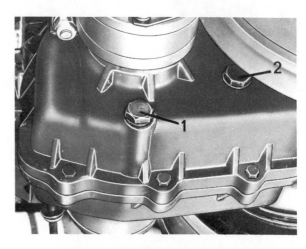

Fig. 6.19 Drain (1) and filler (2) plugs of the secondary transmission unit (except Daf 55 models)

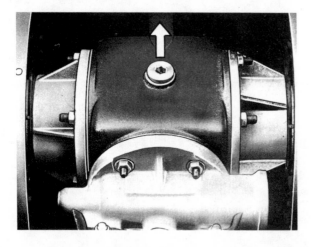

Fig. 6.20 Primary transmission unit drain plug location on Volvo 343 models

Fig. 6.21 Removing the side cover lockring

Fig. 6.22 Removing the transmission inner fixed disc

Fig. 6.23 Extracting the pinion shaft oil seal

Fig. 6.24 Extracting the sealing ring oil seal

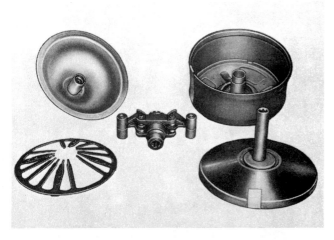

Fig. 6.25 The balanced components of the primary sliding disc

Fig. 6.26 Installing the primary diaphragm spring showing prong (1), recess (2), and balance marks (3)

transmission units, they can be removed together as a complete assembly.

2 Follow the instructions given in Section 5, paragraphs 1 to 6 inclusive (photo).

3 On Daf 66 and Volvo 66 models, disconnect the handbrake cable at the compensator and mounting (photo).

4 Disconnect the selector linkage from the primary unit by removing the clevis pin.

5 Disconnect the reversing light switch wires.

6 Support the transmission units with two trolley jacks and suitable lengths of wood.

7 Unscrew and remove the transmission frame mounting nuts (photo).

8 Carefully lower the front trolley jack then move the assembly forwards and lower the rear of the frame clear of the handbrake cables. Finally lower the transmission to the ground.

9 Refitting is a reversal of removal, but the following additional points should be noted:

   (a) *Make sure that the handbrake cable lies beneath the front crossmember before tightening the mounting nuts*
   (b) *Fit new gaskets to the driveshaft flanges*
   (c) *Renew all self locking nuts and tighten them to the correct specified torque wrench settings*
   (d) *Clean the driveshaft of any grease or foreign matter which could contaminate the drive pulleys*

7 Primary variomatic transmission unit – overhaul

1 Before starting work check that spares are readily available; if not a new or good secondhand unit will have to be fitted.

2 Remove the primary transmission unit as described in Section 3, then drain the oil into a suitable container (photo).

3 Mount the unit in a vice with the vacuum units in the vertical plane; the use of two shaped blocks of wood will be helpful to clamp the pinion shaft end of the transmission housing.

4 Using masking tape or paint, mark the discs and end covers in relation to each other and in relation to the left or right-hand side of the transmission case. This is most important because the transmission is balanced to a fine degree on initial assembly.

5 Using a screwdriver, prise the lockring from the upper side cover (photo).

6 Gently tap the cover with a soft head hammer and lift the cover away (photo).

7 Unscrew and remove the nut from the sealing sleeve; to do this have an assistant hold the diaphragm disc stationary with an old drive belt used in a tourniquet fashion. Alternatively move the selector lever to engage forward or reverse gear and hold the pinion shaft stationary being careful not to damage the splines.

8 Remove the sealing sleeve, then mark the diaphragm plate and threaded end of the cross-shaft in relation to the previous made marks on the discs.

9 Lift the diaphragm away making sure that the centrifugal weight and carrier remain on the cross-shaft.

10 Remove the diaphragm support ring.

11 Mark the diaphragm spring and centrifugal weight in relation to the previously made marks on the disc.

12 Remove the centrifugal weights and the diaphragm spring (photo).

13 Lift the outer sliding disc from the cross-shaft.

14 Using a three leg puller, pull the inner fixed disc from the cross-shaft; under no circumstances use a hammer to free the disc as the cross-shaft bearings will be displaced and possible damaged.

15 Invert the primary transmission in the vice and remove the remaining discs in the same way (photo).

16 Using a screwdriver, prise the oil seals from the transmission side covers, and remove the O-rings from the outer disc bores.

17 Prise the pinion shaft oil seal from the housing; on some models a dust cover must first be removed from the shaft (photo).

18 Unscrew and remove the pinion shaft retaining nut whilst holding the shaft stationary in a soft jawed vice, then remove the collar and O-ring (photo).

19 From the rear of the transmission, unscrew and remove the rear cover retaining nuts and withdraw the rear cover complete with selector arm (Volvo models) and gasket.

20 Using a screwdriver, prise the sealing rings from the sealing ring housings.

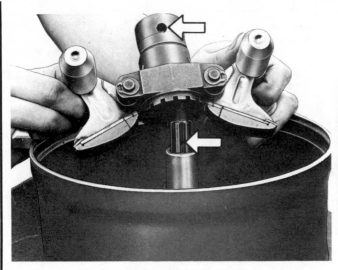

Fig. 6.27 Centrifugal weight air hole alignment

Fig. 6.28 Installing the primary diaphragm showing balance marks

Fig. 6.29 Diaphragm compressing tool – primary variomatic transmission unit

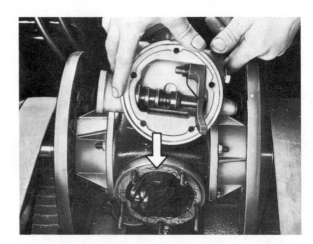

Fig. 6.30 Installing a new primary rear cover gasket

Fig. 6.31 Primary transmission connecting pipe components

21 Using circlip pliers, extract the circlips from the diaphragm side covers followed by the spacer rings, then drive the connecting pipe assemblies from the end covers.

22 Drive the bearings from the side covers with a suitable soft metal drift.

23 Further dismantling of the primary transmission is not recommended as it involves the use of specialised tools and equipment not available to the home mechanic. Should any of the internal bearings on bevel gear teeth be worn or exhibit any signs of roughness, an exchange unit should be obtained.

24 Clean all the components so far dismantled with paraffin and dry them with a lint-free cloth. Examine the components for damage and deterioration and renew them where necessary. In particular check the side cover rims for warping and check the diaphragms for splitting and perishing. Temporarily reassemble the inner and outer discs and check that there is no excessive play between the two components. If either of the components which were previously marked for balance require renewal, the complete primary unit must be renewed otherwise unbalance will occur resulting in excessive vibration in the car. Check the side cover bearings for wear and renew them if necessary, and obtain a complete set of oil seals and gaskets.

25 Start reassembly by pressing new oil seals into the transmission side bearing housings using suitable diameter tubing; note that the left-hand side seal is coloured blue.

26 Fill the grease cavities in each outer disc with 7 cc of a lithium based grease, then install the new O-rings and press the grease retainers into position. Similarly press the new O-ring and oil seal into the inner end of the outer disc.

27 Fill each outer disc assembly with 100 cc of the specified fluid.

28 Lightly grease the transmission side bearing housing oil seal and the oil seals in the outer disc assembly, then fit the fixed and sliding discs to the cross-shaft with the unit mounted in a soft jaw vice (photo). Be careful to align the previously made marks.

29 Fit the diaphragm spring making sure that the marks are aligned and that the driving prongs engage the recesses in the disc.

30 Lower the centrifugal weight over the cross-shaft making sure that the marks are aligned and that the air supply holes in the cross-shaft and weight carrier are also aligned (photo).

31 Fit the diaphragm support ring, then install the diaphragm over the cross-shaft with the marks in alignment.

32 Press a new seal into the sealing sleeve until its closed end is flush with the top of the sleeve.

33 Have an assistant press the diaphragm downwards then fit the sealing sleeve, washer and nut. Alternatively a lever similar to that shown in Fig. 6.29 should be constructed to compress the diaphragm.

34 Using an old drivebelt or similar material as a tourniquet, hold the outer disc stationary and tighten the nut onto the cross-shaft to the correct torque wrench setting.

35 Fit a new oil seal to the connecting pipe with the lip facing outwards, then install the retaining circlip.

36 Apply a lithium based grease to the side cover bearings then drive them into the side cover.

37 Carefully drive the connecting pipe assembly through the bearings and install the inner circlip.

38 Fit the packing ring and inner oil seal with the sealing lip facing the bearing.

39 Smear a small amount of grease to the sealing sleeve lip then install the side cover to the outer disc assembly making sure that the marks are aligned.

40 Tap the cover with a soft head hammer to centralise it, then, while an assistant presses on the cover, fit the lockring into the groove in the outer disc. If a vacuum pump is available, connect this to the outer chamber connecting pipe to facilitate fitting the lockring. Alternatively use mole grips to hold the lockring in position then tap the ring into the groove using a suitable soft metal drift.

41 Repeat the procedure given in paragraphs 28 to 40 inclusive for the remaining side of the transmission.

42 Fit a new seal to the pinion shaft followed by the collar with the chamfered edge facing the seal.

43 Tighten the nut onto the pinion shaft to the correct torque wrench setting; then lock it into position with a centre punch (photo).

44 Install the new pinion shaft oil seal using suitable diameter tubing; then fit the dust cover where applicable.

45 Install a new rear cover gasket and fit the rear cover to the transmission (photo) tightening the retaining nuts in diagonal sequence to the correct torque wrench setting.

46 Refill the primary transmission to the bottom of the filler plug aperture with the correct grade of oil; the filler plug is located on the rear cover (photo).

8 Secondary variomatic transmission unit (Daf 55 models) — overhaul

1 Before starting work check that spares are readily available; if not, a new or good secondhand unit will have to be fitted.

2 Remove the secondary variomatic transmission unit as described in Section 4.

3 Mount the unit in a soft jaw vice, and use masking tape or paint to mark the inner and outer discs and side cover in relation to each other. Failure to take this precaution will result in unbalance on reassembly giving rise to excessive vibration of the unit during operation.

4 Obtain the special tool (Daf No 8-99-535454) and adaptor (Daf No 8-99-535367) from a tool agent or Daf garage and secure it to the outer sliding disc.

5 Temporarily install the driveshaft and brake drum and hold them stationary with a length of rod, then unscrew and remove the nut from the pinion shaft.

6 Withdraw the sliding disc from the fixed disc.

7 Withdraw the fixed disc from the pinion shaft splines; if necessary use a three leg puller. To retain the transmission balance, mark the pinion shaft end in relation to the mark on the fixed disc.

8 Prise the oil seal from the reduction gear outer case.

9 Using a suitable soft metal drift, drive out the location dowels from the reduction gear case halves.

10 Unscrew and remove the retaining nuts and lift the outer case half from the main case.

11 Mark the position of the gearwheel in relation to the axle tube then remove it.

12 Place the axle tube on the workbench and heat the area around the inner bearing until the bearing can be extracted. Where taper-roller bearings are fitted the outer race should be removed in the same manner. Similarly remove the driveshaft outer bearing or race from the axle tube.

13 Extract the oil seal from the axle tube.

14 Heat the outer case half around the pinion bearing and drive out the bearing or outer race as applicable, then prise it out the oil seal.

15 Clean all components with paraffin and dry them with a lint-free cloth then examine them for damage, wear and deterioration. Check the bearings for wear; if ball bearings are fitted, spin the bearings and observe whether there is any roughness; with taper-roller bearings, examine the roller and race surfaces for pitting and grooving. Renew any worn bearings and obtain new oil seals and an O-ring.

16 If on checking the fixed disc, as described in paragraph 37, it is decided that renewal is required, check whether the existing disc has a welded or riveted hub. If it is riveted and the new disc is welded, the outer case half must be remachined to the dimensions shown in Fig. 6.34.

17 Start reassembly by installing the oil seal into the axle tube with the sealing lip facing the gearwheel position.

18 Using suitable diameter tubing drive the bearings or outer races as applicable into the axle casing.

19 Similarly drive the bearings and outer races into the outer case, and then install the oil seal to the outer case with the sealing lip facing inwards.

20 Where taper-roller bearings are fitted, use a suitable puller to remove the inner races from the gearwheel, then drive the new races into position without any shims.

21 Similarly remove the inner races from the pinion shaft and drive the new races into position without any shims.

22 Note that the gearwheel and drive pinion are matched sets and cannot therefore be renewed separately.

23 Remove any burrs from the mating faces of the axle tube and outer case.

24 The bearing pre-loads must now be determined and shims installed in the locations shown in Fig. 6.37.

25 First install the gearwheel into the axle tube with the outer bearing in position on the gearwheel. Measure the distance (A) from the axle tube mating face to the outer edge of the outer bearing. Now measure the distance (B) from the outer case mating face to the shoulder in the case on which the outer bearing abuts. Shims must now be added to the gearwheel to obtain the necessary pre-load in accordance with the

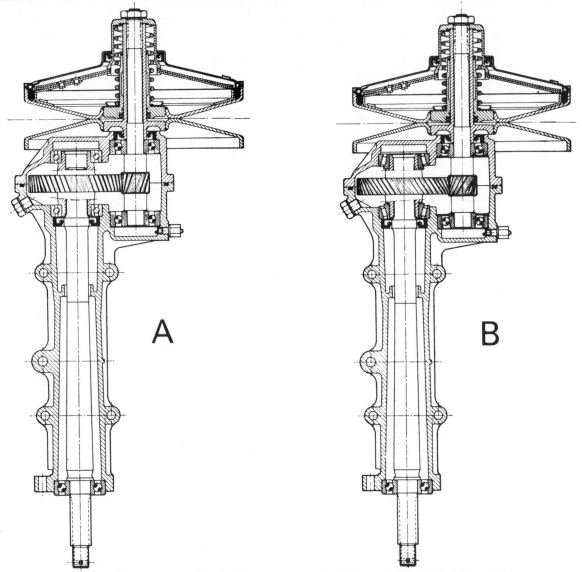

Fig. 6.32 Cross-section view of the secondary transmission unit fitted to Daf 55 models

(A) Pre chassis No 561257
(B) Chassis No 561257 onwards

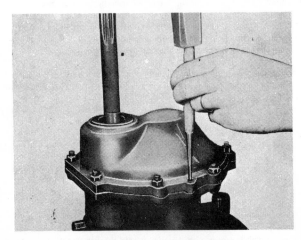

Fig. 6.33 Removing the location dowels from the secondary transmission (Daf 55 models)

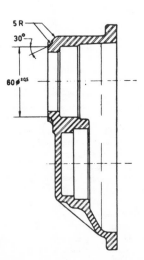

Fig. 6.34 Secondary outer case modification dimensions for Daf 55 models

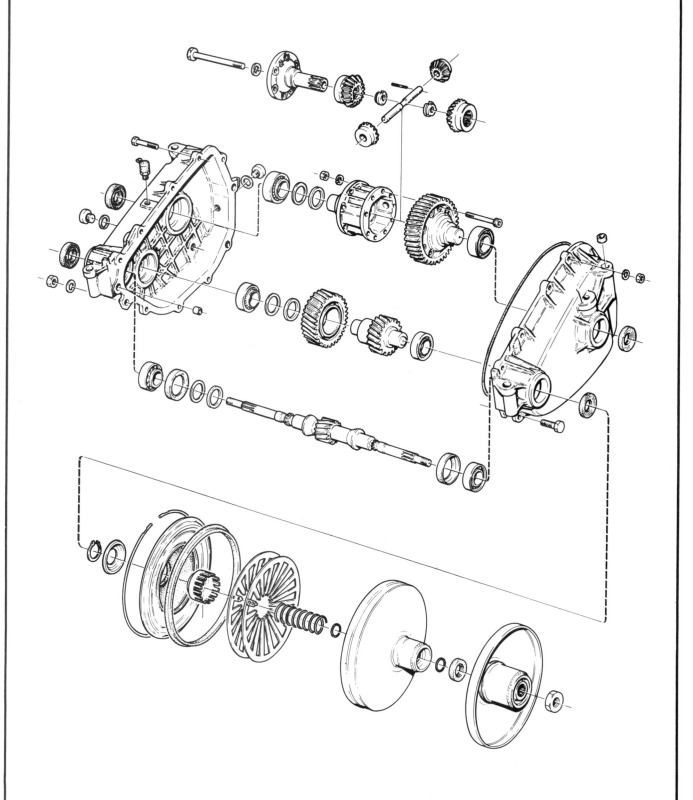

Fig. 6.35 Exploded view of the secondary transmission unit fitted to Daf 66, Volvo 66, and Volvo 343 models

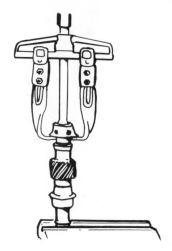

Fig. 6.36 Removing the pinion shaft inner races on Daf 55 models

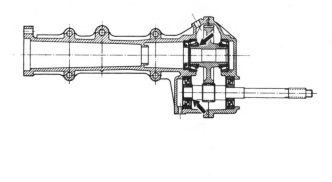

Fig. 6.37 Shim locations on the Daf 55 secondary unit

following formula: Thickness of shims required = Dimension (B) − Dimension (A) + 0.008 in (0.2 mm). After installing the shims, drive the outer race into the outer case where taper roller bearings are fitted.

26 Install the pinion into the axle tube bearing, and fit the outer case without the gearwheel. Using a dial gauge measure the bearing clearance by moving the pinion shaft in and out. The correct shims to fit will be of this dimension plus a further 0.004 in (0.1 mm) to give the necessary pre-load. Fit the shims behind the pinion shaft inner race.

27 Apply a lithium based grease to the bearings then install the gearwheel and pinion shaft into the axle tube casing.

28 Fit the O-ring and locate the outer case onto the axle tube.

29 Drive the locating dowels into position then tighten the nuts in diagonal sequence to the specified torque wrench setting.

30 Turn the pinion shaft to settle the bearings and check for freedom of movement.

31 Working on the sliding disc assembly, use a screwdriver to prise the seal from the inner disc face.

32 Using a long bolt and nut, tighten the disc and remove the clamp.

33 Prise the lockring from the outer cover and tap the cover face.

34 Drive the seal from the outer cover.

35 Prise the rubber ring from the outer disc.

36 Mark the diaphragm spring and outer sleeve in relation to the disc, then unscrew the clamp nut and remove the sleeve and springs.

37 Clean the sliding disc components with paraffin and dry with lint-free cloth, then examine them for damage and deterioration. Check the outer cover for warping, then temporarily assemble the inner and outer discs and check that there is no excessive play between the two components. If either of the disc components requires renewal, the complete disc must be renewed otherwise imbalance will occur resulting in excessive vibration in the car. Obtain a complete set of oil seals.

38 Fill the cavity in the sliding disc hub with grease, then install the O-rings and finally the oil seal with the sealing lip facing inwards.

39 Using suitable diameter tubing drive the oil seal into the outer cover with the sealing lip facing inwards.

40 Smear grease onto the new rubber ring and press it into the outer disc recess with the convex side facing inwards.

41 Pour 75 cc of the specified fluid into the outer disc.

42 Install the springs and sleeve with marks aligned, then tighten the clamp bolt into position.

43 Fit the outer cover, making sure that the previously made marks are aligned.

44 Press the outer cover onto the rubber ring and install the lockring using a soft metal drift to force it into the groove.

45 Assemble the clamp tool to the sliding disc and remove the clamp bolt.

46 Slide the fixed inner disc over the pinion shaft followed by the outer disc.

47 Pre chassis No 716706 fit the wave washer and tighten the nut to the correct torque wrench setting while holding the pinion shaft stationary using the method described in paragraph 5.

48 Post chassis No 716706 do not fit a wave washer but use a liquid

locking agent in the pinion shaft threads, then tighten the nut to the correct torque wrench setting.

49 Remove the disc clamp tool and clean the disc faces with methylated spirit.

9 Secondary variomatic transmission unit (Daf 66, Volvo 66 and Volvo 343 models) – overhaul

1 Note that the pulley discs, gear case oil seals and drive flange oil seals can if necessary be renewed without removing the secondary transmission unit, although due to limited access, removal of the unit is recommended.

2 Refer to Section 5 for the removal procedure for the secondary transmission unit.

3 Using masking tape or paint, mark the inner and outer discs, driveshaft and diaphragm in relation to each other. This precaution is necessary to prevent imbalance on reassembly, which will cause excessive vibration of the unit during operation. Make sure that each component is also marked *left* or *right* as appropriate.

4 In order to prevent damage to the rubber diaphragm, obtain the special tool (Daf/Volvo No 5935) or construct a similar tool, and locate it over the inner disc.

5 Unscrew and remove the cross-shaft nut; the outer disc must be held stationary to do this by using special tool No 5885 (260508) clamped to the outer disc hub.

6 With the tool still attached to the outer disc, use a two leg puller to withdraw the outer disc from the pinion shaft.

7 Withdraw the inner sliding disc from the pinion shaft and place it on the bench with the diaphragm uppermost; failure to do this will result in the loss of oil from the unit.

8 Using a long bolt and nut, clamp the inner disc together and remove the special tool while still keeping the diaphragm uppermost (photo).

9 Extract the circlip from the inner disc hub and remove the clamping plate.

10 Using a screwdriver, prise out the lockring then lift the rubber diaphragm from the disc (photos).

11 Mark the diaphragm, springs and locating collar in relation to the disc, then remove the clamp bolt.

12 Prise out the rubber sealing ring then withdraw the collar, diaphragm springs and coil spring.

13 Discard the oil from the sliding disc.

14 Prise the oil seal and O-rings from the bore of the sliding disc.

15 Carry out the procedure described in paragraphs 4 to 14 inclusive on the remaining pulley assembly.

16 Unscrew and remove the drive flange retaining bolts whilst holding the flange stationary (use a length of metal between two flange bolts which have been temporarily replaced).

17 Remove both flanges (photo) then use a screwdriver to prise out the oil seals from the gear-case.

9.8 Method of compressing the secondary transmission sliding disc components (Daf 66 models)

9.10A Removing the secondary transmission lockring (Daf 66 models)

9.10B Removing the secondary transmission diaphragm (Daf 66 models)

9.17 Secondary transmission drive flange removal (Daf 66 models)

9.18 Secondary transmission unit ready for separation (Daf 66 models)

9.19 Secondary transmission internal gears (Daf 66 models)

9.20A Secondary transmission idler gear (Daf 66 models)

9.20B Secondary transmission differential unit (Daf 66 models)

9.23 Secondary transmission pinion shaft (Daf 66 models)

9.30 Refilling the secondary transmission with fluid (Daf 66 models)

9.32A Installing the diaphragm clamping plate (Daf 66 model secondary transmission)

9.32B Clamping plate circlip location (Daf 66 model assembly transmission)

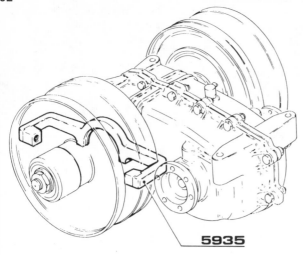

Fig. 6.38 Secondary transmission inner disc retaining tool

Fig. 6.39 Using the special tool when unscrewing the cross-shaft nut

Fig. 6.40 Removing the disc rubber sealing ring (secondary transmission)

Fig. 6.41 Removing the O-ring (secondary transmission)

Fig. 6.42 Installing the diaphragm clamping plate showing correct location of holes 1 and 2

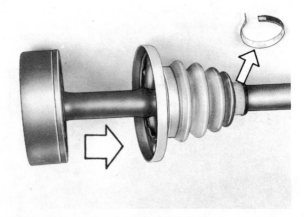

Fig. 6.43 Removing the halfshaft bellows

9.37 Tightening the secondary transmission fixed disc (Daf 66 models)

10.4 Halfshaft homokinetic joint (Daf 66 models)

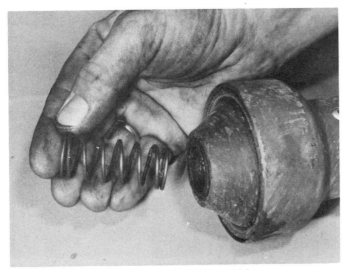

11.1 Propeller shaft spring location (Daf 66 models)

18 Place the right-hand side of the gear-case on the bench, then unscrew and remove the case retaining nuts in diagonal sequence (photo).

19 Lift the case half away and prise the rubber O-ring from the lower case (photo).

20 Withdraw the pinion shaft, idler gear and differential unit from the lower case noting which way round they are fitted (photos).

21 Prise the oil seals from the pinion shaft apertures in the gearcases.

22 Thoroughly clean all components with paraffin and dry them with lint-free cloth. Examine all the components for wear, damage and deterioration. Inspect the taper rollers and races for signs of scoring and pitting, then examine the pinion and gearwheel teeth for wear; if evident it will be more economical to obtain a new secondary transmission rather than renew a number of components. If wear is minimal, obtain new oil seals and an O-ring. Check the disc assemblies for wear by temporarily assembling the inner and outer discs and observing any excessive play between the two components. Examine the rubber diaphragms for splits and fractures. If either of the disc components require renewal, the complete pulley must be renewed otherwise imbalance will occur resulting in excessive vibration in the car.

23 Start reassembly by installing the pinion shaft followed by the idler gear and differential unit (photos).

24 Locate the O-ring in the right-hand side case making sure that it is kept dry, then install the left-hand side case over the pinion shaft and tighten the retaining nuts in diagonal sequence to the correct torque wrench setting.

25 Using suitable diameter tubing, insert the drive flange and pinion shaft oil seals into the gear case until they are flush with the case.

26 Lightly grease the outer periphery of the drive flanges then insert them into the differential unit and oil seals. Install the retaining bolts and tighten them to the correct torque wrench setting while holding the flanges stationary using the method described in paragraph 16.

27 Install new O-rings into the sliding disc bore then drive the new oil seal into the recess until it is flush with the end of the inner disc.

28 Install the coil spring, diaphragm springs and collar into the sliding disc, then clamp the springs into the disc using the long bolt and nut as in the removal procedure. Make sure that the previously made marks are aligned.

29 Insert a new rubber sealing ring into the disc making sure that the lugs locate in the disc recesses.

30 Fill the sliding disc with 75 cc of the specified fluid (photo).

31 Install the diaphragm making sure that the previously made marks are aligned, then fit the lockring into the groove using pliers to ensure that it is fully seated.

32 Fit the clamping plate over the diaphragm with the hole opposite the hole in the spring collar (ie not aligned), then fit the circlip to the inner disc hub (photos).

33 Locate the tool used in paragraph 4 over the sliding disc and remove the clamp bolt.

34 Assemble the sliding disc unit over the pinion shaft making sure that it is on the correct side as previously marked. The inner bore cavity should be filled with grease prior to assembly.

35 Install the fixed disc over the pinion shaft making sure that the previously made marks are aligned; use a soft head hammer or mallet to top it onto the splines.

36 Clean the pinion shaft threads with a cold solvent then apply a liquid locking agent to the threads and fit the nut.

37 Using the tool described in paragraph 5 hold the outer disc stationary and tighten the retaining nut to the specified torque wrench setting (photo).

38 Remove the clamp from the sliding disc.

39 Repeat the procedure given in paragraphs 27 to 38 inclusive on the remaining pulley assembly then thoroughly clean the disc faces with methylated spirit.

10 Halfshaft (Daf 66, Volvo 66, and Volvo 343 models) – removal, inspection and refitting

1 Jack up the rear of the car and support it adequately with axle-stands.

2 Unscrew the retaining screws and remove the guard panel from the variomatic transmission.

3 Mark the drive flanges and halfshaft in relation to each other,

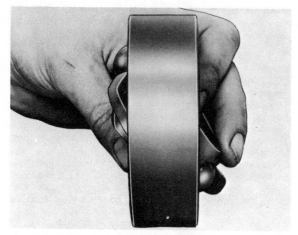

Fig. 6.44 Method of removing and installing the halfshaft joint balls

Fig. 6.45 Halfshaft joint assembly

Fig. 6.46 Alignment of the halfshaft joint inner and outer races

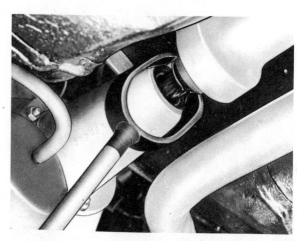

Fig. 6.47 Using the special tool to remove the propeller shaft (Volvo 343 models)

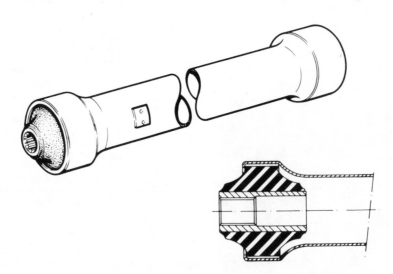

Fig. 6.48 Diagrammatic view of the propeller shaft

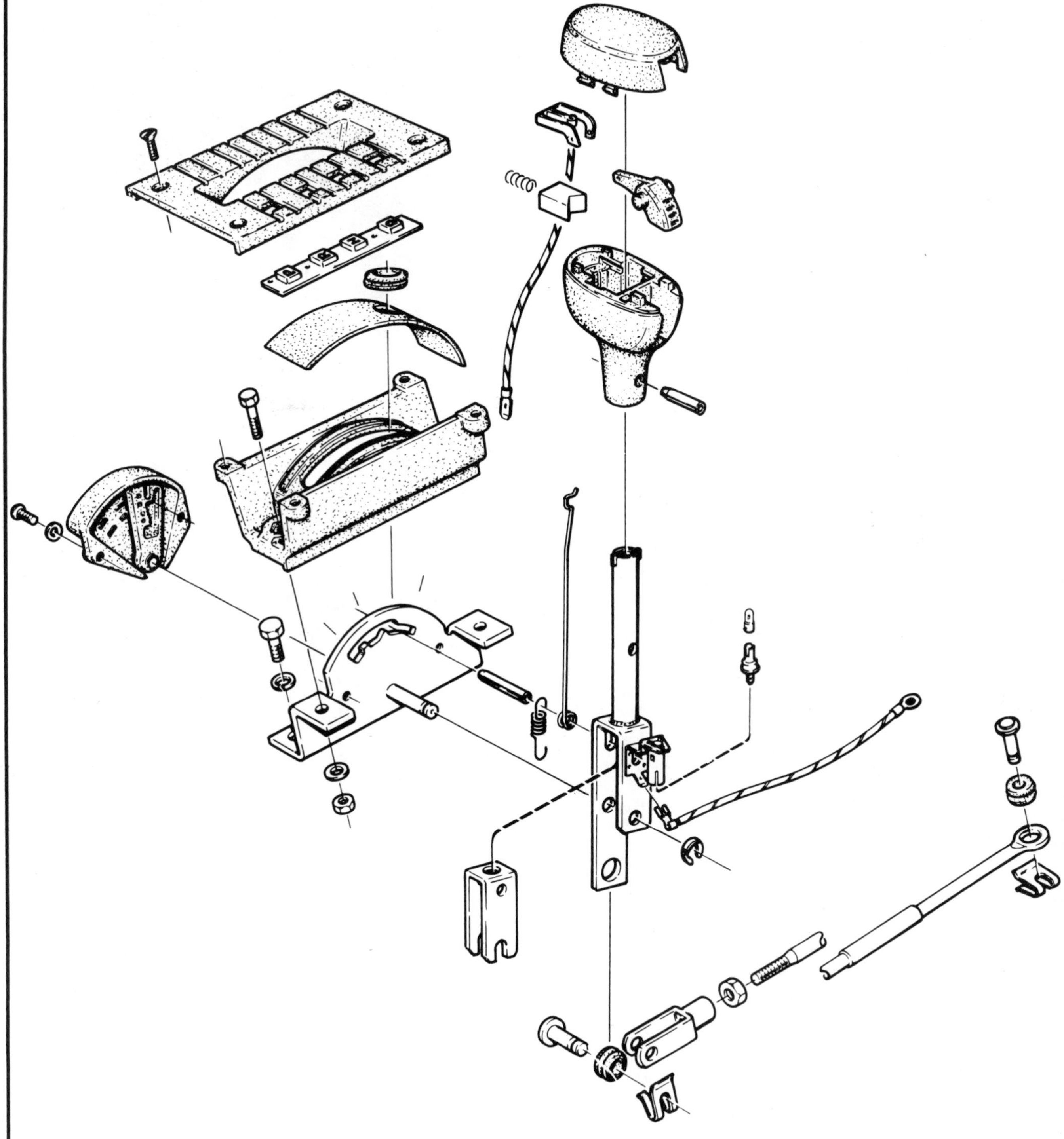

Fig. 6.49 Exploded view of the selector lever (early Volvo 343 models)

using an Allen key, unscrew and remove the inner and outer flange bolts.

4   Withdraw the halfshaft from the car (photo).

5   Using circlip pliers, extract the circlip from the halfshaft groove.

6   Remove the clip from the small diameter of the rubber bellows and slide the bellows along the shaft.

7   Support the inner race of the joint and press or drive out the half-shaft; the rubber bellows can now be removed from the shafts, together with the gasket.

8   If necessary the homokinetic joint may be dismantled by turning the inner race diagonally to the outer race and removing the bolts. Clean the components in paraffin and when dry examine the balls and races for wear and pitting; if evident a new joint should be obtained. If the components are serviceable reassemble the joint using a reversal of the dismantling procedure but make sure that the recess in the outer race and the spline run-out on the inner race face the same way, also ensure that the assembled position of the inner and outer races is as shown in Fig. 6.46.

9   The remaining reassembly and refitting of the half-shaft is a reversal of the dismantling and removal procedure, but the following additional points should be noted:

(a) *Pack the joints with a lithium based grease*

(b) *Fit new gaskets to the joint and flange faces; if necessary use glue to hold them in position*

(c) *Tighten the flange bolts to the specified torque wrench setting*

(d) *Wipe away any excess grease or foreign matter which could contaminate the transmission pulleys*

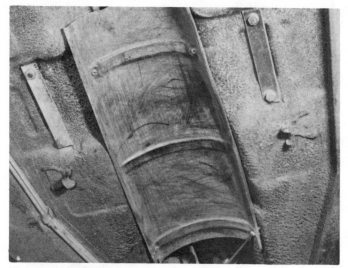

11.4 Exhaust system heat shield location (Volvo 343 models)

11 Propeller shaft – removal and refitting

1   Removal of the propeller shaft on Daf 55, Daf 66 and Volvo 66 models necessitates the removal of the engine or primary variomatic transmission unit; these procedures are described in Chapter 1 and Section 3 of this Chapter. Before installing the propeller shaft, lightly grease the splines of the clutch output shaft and the primary transmission pinion shaft; also make sure that the spring is located on the pinion shaft before engaging the propeller shaft (photo).

2   To remove the propeller shaft on Volvo 343 models, jack up the rear of the car and support it adequately on axle-stands.

3   Unscrew the retaining screws and remove the transmission guard panel.

4   Remove the heat shield located above the exhaust silencer after unscrewing the retaining screws (photo).

5   Obtain the tool (Volvo tool No 5948) or construct a similar tool and use it to lever the propeller shaft from the clutch output shaft splines.

6   Move the propeller shaft forwards and withdraw it from the car.

7   Refitting is a reversal of removal but lightly grease the splines and ensure that the spring is located correctly.

12 Selector lever and rod (Daf 55, Daf 66 and Volvo 66 models) – removal, refitting and adjusting

1   Jack up the front and rear of the car and support it adequately on axle-stands.

2   Disconnect the fork from the bottom of the selector lever by removing the clamp and clevis pin (photo).

3   Unscrew and remove the retaining screws and withdraw the right-hand console panel together with the cover plate and padding.

4   Disconnect the battery negative terminal.

5   Unscrew and remove the mounting bolts and detach the lever mounting assembly from the propeller shaft tunnel.

6   Withdraw the selector lever from the console.

7   Drive out the locking pin, noting the location of the return spring then detach the earth lead and slip contact holder (when fitted).

8   To remove the selector rod, first remove the transmission guard panel then remove the clevis pin and disconnect the rear of the selector rod from the selector lever (photos).

9   Remove the selector rod from the car, and examine the rubber grommets for deterioration; renew them if necessary.

10   Check the selector lever lower rubber gaiter for deterioration and renew it if necessary.

11   Refitting is a reversal of removal, but the selector rod must be

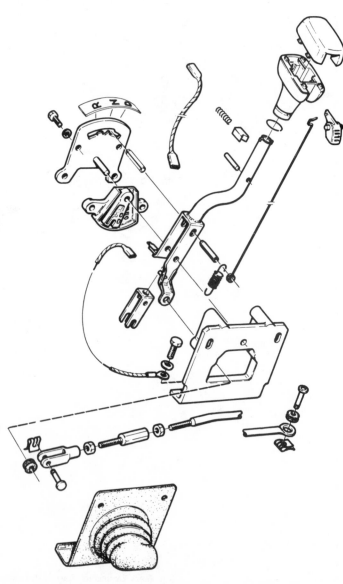

Fig. 6.50 Exploded view of the selector lever (Daf 55, Daf 66, and Volvo 66 models)

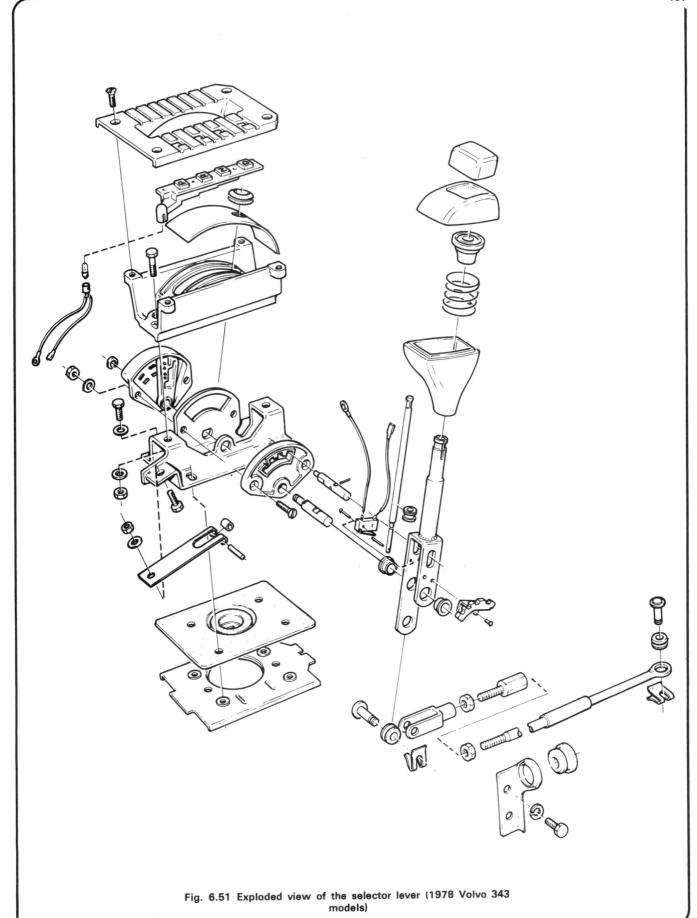

Fig. 6.51 Exploded view of the selector lever (1978 Volvo 343 models)

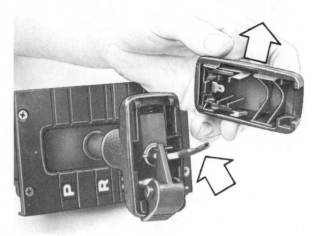

Fig. 6.52 Removing the selector lever cover (early Volvo 343 models)

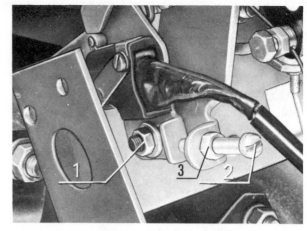

Fig. 6.53 Vacuum control micro-switch location (except Volvo 343 models)

(1) Retaining bolt   (3) Locknut
(2) Adjusting screw

Fig. 6.54 Vacuum control micro-switch location (Volvo 343 models pre 1978)

1   Adjusting screw   2   Steady screw

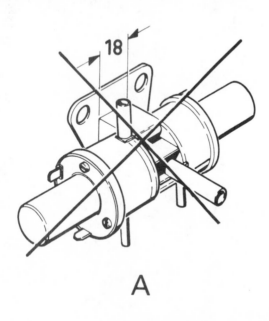

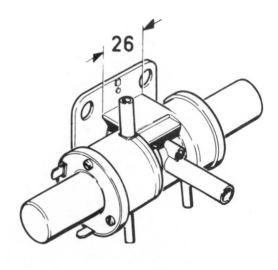

A

B

Fig. 6.55 Alternative types of vacuum control valve fitted to Daf 55 models (dimensions in mm)

Type A – Pre chassis No 713176 (no longer available as a replacement)
Type B – Chassis No 713176 onwards

adjusted as follows.

12 Place the selector lever in neutral and check that the primary transmission lever is also in the neutral position. Adjust the length of the selector rod until the clevis pin can be inserted without moving the levers, but make sure that the union nut is threaded onto the selector rod at least three or four threads.

13 Tighten the lock nuts after the adjustment is completed.

13 Selector lever and rod (Volvo 343 models pre 1978) – removal, refitting and adjusting

Note: The 1978 model selector lever differs from the previous design, refer to Fig. 6.51.

1 Jack up the front and rear of the car and support it adequately on axle-stands.

2 Remove the propeller shaft as described in Section 11.

3 Disconnect the fork from the bottom of the selector lever by removing the clamp and clevis pin.

4 Similarly disconnect the selector rod from the primary transmission lever and remove it from the car.

5 Prise the tray from the front of the console.

6 Disconnect the battery negative lead.

7 Prise the two switches from the console and disconnect the wires noting their locations.

8 Move the selector lever to position R, then unscrew and remove the retaining screws and withdraw the console; the screws are located beneath the plastic covers.

9 Detach the contact holder and sliding contact.

10 Disconnect the illumination supply wire, then unbolt the selector lever and gate.

11 Prise the cover from the top of the lever and disconnect the wire.

12 Detach the detent button and remove the spring and centering block.

13 Using a soft metal drift, drive the pin from the selector lever

handler after removing the retaining spring then withdraw the knob.

14 Unscrew and remove the retaining screws and withdraw the selector scale and dust cover.

15 Remove the selector lever housing and detach the earth cable and illumination fitting.

16 Prise out the clip then remove the selector gate and return spring.

17 Drive out the spring pin, remove the stop bracket and remove the pull rod after disconnecting the cable.

18 Check the selector lever grommet and selector rod bushes for deterioration and renew them if necessary.

19 Refitting is a reversal of removal, but the following additional points should be noted:

(a) The spring pin must protrude from the selector lever by 0.16 ± 0.001 in (4.0 ± 0.3 mm) plus the thickness of the selector gate

(b) Adjust the length of the selector rod so that with the selector lever and primary transmission lever in the neutral position, the clevis pin can be inserted without moving the levers; tighten the locknuts when the adjustment is completed

(c) Refit the propeller shaft with reference to Section 11

14 Vacuum control micro-switch – adjustment

1 Start the engine and allow it to reach the normal operating temperature, then adjust the idling speed as described in Chapter 3.

2 Using a T-connection and additional hose, connect a vacuum gauge into the primary transmission outer (overdrive) chamber supply hose between the control valve and the transmission (photo).

3 Apply the handbrake and move the selector lever to *neutral* then connect up an engine revolution counter (tachometer).

4 On Daf 55, Daf 66 and Volvo 66 models, loosen the micro-switch mounting nut and adjustment locknut, unscrew the adjustment screw and pull the switch forward as far as possible (photo).

12.2 Selector lever lower joint (Daf 66 models)

12.8A Selector rod rear joint (Daf 66 models)

12.8B Selector lever mechanism (Daf 66 models)

14.2 Checking the transmission vacuum control switch adjustment with a vacuum gauge

14.4 Vacuum control microswitch location (Daf 66 models)

5   On Volvo 343 models unscrew the adjustment bolt fully and pull back the micro-switch.
6   Start the engine and increase its speed to 2900 rpm (Daf 55 models prior to chassis No 713176) or 2650 rpm (all other models). Refer to Fig. 6.55.
7   Tighten the adjustment screw until the vacuum gauge returns to zero, then tighten the locknut and mounting nut on all but Volvo 343 models.
8   The micro-switch is now adjusted, but check its operation by gradually increasing the engine speed to the speeds given in paragraph 6, at which time the vaccum gauge should start indicating.
9   Remove the tachometer and vacuum gauge.

15 Fault diagnosis – transmission and final drive

Symptom	Reason/s
Lack of drive	Broken drivebelts
	Drivebelts out of adjustment or contaminated with oil
	Selector rod disconnected or selector mechanism faulty
Lack of drive on one rear wheel and tendency to wander on acceleration (Daf 55 models)	Broken drivebelt
	Seized secondary transmission
Excessive vibration and whine	Drivebelts out of adjustment
	Old, congealed oil in primary sliding discs
	Worn bearings or gear teeth
	Worn drivebelts
	Worn propeller shaft splines
Engine over-revs – transmission fails to change up correctly	Vacuum hoses broken or blocked
	Vacuum control valve or micro-switch faulty
	Primary sliding disc diaphragm broken or not sealing
Low ratio hold inoperative	Vacuum control valve faulty
	Low ratio switch faulty

Chapter 7 Braking system

Contents

Specifications

System type ....   Four wheel hydraulic, discs or drums at front, drums at rear (self-adjusting on Volvo models), dual circuit. Mechanical handbrake to rear wheels

Front brakes
Discs
Diameter:

Daf 55, Daf 66, Volvo 66	9.76 in (248 mm)
Volvo 343	9.16 in (232.7 mm)
Thickness when new (all models)	0.41 in (10.5 mm)
Minimum thickness after resurfacing	0.37 in (9.5 mm)
Maximum run-out	0.008 in (0.2 mm)

Drums

Diameter	7.87 in (200 mm)
Maximum diameter when reconditioned	+ 0.04 in (+ 1.0 mm)

Rear brakes
Drum diameter:

Daf 55	7.87 in (200 mm)
Daf 66	7.00 in (178 mm)
Volvo 66 and 343	8.00 in (203 mm)
Maximum diameter when reconditioned	+ 0.04 in (+ 1.0 mm)

Master cylinder
Bore:

Daf 55, Daf 66 DL	0.69 in (17.46 mm)
Daf 66 (except DL)	0.81 in (20.64 mm)
Volvo 66	0.87 in (22.2 mm)
Volvo 343	0.75 in (19.05 mm)
Brake pedal free travel (Daf 55 and Daf 66 models)	0.12 to 0.20 in (3 to 5 mm)

Brake fluid ....   SAE J 1703 (DOT 3 – DOT 4)

Torque wrench settings

	lbf ft	Nm
Wheel nuts	58 to 65	80 to 90
Master cylinder retaining nuts	11	15
Master cylinder retaining bolts	17	23
Bleed nipples	7.35	10
Brake lines	6 to 8	8 to 11
Caliper retaining bolts	28 to 33	38 to 45
Servo unit retaining bolts	15 to 19	21 to 26
Rear hub nut (Daf 55 models)	152 to 208	210 to 290
Disc-to-hub bolts	34	47

1 General description

The four wheel braking system is of dual circuit, hydraulic type with discs or drums at the front and drum brakes at the rear. On Volvo models the rear brakes are self-adjusting. A vacuum servo unit is fitted to most models as standard equipment. The handbrake is mechanically operated on the rear wheels only.

A pressure regulating valve is installed in the hydraulic circuit on Volvo 343 models to prevent the rear wheels locking in advance of the front wheels during heavy braking. On 1978 Volvo 343 models the master cylinder is provided with a high pressure switch which operates the transmission low ratio hold during excessive braking.

2 Drum brakes – adjustment

Front drums

1 Jack up the front of the car and support it adequately on axle-stands.
2 Two adjustment bolts are provided on the brake shoe backplate; the top bolt adjusts the upper brake shoe and the bottom bolt adjusts the lower brake shoe.
3 Using an open ended spanner turn each bolt towards the wheel cylinder (see Fig. 7.1) until the wheel can be turned freely.
4 Turn one adjustment bolt away from the wheel cylinder until the wheel is locked, then turn the bolt in the opposite direction until the wheel is just free to turn.
5 Repeat the procedure on the remaining adjustment bolt.
6 Carry out the procedure described in paragraphs 4 and 5 on the remaining wheel.
7 Lower the car to the ground.

Rear drums

8 Adjustment of the rear brakes is only possible on Daf 55 and 66 models.
9 Jack up the rear of the car and support it adequately on axle-stands.
10 On Daf 55 models two adjustment bolts are provided on the inside of the brake shoe backplate; on Daf 66 models there is only one adjuster (photo).
11 Fully release the handbrake. Working on one wheel, fully release the adjustment until the wheel turns freely. On Daf 55 models the two adjusting bolts must be turned towards the wheel cylinder; on Daf 66

models the single adjustment must be turned anti-clockwise when viewed from the inside.
12 On Daf 55 models turn one adjustment bolt in the opposite direction until the wheel is locked, then back it off until the backlash on the rear wheel reduction gears can just be felt. Repeat this procedure on the remaining adjusting bolt.
13 On Daf 66 models turn the adjustment clockwise until the wheel is locked, then back it off until the wheel is just free to rotate.
14 Carry out the procedure described in paragraphs 11 to 13 inclusive on the remaining wheel.
15 Lower the car to the ground.

3 Front brake shoes – inspection and renewal

1 Front drum brakes are only fitted to Daf 66 DL models and the following paragraphs are therefore only applicable to this model.
2 Jack up the front of the car and support it adequately on axle-stands.
3 Mark the roadwheel in relation to the wheel studs, then remove it.
4 Fully back off the front brake adjustment bolts (see Section 2).
5 Carefully tap off the hub dust cap; the speedometer cable adaptor is an integral port of the left-hand side dust cap.
6 Unscrew and remove the hub adjusting locknut and withdraw the brake drum from the stub axle.
7 Brush away any accumulated dust and inspect the linings; if they are worn down to within 0.04 in (1 mm) of the rivets or if the total thickness is under 0.08 in (2 mm), renew the shoes as a complete set. If the linings are in good condition, clean the interior of the brake drum and refit it.
8 Where the shoes must be renewed, obtain new or reconditioned units.
9 Unhook the large rear spring from both brake shoes noting the location holes in the shoe webs.
10 Note the location of the front return spring, then carefully lift the shoes from the wheel cylinder and detach the spring.
11 Clean the brake backplate and check the wheel cylinder for leaks; if evident, renew or overhaul the wheel cylinder as necessary.
12 Do not touch the brake pedal while the shoes are removed.
13 If the adjusting bolts are seized they must be freed by using penetrating oil. Smear a little brake grease on the ends of the shoe webs which will contact the wheel cylinder and anchor block.
14 Rotate the adjusting bolts to their retracted positions, then refit the brake shoes using a reversal of the removal procedure. Make sure that the centre section of the front return spring rests against the

2.10 Rear brake adjustment (Daf 66 models)

4.4 Removing the disc pad retaining pins (Daf 66 models)

4.6 Removing the disc pads

Fig. 7.1 Location of adjustment bolts on front drum brakes (release direction arrowed)

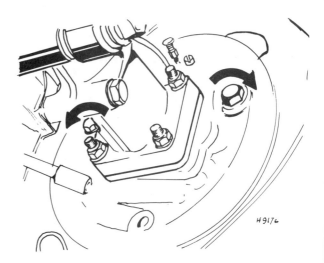

Fig. 7.2 Location of rear brake adjustment on Daf 55 models (lock direction arrowed)

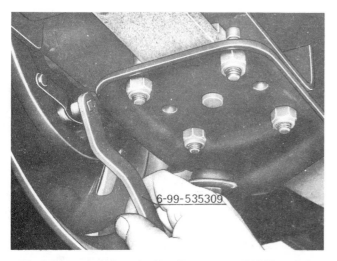

Fig. 7.3 Location of rear brake adjustment on Daf 66 models

Fig. 7.4 Front drum brake return spring (1 and 2)

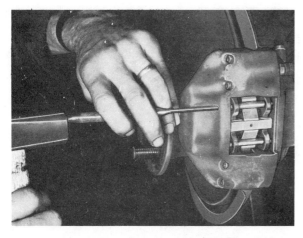

Fig. 7.5 Removing the disc pad retaining pin (Daf 55 and 66 models)

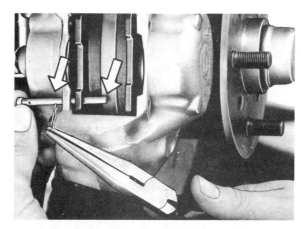

Fig. 7.6 Removing the disc pad retaining pin (Volvo 343 models)

wheel cylinder.

15 Check that the linings are free of dirt or finger marks, using sand-paper if necessary to remove any contamination.

16 Refit the hub and brake drum and tighten the adjusting nut until the circlip beneath it can just be moved. Use a suitable punch to lock the adjusting nut onto the stub axle.

17 Refit the dust cap and the roadwheel.

18 Adjust the brake shoes as described in Section 2, then lower the car to the ground.

4 Disc pads – inspection and renewal

1 Every 12 000 miles (20 000 km) the disc pads should be inspected for wear.

2 Jack up the front of the car and support it adequately on axle-stands.

3 Mark the roadwheel in relation to the wheel studs then remove it.

4 On Daf 55, Daf 66, and Volvo 66 models, drive out the disc pad retaining pins with a suitable drift and withdraw the four blade retaining spring (photo).

5 On Volvo 343 models, use long nose pliers to extract the spring clips from the retaining pins, then pull the pins out from the caliper using a suitable drift if necessary.

6 Withdraw the two disc pads noting from which side of the disc they were removed (photo). If they are difficult to remove, use a pair of pliers and ease the pads from the disc to allow room for any rust to be dislodged. In extreme cases make up a tool similar to that shown in Fig. 7.7.

7 Brush any dust or dirt from the disc pad recessed in the caliper (do not inhale the dust), then use a flat piece of wood to press the two pistons into the caliper to accommodate the extra thickness of new pads.

8 Inspect the thickness of the friction material on the disc pads and if less than 0.08 in (2 mm) on any single pad, a complete set of new pads must be fitted.

9 On all but Volvo 343 models the caliper pistons must be located with the cut out facing downward and a little to the rear in order to prevent the disc pads squeaking. If necessary a gauge should be borrowed from a tool agent or Volvo garage to check the piston setting.

10 Install the new friction pads making sure that the friction surface is towards the disc, and that the retaining springs and pins are fitted correctly.

11 Finally give the footbrake pedal several hard applications to bring the disc pads to their correct positions.

12 Fit the roadwheel then lower the car to the ground and tighten the wheel nuts to the correct torque wrench setting.

13 Check the disc pads on the remaining wheel.

5 Rear brake shoes (manual adjusting) – inspection and renewal

1 Jack up the rear of the car and support it adequately on axle-stands.

2 Mark the roadwheel in relation to the wheelstuds then remove it.

3 Fully release the handbrake and back off the brake shoe adjustments with reference to Section 2.

4 On Daf 55 models extract the split-pin, unscrew and remove the castellated nut and remove the brake drum and spacer ring. To do this it will be necessary to obtain a hub puller from a tool agent or the special extractor (tool No 6-99-535017) from a Daf garage.

5 On Daf 66 models tap the brake drum from the axleshaft with a soft headed mallet (photo).

6 Brush away any accumulated dust and inspect the linings; if they are worn down to within 0.04 in (1 mm) of the rivets or if the total thickness is under 0.08 in (2 mm), renew the shoes as a complete set. If the linings are in good condition, clean the interior of the brake drum and refit it.

7 Where the shoes must be renewed, obtain new or reconditioned units.

8 Note the location of the return springs to ensure correct refitting.

9 On Daf 55 models unlock the large curved spring from the brake shoes and anchor block, detach the shoes from the upper wheel cylinder, and disconnect the handbrake cable. The two shoes can then be removed from the backplate and the link removed followed by the return spring.

10 On Daf 66 models use a screwdriver to prise the brake shoes from

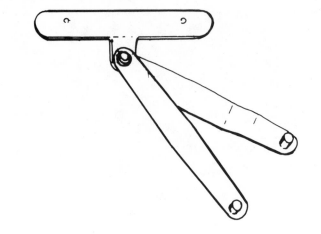

Fig. 7.7 Disc pad removing tool

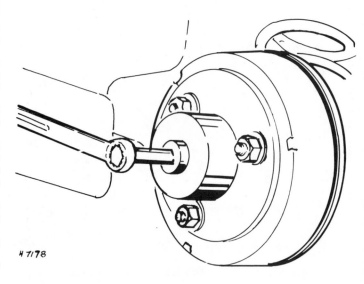

H 7/78

Fig. 7.8 Extracting the rear hub and brake drum (Daf 55 models)

1

Fig. 7.9 Removing the large brake shoe retaining spring (1) on Daf 55 models

5.5 Rear brake drum (Daf 66 models)

8.15 Caliper piston angled recess

11.1 Brake master cylinder (Daf 66 models)

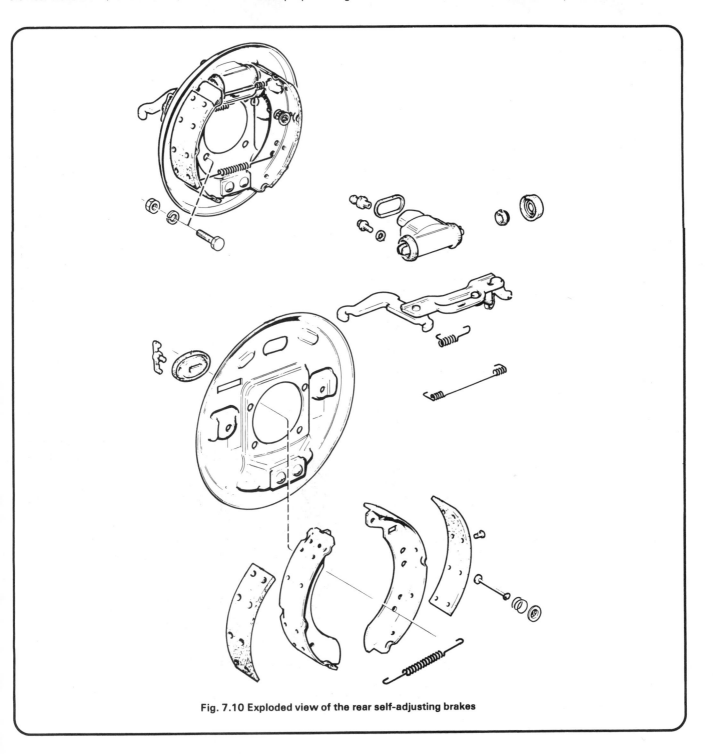

Fig. 7.10 Exploded view of the rear self-adjusting brakes

Fig. 7.11 Removing the handbrake lever stop pad

Fig. 7.12 Detaching the trailing shoe retaining spring (self-adjusting brakes)

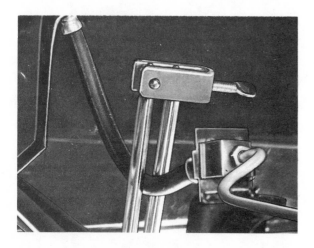

Fig. 7.13 Using a brake hose compressor

Fig. 7.14 Removing the wheel cylinder pistons (Volvo 343 models)

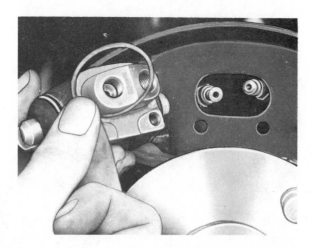

Fig. 7.15 Location of wheel cylinder gasket (late models)

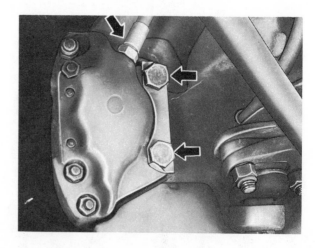

Fig. 7.16 Location of the caliper retaining bolts and hose connection

the wheel cylinder and adjuster, then unhook the return springs and remove the brake shoes. Note that the upper return spring is coloured red.

11 Clean the brake backplate and check the wheel cylinder for leaks; if evident, renew or overhaul the wheel cylinder as necessary.

12 Do not touch the brake pedal while the shoes are removed.

13 Check the adjusting bolts or quadrant for freedom of movement, using penetrating oil as necessary. Smear a little brake grease on the ends of the shoe webs which will contact the wheel cylinder and anchor block or adjuster.

14 Rotate the adjusters to their restricted positions, then refit the brake shoes using a reversal of the removal procedure. On Daf 55 models make sure that the link is mounted correctly between the two shoes, and on Daf 66 models, hook the upper rod spring onto the shoes first and locate them onto the wheel cylinder, then locate the lower spring and shoes; rotate the hub as necessary to the most favourable position during this operation.

15 Check that the linings are free of dirt or finger marks, using fine sandpaper if necessary to remove any contamination.

16 Refit the brake drum and roadwheel, on Daf 55 models make sure that the spacer ring is between the drum and the axleshaft and tighten the castellated nut to the correct torque wrench setting before inserting a new split-pin.

17 Adjust the brake shoes as described in Section 2, then lower the car to the ground.

6 Rear brake shoes (self-adjusting) – inspection and renewal

1 Jack up the rear of the car and support it adequately on axle-stands.

2 Mark the roadwheel in relation to the wheelstuds, then remove it.

3 Fully release the handbrake lever.

4 Using a wooden or soft head mallet, tap the brake drum from the hub and wheelstuds. If difficulty is experienced as a result of worn brake drums, loosen the handbrake adjustment at the handbrake lever (see Section 17), then using a screwdriver, lever the handbrake operating lever away from the backplate and pull the nylon stop from the rubber boot of the lever. On release of the lever the brake shoes will retract enough to allow the brake drums to be removed.

5 Brush away any accumulated dust and inspect the linings; if they are worn down to within 0.04 in (1 mm) of the rivets or if the total thickness is under 0.08 in (2 mm), renew the shoes as a complete set. If the linings are in good condition, clean the interior of the brake drum and refit it.

6 Where the shoes must be renewed, obtain new or reconditioned units.

7 Note the location of the return and retaining springs to ensure correct refitting.

8 Remove both shoe steady posts. To do this, grip the dished washer with a pair of pliers, depress it and rotate it through 90°, then release it and withdraw the washer and spring from the T-shaped post.

9 Using a screwdriver or adjustable spanner, prise the two shoes from the lower anchor block and unhook the lower return spring.

10 Prise the front shoe from the groove in the wheel cylinder and detach it from the self-adjusting mechanism quadrant. Unhook the upper return spring from the trailing shoe and withdraw the leading shoe forwards.

11 Unhook the remaining return spring from the trailing shoe and withdraw the shoe rearwards.

12 Clean the backplate and check the wheel cylinders for leaks; if evident, renew or overhaul the wheel cylinder as necessary.

13 Do not touch the brake pedal while the shoes are removed.

14 Check the self-adjusting mechanism for free movement and lubricate it sparingly, being careful to wipe any excess oil away. Smear a little brake grease on the ends of the shoe webs which will contact the wheel cylinder and anchor block. Place the self-adjusting mechanism in its *start* position.

15 Refitting the brake shoes is a reversal of the removal procedure but the following additional points should be noted:

(a) *The arrows marked on new shoes should point upwards towards the wheel cylinder*

(b) *Make sure that all the springs are fitted correctly; in particular check that the steady spring T-posts are at right angles to the slots in the dished washer*

(c) *Refit the handbrake lever nylon stop as necessary*

(d) *Refit the brake drum and wheel, then depress the footbrake several times to operate the self-adjusting mechanism, and adjust the handbrake as described in Section 17.*

16 Lower the car to the ground.

7 Wheel cylinder – removal, servicing, and refitting

1 Jack up the front or rear of the car as necessary and support it adequately on axle-stands.

2 Remove the brake shoes as described in Sections 3, 5, and 6.

3 Remove the cap from the master cylinder reservoir and place a piece of polythene sheeting over the opening, then refit the cap. This will create a vacuum and prevent loss of hydraulic fluid in subsequent operations. Alternatively use a brake pipe compressor to pinch the flexible hose to the wheel cylinder.

4 Place a small container beneath the wheel cylinder and extract the two pistons noting from which side they were removed. On Volvo 343 models, also remove the interior spring.

5 Using methylated spirit, clean the interior of the wheel cylinder thoroughly and check the bore surfaces for scoring or bright wear areas. Similarly clean the pistons and check them for wear.

6 If the components are in good condition, discard the rubber seals and obtain new ones in the form of a repair kit. Install the new seals using the fingers only to manipulate them into position. Dip the pistons in clean hydraulic fluid before installing them and then fit the dust excluders.

7 If the components are excessively worn, the wheel cylinder must be renewed. To remove it, unscrew and remove the hydraulic supply line(s) and bleed nipple, then unscrew and remove the retaining bolts and withdraw the wheel cylinder from the backplate. On late models note the gasket fitted between the wheel cylinder and backplate.

8 Refitting is a reversal of removal but the following additional points should be noted:

(a) *When renewing the wheel cylinder on late models, make sure that the gasket is located correctly against the backplate.*

(b) *Tighten all nuts and bolts to the correct torque wrench setting*

(c) *After removing the plastic sheeting from the master cylinder, adjust the brakes then bleed the hydraulic system as described in Section 16*

(d) *Make sure that the dust cap retaining springs are fully engaged in the cylinder grooves where applicable*

8 Disc caliper – removal, servicing and refitting

1 Jack up the front of the car and support it adequately on axle-stands.

2 Withdraw the disc pads as described in Section 4.

3 Remove the cap from the master cylinder reservoir and place a piece of polythene sheeting over the opening, then refit the cap. This will prevent excessive loss of hydraulic fluid during subsequent operations. Alternatively use a brake pipe compressor to pinch the flexible hose leading to the caliper.

4 Loosen the brake hose union at the caliper a quarter of a turn.

5 Unscrew and remove the two caliper retaining bolts after bending back the lock tabs, but do not allow the caliper to hang by the hydraulic hose.

6 Unscrew the caliper from the hose and seal the apertures with masking tape to prevent the ingress of foreign matter.

7 Place the caliper in a soft jaw vice with the bleed nipple uppermost; this will facilitate adjustment of the pistons in subsequent operations.

8 Clean the external surfaces of the caliper with methylated spirit. On no account loosen the nuts that secure the two halves of the caliper body together.

9 Extract the spring retaining rings and dust excluders from the ends of the caliper pistons.

10 Using two screwdrivers as levers and taking care not to scratch the pistons, prise the pistons from the caliper body. Mark each piston in relation to its respective bore. An alternative method of removing the pistons is by using a tyre pump connected to the inlet aperture

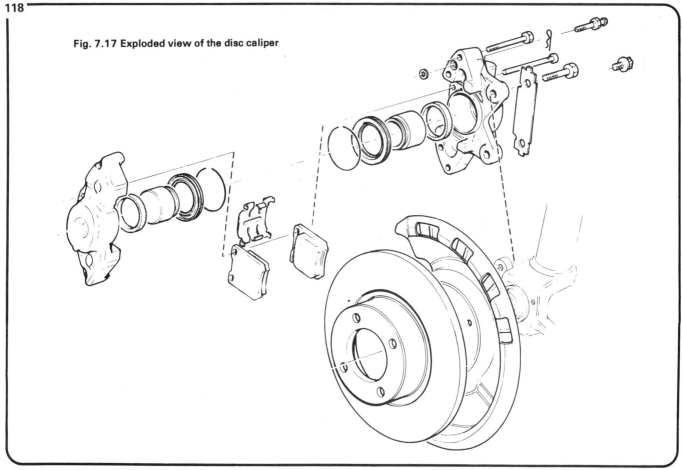

Fig. 7.17 Exploded view of the disc caliper

11.8 Removing the master cylinder fluid filter

16.7A Removing the bleed nipple cover

16.7B Bleeding the brake caliper (Daf 66 models)

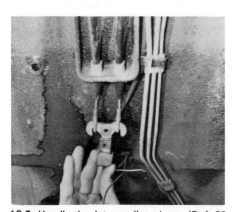

18.3 Handbrake intermediate lever (Daf 66 models)

18.4 Handbrake rear section lever connection (Daf 66 models)

22.2 Removing the vacuum servo unit air filter (RHD Daf 66 models)

Fig. 7.18 Removing the caliper piston dust excluder and spring

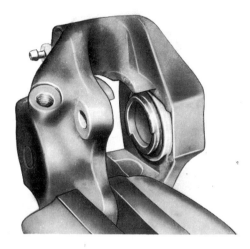

Fig. 7.19 Correct location of the caliper piston recess

with the bleed nipple closed; wrap the caliper in rag and restrain one piston while the other piston is being removed, then seal the piston aperture and remove the remaining piston.

11 Using a plastic or copper needle, prise the sealing rings from the caliper bores.

12 Clean the pistons and caliper bores with methylated spirit and inspect the surfaces for scoring, rust and bright wear areas; if evident the complete caliper must be renewed.

13 If the components are in good condition, discard the seals and obtain a repair kit.

14 Install the new seals using the fingers only to manipulate them into their grooves.

15 Dip the assembled pistons in clean hydraulic fluid and insert them squarely into their cylinder bores. Where the pistons have angled recesses, remember to install them with the cutout facing downwards and a little to the rear of the caliper. When correctly positioned, an imaginary line through the recessed edges of the pistons should be in line with the lower retaining pin bore (photo).

16 Install the new dust excluders and spring retainers; apply the special grease supplied with the kit to the inside surfaces of the dust excluders.

17 Refitting the caliper is now a reversal of removal but the following additional points should be noted:

  (a) Tighten all nuts and bolts to the correct specified torque wrench settings
  (b) After removing the plastic sheeting from the master cylinder or the brake hose clamp, bleed the hydraulic system as described in Section 16

9 Brake disc – examination, removal and refitting

1 Detach the caliper from the stub axle and tie it up out of the way as described in the preceding Section, paragraphs 1, 2 and 5.

2 The disc should now be examined for deep scoring or grooving (light scoring is normal). If severe, the disc should be removed and either renewed or ground within limits (see Specifications) by a suitably equipped engineering works.

3 Check the disc for run-out with a dial gauge, or alternatively with a fixed stand and a feeler gauge by taking readings at various points around the disc.

4 To remove the disc, first withdraw the hub assembly as described in Chapter 9.

5 Unscrew and remove the four bolts securing the disc to the hub. To do this fit the hub to a wheel and tighten the wheel nuts. Place the wheel flat on the ground and loosen the four bolts; an Allen key will be required on late models.

6 Use a wooden or soft head mallet to carefully remove the disc from the hub.

7 Clean the disc guard plate and if the original disc is being refitted,

clean it thoroughly of any rust or foreign matter. The contact surface of the hub should also be thoroughly cleaned.

8 Refitting is a reversal of removal but the following additional points should be noted:

  (a) Tighten the retaining bolts to the correct specified torque wrench setting
  (b) Refit and adjust the hub bearings as described in Chapter 9
  (c) Check that the disc run-out is within limits. If it is not, it may be possible to correct it by moving the disc half a turn on the hub
  (d) To prevent the car pulling to one side it is recommended that both front discs are renewed or reground at the same time

10 Brake drum – inspection and renovation

1 Whenever the brake drums are removed, they should be examined for deterioration and cracking.

2 After high mileage the drums may become slightly oval internally and may also be excessively scored. If this is evident the drums should be renewed or surface ground within limits (see Specifications).

11 Master cylinder (Daf 55 and Daf 66 models) – removal, servicing and refitting

1 The master cylinder is of the tandem type and is mounted on the bulkhead on models without servo-assistance. On servo-assisted models the master cylinder is mounted on the bulkhead on right-hand drive cars (photo), and on the front of the servo unit on left-hand drive cars.

2 Disconnect the battery negative terminal and remove the spare wheel.

3 Disconnect the two wires from the stoplight switch mounted on the end of the master cylinder.

4 Place a small container beneath the master cylinder and if possibly syphon the brake fluid from the reservoir.

5 Unscrew and remove the unions securing the hydraulic lines to the master cylinder and carefully pull them clear.

6 Plug the cylinder apertures and pipe ends to prevent the ingress of foreign matter.

7 Working inside the car, disconnect the master cylinder operating rod from the brake pedal on all models except LHD servo-assisted models.

8 Unscrew and remove the retaining nuts and washers and withdraw the master cylinder; empty the hydraulic fluid from the reservoir and discard it (photo).

9 Clamp the master cylinder in a soft jaw vice and withdraw the reservoir by tilting it, then extract the sealing plugs.

Fig. 7.20 Removing the caliper retaining bolts (late models)

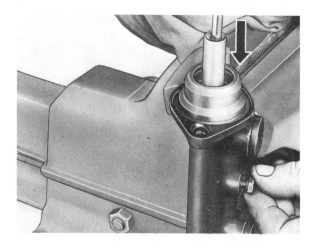

Fig. 7.21 Removing the stop bolt on Daf 55 and 66 models

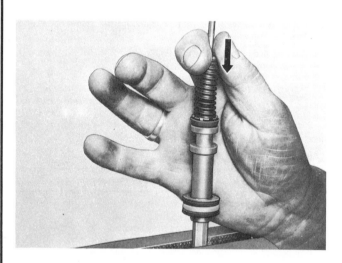

Fig. 7.22 Removing the primary piston spring (Daf 55 and 66 models)

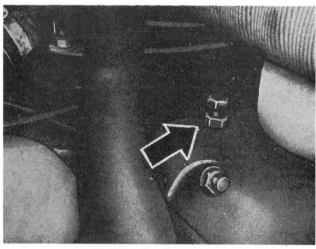

Fig. 7.23 Brake pedal free play adjusting bolt fitted to some models

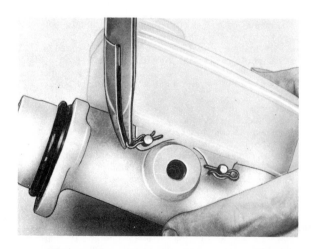

Fig. 7.24 Extracting the reservoir pin retaining clips (Volvo models)

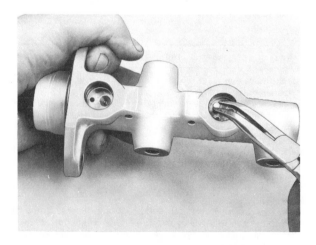

Fig. 7.25 Removing the primary piston stop pin (Volvo models)

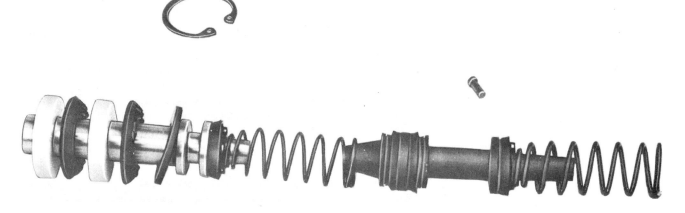

Fig. 7.26 Master cylinder internal components (Volvo models)

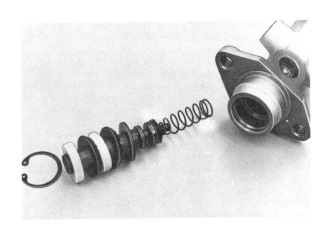

Fig. 7.27 Primary piston components removed from the master cylinder (Volvo models)

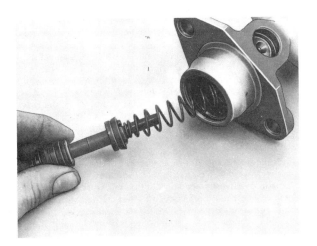

Fig. 7.28 Removing the secondary piston components from the master cylinder (Volvo models)

10 Depress the primary piston and unscrew and remove the stop bolt and washer.

11 With the primary piston still depressed, use circlip pliers to remove the circlip from the mouth of the cylinder bore. On some models a spring clip is fitted and it will then be necessary to prise it out with a screwdriver.

12 Extract the primary and secondary pistons together with the springs noting the extact order of removal. Tap the end of the cylinder on a block of wood if any of the components are difficult to remove.

13 Unscrew and remove the stoplight switch and washer.

14 Clean all components in methylated spirit and allow them to dry, then examine the piston and cylinder bore surfaces for scoring or bright wear areas. Where these are evident the master cylinder must be renewed.

15 If the components are in good order, discard the seals and obtain a repair kit. To remove the rear seal from the primary piston, slightly compress the spring and remove the retaining screw.

16 Install the new seals using the fingers only to manipulate them into position. Make sure that the sealing lips are facing the correct way, and compress the primary piston spring before tightening the retaining screw.

17 Dip the components in clean hydraulic fluid then assemble them to the bore of the master cylinder using a reversal of the removal procedure.

18 Depress the primary piston and fit the stop bolt and washer.

19 Refitting the master cylinder is a reversal of removal, but it will then be necessary to top-up the hydraulic fluid and bleed the system as described in Section 16. Where the master cylinder is fitted directly to the servo unit, a new rubber sealing ring should be installed.

20 Check that the free-play of the brake pedal is within the limits given in Specifications. If necessary turn the adjusting screw located on the bulkhead in the engine compartment until the clearance is correct.

21 Finally check that the dust cap is correctly located in the operating rod groove.

12 Master cylinder Volvo 66 and Volvo 343 models – removal, servicing and refitting

1 The master cylinder is of the tandem type and on RHD Volvo 66 models is mounted directly onto the bulkhead; on LHD Volvo 66 and all Volvo 343 models the cylinder is mounted on the front of the servo unit.

2 Disconnect the battery negative terminal, and remove the spare wheel.

3 Disconnect the two wires from the stoplight switch mounted on the end or side of the master cylinder, and also disconnect the wires from the brake level warning switch located in the filler cap.

4 Place a small container beneath the master cylinder and if possible syphon the brake fluid from the reservoir.

5 Unscrew and remove the unions securing the hydraulic lines to the master cylinder and carefully pull them clear.

6   Plug the cylinder apertures and pipe ends to prevent the ingress of foreign matter.

7   On RHD Volvo 66 models disconnect the master cylinder operating rod from the brake pedal.

8   Unscrew and remove the retaining nuts or bolts as applicable together with the washers, and withdraw the master cylinder; empty the hydraulic fluid from the reservoir and discard it.

9   Clamp the master cylinder in a soft jaw vice and remove the reservoir by extracting the locking clips and withdrawing the two retaining pins.

10 Where the master cylinder is fitted directly to a servo unit, remove the sealing ring from the rear face.

11 Prise the reservoir seals from the two ports.

12 Unscrew and remove the stoplight switch and washer.

13 Depress the primary piston and extract the stop pin from the front port with a pair of long nose pliers.

14 Remove the dust cover where necessary and, with the primary piston still depressed, use circlip pliers to extract the circlip from the mouth of the cylinder bore.

15 Extract the primary and secondary pistons together with the springs, noting the exact order of removal. Tap the end of the cylinder on a block of wood if any of the components are difficult to remove.

16 Clean all the components in methylated spirit and allow them to dry, then examine the piston and cylinder bore surfaces for scoring or bright wear areas. Where these are evident the master cylinder must be renewed.

17 If the components are in good order, discard the seals and obtain a repair kit.

18 Install the new seals using the fingers only to manipulate them into position. Make sure that the sealing lips are facing the correct way.

19 Lubricate the internal components of the master cylinder with the paste supplied with the repair kit or alternatively dip them in clean hydraulic fluid, then assemble them to the bore of the master cylinder using a reversal of the removal procedure.

20 Depress the primary piston in order to fit the stop pin and circlip.

21 Refitting the master cylinder is a reversal of removal but it will then be necessary to top-up the hydraulic fluid and bleed the system as described in Section 16. Where the master cylinder is fitted directly to the servo unit, a new rubber sealing ring should be installed.

13 Pressure conscious reducing valve – description, removal and refitting

1   This unit is fitted to Volvo 343 models. A spring tensioned plunger is included in the rear braking circuit and effectively limits the braking effort that can be applied to the rear wheels. The device ensures that under extreme braking the greatest percentage of braking effort is applied to the front wheels, and rear wheel locking is prevented.

2   If the front brake circuit should fail a pressure differential sensing plunger will operate, opening a by-pass orifice so that the rear brake pressure reducing valve becomes inoperative.

3   The valve cannot be repaired and, in the event of a fault developing, must be renewed complete.

4   Removal of the valve is simply a matter of disconnecting the hydraulic lines.

5   Refitting is a reversal of removal but it will be necessary to bleed the hydraulic system as described in Section 16.

14 Flexible hoses – inspection, removal and refitting

1   Periodically the flexible hydraulic hoses should be inspected for deterioration and damage. If they are swollen or chafed they must be renewed.

2   To remove a hose, first place some polythene sheeting beneath the reservoir filler cap to prevent excessive loss of hydraulic fluid.

3   Unscrew the unions, being careful to prevent the rigid line connection from turning.

4   Refitting is a reversal of removal, but make sure that the hose is not twisted when the wheels are in the straight-ahead position. The hose must not foul any part of the body or wheel. It will be necessary to bleed the hydraulic system as described in Section 16.

15 Rigid brake lines – inspection, removal and refitting

1   At regular intervals clean the steel brake pipes and examine them

for signs of rust or denting caused by flying stones.

2   Examine the securing clips and adjust them if necessary so that they hold the pipes securely and prevent them from vibrating.

3   Check that the pipes are not touching any adjacent components and bend them away if necessary.

4   If the pipes are corroded badly, they must be renewed. Unscrew the unions from each end of the pipe, using a split ring spanner if possible.

5   Fit the new pipes making sure that bends are kept to a minimum. Bleed the hydraulic system as described in Section 16 after tightening the unions to the correct specified torque wrench setting.

16 Hydraulic system – bleeding

1   Removal of all air from the hydraulic system is essential to the correct working of the braking system. Before starting, check the brake lines and hoses for leakage and make sure that the vent holes in the reservoir filler cap are unrestricted.

2   If regular topping-up of the brake fluid has been necessary, the source of the leak must be found, and this may include checking the wheel cylinders and calipers.

3   Remember that the brake fluid can permanently damage paintwork; any spills or splashes must be washed off *immediately* with cold water.

4   If there is any possibility of incorrect fluid being present in the system, completely drain it and flush through with methylated spirit. Renew all internal seals since these will be affected.

5   A clean jar, a length of tubing which fits tightly over the bleed nipples, and a tin of the correct brake fluid will be required.

6   Where a servo unit is fitted, depress the brake pedal several times in order to exhaust the vacuum which may be present.

7   Bleed the front calipers or wheel cylinders first, followed by the rear wheel cylinders. Connect the tube to the nipple and immerse its open end in a little brake fluid contained in the jar. Keep the open end of the tube submerged throughout the operation (photo).

8   Open the bleed nipple about half a turn and then have an assistant depress the brake pedal fully. The pedal must then be released until fully returned and the procedure repeated three or four times.

9   Check the level of fluid in the reservoir and top-up as necessary.

10 When no more bubbles emerge from the bleed tube, tighten the bleed nipple with the brake pedal fully depressed, then release it.

11 Always discard fluid which has been expelled into the jar and always top-up the reservoir with clean hydraulic fluid which has been stored in an airtight container and remained unshaken for the previous 24 hours.

12 Note that on some models the nipple mounted on one rear wheel cylinder serves to bleed both rear cylinders.

17 Handbrake – adjustment

1   Before adjusting the handbrake, the rear brake shoes must be adjusted as described in Section 2. On self-adjusting rear brake models depress the footbrake pedal several times to ensure the brake shoes are fully adjusted.

2   On Daf 55 models up to chassis No 634000, disconnect the cable yoke located just in front of the transmission unit by extracting the split-pin and removing the clevis pin. Loosen the locknut and turn the yoke so that the handbrake lever is fully applied at three notches. This will require some trial and error, and when completed, the clevis pin and split-pin should be refitted and the locknut tightened. When adequate adjustment cannot be obtained at the yoke, adjust the cable at the lever.

3   On Daf 55 models from chassis No 634000 onwards, Daf 66 and Volvo 66 models, first jack up the rear of the car and support it adequately on axle-stands. Pull the rubber grommet back from the handbrake lever to expose the adjusting nuts, and insert a screwdriver into the slotted end. Loosen the locknut and turn the adjusting nut until it is possible to turn the rear wheels with the handbrake lever applied five notches. When completed tighten the locknut and refit the rubber grommet.

4   On Volvo 343 models jack up the rear of the car and support it adequately on axle-stands. Pull the rubber grommet back from the handbrake lever and loosen the cable locknut. Turn the adjusting nut until it is impossible to turn the rear wheels with the handbrake lever

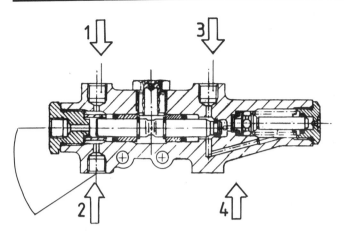

Fig. 7.29 Cross section diagram of the brake pressure conscious reducing valve

1 *Front circuit entry port*   3 *Rear circuit entry port*
2 *Front circuit exit port*   4 *Rear circuit exit port*

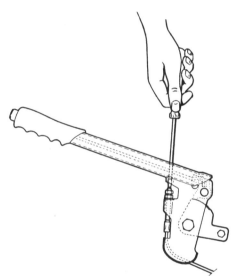

Fig. 7.30 Handbrake adjustment location (late Daf 55, Daf 66, and Volvo 66 models)

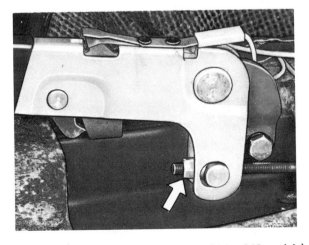

Fig. 7.31 Handbrake adjustment location (Volvo 343 models)

applied three notches. Tighten the locknut and refit the grommet when completed. To provide better access it is recommended that the left-hand seat is moved forwards as far as possible.

18 Handbrake cable – removal and refitting

1   Jack up the rear of the car and support it adequately on axle-stands.
2   Fully release the handbrake lever and pull back the rubber grommet then detach the cable from the lever.
3   Working beneath the car disconnect the front cable from the inter-mediate lever or equaliser, as applicable, and withdraw the cable downwards (photo).
4   To remove the rear handbrake cable on Daf 55 models it will be necessary to remove the rear brake shoes as described in Section 5, and then disconnect it from the intermediate lever (photo). On all other models, detach the cable from the equaliser and prise the retaining clamp apart.
6   Spring the cable suspension hook from the bracket then remove the relevant roadwheel.
7   Prise the cable clamp from the De Dion axle bracket and unhook the cable end from the operating arm. The cable can now be with-drawn from the car.
8   Refitting is a reversal of removal but it will be necessary to adjust the handbrake as described in Section 17.

19 Handbrake lever – removal and refitting

1   On Volvo 343 models only, move the left-hand seat forwards as far as possible.
2   On all models pull the rubber grommet away from the lever, and push the floor covering to one side.
3   Disconnect the cable from the lever and where a handbrake warning switch is fitted disconnect the supply lead.
4   Unscrew and remove the handbrake lever retaining bolts and lift the assembly from the mounting plate.
5   Refitting is a reversal of removal, but it will be necessary to adjust the cable as described in Section 17.

20 Vacuum servo unit – description

Some models are fitted with a vacuum servo unit in the brake hydraulic circuit to provide assistance to the driver when the brake pedal is depressed. On LHD models and all Volvo 343 models the unit is fitted directly behind the master cylinder, but on other models it is remotely mounted.

The unit operates by vacuum obtained from the induction manifold and comprises basically a booster diaphragm and a central valve.

Under normal conditions vacuum affects both sides of the internal diaphragm which therefore remains stationary. When the brake pedal is depressed, the internal valve cuts off vacuum to one side of the diaphragm and opens it to atmospheric pressure. The resulting inrush of air pushes the servo piston forward and augments the driver's pressure on the pushrod to the brake master cylinder. A non-return valve retains the vacuum in the servo if the engine cuts out or is switched off. The servo will then provide assistance for 2 or 3 applications of the brakes before it is exhausted, this will be apparent because of the sudden increase in pedal pressure required.

The air entering the unit passes through a small oil filter and the only service operations that should be carried out on the servo unit are to replace the non-return valve (Section 23) and to clean the air filter (Section 22).

Should the unit fail, the braking system will still be operative but extra effort will be required at the foot pedal.

21 Vacuum servo unit – testing, removal and refitting

1   To test the unit, first depress the footpedal several times to

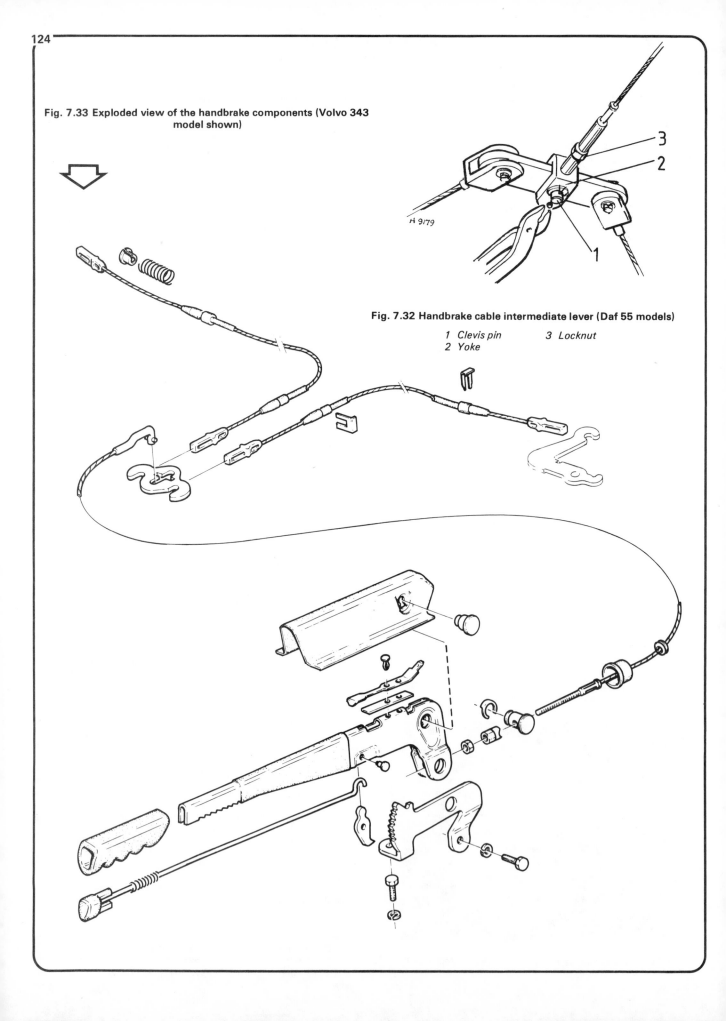

Fig. 7.33 Exploded view of the handbrake components (Volvo 343 model shown)

H 9/79

Fig. 7.32 Handbrake cable intermediate lever (Daf 55 models)

1 Clevis pin   3 Locknut
2 Yoke

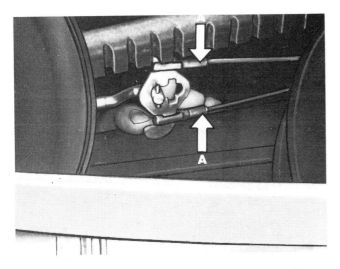

Fig. 7.34 Handbrake cable equaliser and rear cables (A)

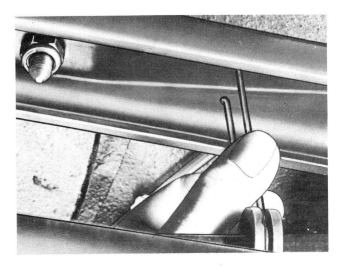

Fig. 7.35 Removing a rear handbrake cable support hook

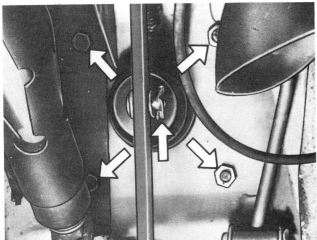

Fig. 7.36 Vacuum servo mounting bolts and pedal connection
(Volvo 343 models)

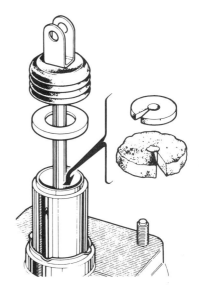

Fig. 7.37 Vacuum servo filter location (bulkhead mounted models)

exhaust the vacuum within the unit, then, with the pedal depressed, start the engine. If the servo unit is functioning correctly the pedal will be forced downwards a little, thus proving the additional assistance. If the servo ceases to function immediately the engine is switched off, the non-return valve is faulty.

2 On LHD models and all Volvo 343 models remove the master cylinder as described in Section 11 and 12. On all other models unscrew the hydraulic line unions from the servo cylinder body, and carefully pull them clear.

3 On LHD models and all Volvo 343 models, disconnect the servo pushrod from the brake pedal by extracting the split-pin and removing the clevis pin.

4 Disconnect the vacuum hose.

5 Unscrew and remove the servo mounting nuts and bolts and lift the unit from the car.

6 On Daf 55 and Daf 66 models with LHD unscrew the pushrod extension and refit it to the new unit so that the distance from the centre of the yoke hole to the servo flange is 10.75 in (273 mm) on Daf 55 models and 10.93 ± 0.04 in (277.5 ± 1 mm) on Daf 66 models.

7 Refitting is a reversal of removal but it will be necessary to bleed the hydraulic system as described in Section 16.

22 Vacuum servo unit air filter – removal and refitting

1 At intervals of 48 000 miles (50 000 km) the servo air filter should be renewed. In dusty climates renew it more frequently.

2 On remote located servo units prise the spring clip from the retainer and extract the pad and filter (photo).

3 When the servo unit is attached to the master cylinder first remove the unit as described in Section 21.

4 Pull back the dust cover and prise the end cover out with a screwdriver.

5 Extract the filter elements and discard them.

6 Refitting is a reversal of removal.

23 Vacuum servo unit non-return valve – removal and refitting

1 Remove the vacuum hose from the non-return valve.

2 Lower the valve from its seating grommet using the blade of a screwdriver. Remove the grommet from the servo housing.

3 Refitting is a reversal of removal. A little rubber grease or brake fluid should be used to facilitate the assembly of the valve into the grommet.

24 Fault diagnosis – braking system

Symptom	Reason/s
Excessive pedal travel before brakes operate	Brake fluid level too low Leaking caliper or wheel cylinder Leaking master cylinder (bubbles in reservoir) Fractured hose or brake line Loose brake system unions Brake shoes excessively worn or out of adjustment Faulty master cylinder seals
Brake pedal feels springy	New linings not yet bedded-in Brake discs or drums badly worn or cracked Master cylinder securing nuts and bolts loose
Brake pedal feels spongy	Caliper or wheel cylinder leaking Leaking master cylinder (bubbles in reservoir) Fractured hose or brake line Loose brake system unions
Excessive effort required to stop car	Faulty vacuum servo unit Badly worn pad or shoe linings New linings not yet bedded-in Incorrect linings fitted (too hard) Oil or fluid contaminated linings
Brakes uneven and pulling to one side	Tyre pressures unequal and incorrect Incorrect linings or contaminated with oil or fluid Suspension or steering joints loose Loose caliper Brake discs or drums badly worn or cracked
Brakes bind or drag	Seized caliper or wheel cylinder Air in system Seized handbrake cables Handbrake over-adjusted

Chapter 8 Electrical system

Contents

Specifications

System type .... 12 volt negative earth

Battery capacity .... 36 amp/hr (at 20 hr discharge rate)

Dynamo
Type .... Ducellier 7267
Output .... 24 amp
Minimum brush length .... 0.35 in (9 mm)

Dynamo voltage regulator
Type .... Ducellier 8361
Maximum cut-in speed (engine) .... 1940 rpm

Alternator
Daf 55 models:
    Type .... SEV Motorola
    Output .... 40 amp
Except Daf 55 models:
    Type .... Ducellier 7550
    Output .... 36 amp

Alternator voltage regulator
Daf 55 models:
    Type .... SEV Motorola
    Control voltage (D + terminal) .... 15.3 ± 0.15 volts
Except Daf 55 models:
    Type .... Ducellier 8371 A
    Control voltage .... 13.4 to 14.4 volts at 30 amps

Starter motor
Type:

Daf 55 and Daf 66/1100 models	Ducellier 6172 or 6172 B pre-engaged
Volvo 66/1100 models	Ducellier 6227 A pre-engaged
Volvo 66/1300 and Volvo 343 models	Ducellier 6231 A pre-engaged
Minimum brush length	0.28 in (7 mm)
Armature endfloat	0.02 in (0.5 mm)

Fuses

Daf 55 and Daf 66 models	8 x 8 amp
Volvo 66 models	4 x 8 amp, 6 x 5 amp, 2 x 16 amp
Volvo 343 models	1 x 5 amp, 14 x 8 amp, 1 x 16 amp

Bulbs

Unit	Wattage
Headlamps	45/40
Parking light	4
Spot lights	55
Direction indicator/parking (Daf 55 models)	25/5
Direction indicator (except Daf 55 models)	21
Number plate lamp (except Volvo 343 models)	5
Number plate (Volvo 343 models)	10
Courtesy light	5
Instrument panel warning lamps	1.2
Stop lamp	21
Tail lamp	5
Reversing lamp (except Volvo 343 models)	18
Reversing lamp (Volvo 343 models)	21
Boot light	5
Selector lever (Volvo 66 models)	1.2
Selector lever (Volvo 343 models)	2
Low ratio hold (Volvo 66 models)	2

Torque wrench settings

	lbf ft	Nm
Alternator pulley nut	29	40
Temperature sender unit	24	33

---

1 General description

The electrical system is of 12 volt negative earth type. The battery is charged by a belt-driven dynamo or alternator with a remote regulator mounted on the engine compartment side panel (photo).

Although repair procedures are fully described in this Chapter, in view of the long life of the major electrical components it is recommended that consideration be given to exchanging the unit for a factory reconditioned assembly when a fault does develop.

2 Battery – removal and refitting

1 The battery is located at the front of the engine compartment, on the right-hand side for Volvo 343 models and the left-hand side for all other models.

2 Disconnect the lead from the negative (-) terminal followed by the positive (+) terminal. On some later models access to the positive terminal is gained by lifting the plastic cover.

3 Remove the battery clamp and lift the battery from its mounting

1.1 Remote type regulator fitted to Daf 66 models

2.3 Battery clamp location

platform, taking care not to spill any electrolyte on the bodywork (photo).

4   Refitting is a reversal of removal but make sure that the polarity is correct before connecting the leads, and do not overtighten the clamp bolts.

3   Battery – maintenance

1   Carry out the regular weekly maintenance described in the Routine Maintenance Section at the front of the Manual.

2   Clean the top of the battery, removing all dirt and moisture.

3   As well as keeping the terminals clean and covered with petroleum jelly, the top of the battery, and especially the top of the cells, should be kept clean and dry. This helps prevent corrosion and ensures that the battery does not become partially discharged by leakage through dampness and dirt.

4   Once every three months remove the battery and inspect the battery securing bolts, the battery clamp plate, tray, and battery leads for corrosion (white fluffy deposits on the metal which are brittle to touch). If any corrosion is found, clean off the deposits with ammonia and paint over the clean metal with an anti-rust/anti-acid paint.

5   At the same time inspect the battery case for cracks. If a crack is found, clean and plug it with one of the proprietary compounds marketed for this purpose. If leakage through the crack has been excessive then it will be necessary to refill the appropriate cell with fresh electrolyte as detailed later. Cracks are frequently caused to the top of the battery case by pouring in distilled water in the middle of winter *after* instead of *before* a run. This gives the water no chance to mix with the electrolyte and so the former freezes and splits the battery case.

6   If topping-up the battery becomes excessive and the case has been inspected for cracks that could cause leakage, but none are found, the battery is being overcharged and the voltage regulator will have to be checked and reset.

7   With the battery on the bench at the three monthly check, measure the specific gravity with a hydrometer to determine the state of charge and condition of the electrolyte. There should be very little variation between the different cells and if a variation in excess of 0.025 is present it will be due to either:

   a) *Loss of electrolyte from the battery sometimes caused by spillage or a leak resulting in a drop in the specific gravity of the electrolyte, when the deficiency was replaced with distilled water instead of fresh electrolyte*

   b) *An internal short circuit caused by buckling of the plates or a similar malady pointing to the likelihood of total battery failure in the near future*

8   The specific gravity of the electrolyte for fully charged conditions at the electrolyte temperature indicated, is listed in Table A. The specific gravity of a fully discharged battery at different temperatures of the electrolyte is given in Table B.

Tabe A

Specific gravity – Battery Fully Charged
1.268 at 100°F or 38°C electrolyte temperature
1.272 at 90°F or 32°C electrolyte temperature
1.276 at 80°F or 27°C electrolyte temperature
1.280 at 70°F or 21°C electrolyte temperature
1.284 at 60°F or 16°C electrolyte temperature
1.288 at 50°F or 10°C electrolyte temperature
1.292 at 40°F or 4°C electrolyte temperature
1.296 at 30°F or -1.5°C electrolyte temperature

Table B

Specific gravity – Battery Fully Discharged
1.098 at 100°F or 38°C electrolyte temperature
1.102 at 90°F or 32°C electrolyte temperature
1.106 at 80°F or 27°C electrolyte temperature
1.110 at 70°F or 21°C electrolyte temperature
1.114 at 60°F or 16°C electrolyte temperature
1.118 at 50°F or 10°C electrolyte temperature
1.122 at 40°F or 4°C electrolyte temperature
1.126 at 30°F or -1.5°C electrolyte temperature

4   Electrolyte – replenishment

1   If the battery is in a fully charged state and one of the cells maintains a specific gravity reading which is 0.025 or more lower than the others, and a check of each cell has been made with a voltmeter to check for short circuits (a four to seven second test should give a steady reading of between 1.2 to 1.8 volts), then it is likely that electrolyte has been lost from the cell which shows the low reading.

2   Top-up the cell with a solution of 1 part sulphuric acid to 2.5 parts of water. If the cell is already fully topped up, draw some electrolyte out of it with a pipette.

3   When mixing the sulphuric acid and water *never add water to sulphuric acid* – always pour acid slowly into the water in a glass container. *If water is added to sulphuric acid it will explode.*

4   Continue to top-up the cell with the freshly made electrolyte and then recharge the battery and check the hydrometer readings.

5   Battery charging

1   In winter time when heavy demand is placed upon the battery, such as when starting from cold, and much electrical equipment is continually in use, it is a good idea to ocasionally have the battery fully charged from an external source at the rate of 3.5 to 4 amps.

2   Continue to charge the battery at this rate until no further rise in specific gravity is noted over a four hour period.

3   Alternatively, a trickle charger charging at the rate of 1.5 amps can be safely used overnight.

4   Specially rapid boost charges which are claimed to restore the power of the battery in 1 to 2 hours are most dangerous as they can cause serious damage to the battery plates through overheating.

6   Generator – maintenance and special precautions

1   Occasionally wipe away any dirt or grease which has accumulated on the outside of the unit and check the security of the leads.

2   Every 6000 miles (10 000 km) check the tension of the drivebelt and adjust it if necessary as described in Chapter 2.

3   Every 6000 miles (10 000 km) lubricate the dynamo commutator end bush with two or three drops of engine oil through the hole in the end cover. No lubrication is required for the alternator as the bearings are sealed for life.

Note: *Take extreme care when making circuit connections to a car fitted with an alternator. When using jumper leads from another battery always match the correct polarity. Before using electric arc-welding equipment, disconnect the battery terminals and the alternator output leads. Always disconnect the battery terminals before using a mains charger. Never remove the battery with the engine running. Testing of an alternator is best undertaken by an automotive electrician who will have the specialised equipment necessary.*

7   Dynamo – removal and refitting

1   Remove the spare wheel.

2   Loosen the dynamo mounting and adjustment bolts and swivel the unit in towards the engine.

3   Remove the drivebelt from the pulley.

4   Unscrew and remove the terminal nuts, and disconnect the supply wires, noting their locations.

5   Support the dynamo and remove the mounting bolts, then withdraw the unit from the engine compartment.

6   Refitting is a reversal of removal but adjust the drivebelt as described in Chapter 2.

8   Alternator – removal and refitting

1   Disconnect the battery negative terminal.

2   Loosen the alternator mounting and adjustment bolts and swivel the unit in towards the engine (photo).

3   Remove the drivebelt from the pulley.

4   Unscrew and remove the terminal nuts and disconnect the supply wires, noting their locations.

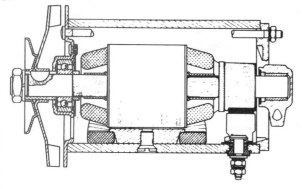

Fig. 8.1 Cross-section view of the dynamo

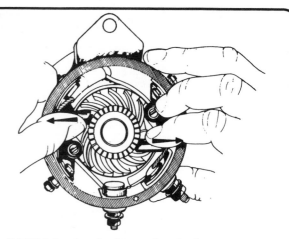

Fig. 8.2 Withdrawing the dynamo housing (arrows indicate direction to pull brushes)

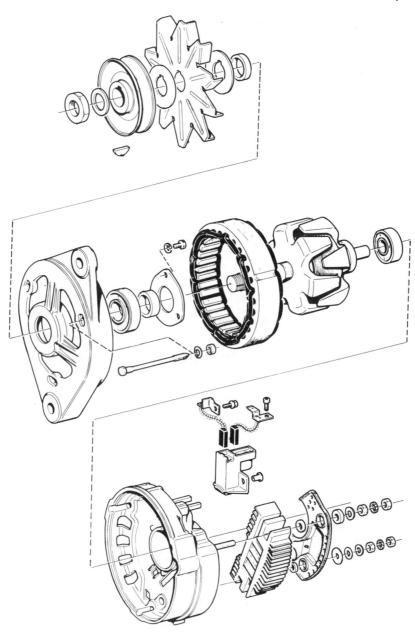

Fig. 8.3 Exploded view of the alternator (Volvo 343 models)

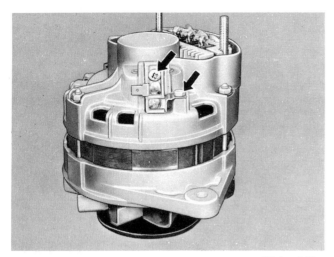

Fig. 8.4 Location of brush holder retaining screws (Volvo 343 models)

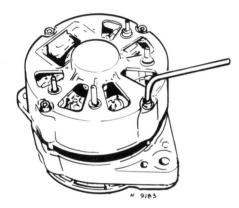

Fig. 8.5 Removing the alternator end cover retaining screws (Daf 55 models)

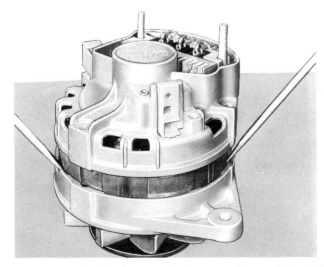

Fig. 8.6 Removing the alternator end cover and stator (Volvo 343 models)

5   Remove the mounting and adjustment bolts and withdraw the alternator from the engine compartment.
6   Refitting is a reversal of removal but adjust the drivebelt as described in Chapter 2.

9 Dynamo – dismantling, servicing and reassembly

1   Remove the dynamo as described in Section 7.
2   Unscrew and remove the commutator end cover retaining nuts and withdraw the end cover.
3   Lift the dynamo housing from the armature at the same time making sure that the brushes are not damaged.
4   Unscrew and remove the terminal retaining nuts as necessary and remove the brushes.
5   Unscrew and remove the pulley retaining nut and withdraw the pulley and shield.
6   Withdraw the bearing retainer from the armature shaft then drive the bearing from the retainer.
7   Do not attempt to remove the dynamo field coils as a special impact screwdriver is required.
8   Clean the components in petrol and thoroughly dry them but do not dip the armature or field coils in the fuel; wipe them with a fuel moistened lint-free cloth.
9   Examine the commutator surface for scoring and pitting; if slight this can be removed with fine glass paper. In extreme cases the commutator must be machined on a lathe.
10 Using a suitable width hack saw blade, undercut the segment insulation to a depth of 0.02 in (0.5 mm).
11 Examine the carbon brushes and if they are less than 0.35 in (9.0 mm) in length obtain new ones.
12 Inspect the armature bearings for wear; if evident it will probably be more economical to obtain a reconditioned or good secondhand dynamo.
13 Accurate testing of the armature and field windings is only possible with specialised instruments but a simple check can be made with a 12 volt battery, testlamp and leads. To test the armature for insulation connect the negative lead to the armature shaft and connect the positive lead to each segment in turn. The test lamp should not glow if the insulation is in good order. To test the armature for open circuit connect the leads to opposite segments; the test lamp should glow if the circuit is in good order.
14 Reassembly of the dynamo is a reversal of dismantling but the following additional points should be noted:

  (a) *Make sure that the brushes are free to move in their holders and if necessary use a fine file to smooth out any irregularities on the sides of the brushes*
  (b) *Check that the tension springs are located correctly on the brushes*
  (c) *Fit the end covers so that the locating pegs engage with the recesses in the housing*
  (d) *Lubricate the bearings sparingly with engine oil*

10 Alternator – dismantling, servicing and reassembly

1   Remove the alternator as described in Section 8.
2   Unscrew and remove the brush holder retaining screws and withdraw the brush holder and brushes.
3   Mark the end cover, stator and housing in relation to each other.
4   Unscrew and remove the retaining bolts and withdraw the end cover and stator together. Use two screwdrivers to prise the assembly away from the housing but make sure that the stator windings are not damaged.
5   Mount the rotor in a soft jaw vice and unscrew the pulley retaining nut.
6   Withdraw the pulley, cooling fan and locating key followed by the end housing.
7   Unscrew and remove the bearing retainer bolts and drive the bearing from the housing using a soft metal drift.
8   Remove the bearing from the commutator end of the rotor; to do this it is preferable to use a two leg puller.
9   Inspect the brush gear for free movement and renew the brushes if they have worn below their minimum specified length of 0.2 in (5.0 mm).

8.2 Alternator location and wiring

12.2 Starter motor front mounting bracket

14.1 Fuse box and fuses (Daf 66 models)

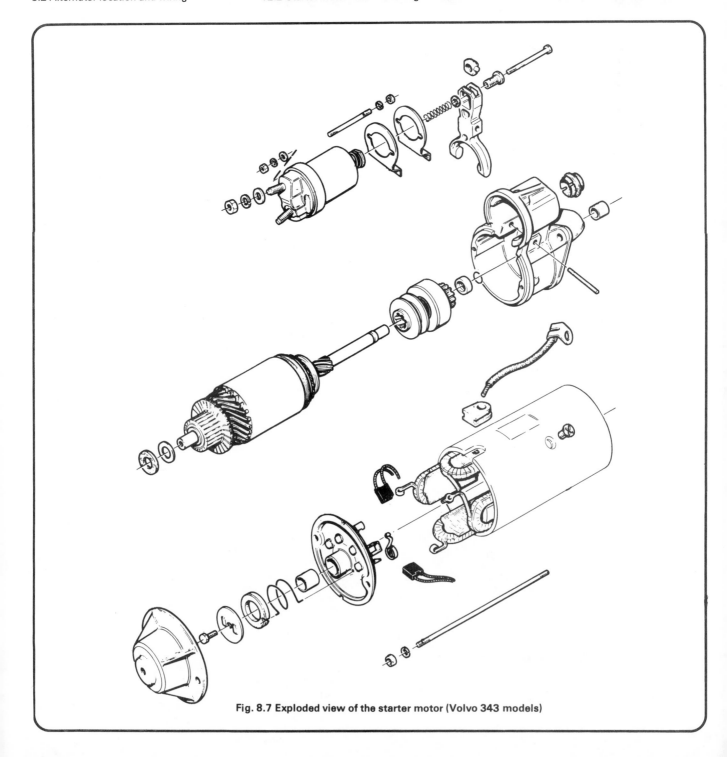

Fig. 8.7 Exploded view of the starter motor (Volvo 343 models)

10 Clean the components in petrol or white spirit and thoroughly dry them, but do not dip the rotor or stator windings in the fuel; wipe them off with a fuel moistened lint-free cloth.

11 Examine the surfaces of the slip rings and if they are deeply scored have them machined on a lathe.

12 To accurately test the rotor and stator windings requires the use of specialised instruments, but a simple check can be made with a 12 volt battery, testlamp and leads. To test the rotor for insulation, connect the negative lead to the rotor shaft and connect the positive lead to each slip ring in turn. The testlamp will not glow if the insulation is in good order. To test the rotor windings for open circuit, connect each lead to separate slip rings; the testlamp will glow if the circuit is not broken.

13 Check the bearings for excessive wear and renew them if necessary.

14 Reassembly is a reversal of dismantling but the following additional points should be noted:

(a) *Make sure that the brushes are free to move in their holders and if necessary use a fine file to smooth out any irregularities on the sides of the brushes*

(b) *Use suitable diameter tubing to drive the bearings into position*

(c) *Tighten the pulley nut to the correct specified torque wrench setting*

11 Starter motor – description

The starter motor is of the pre-engaged type and has two brushes operating on a commutator located on the front of the armature.

A solenoid, mounted on the starter motor drive end housing, engages the pinion with the flywheel ring gear when the ignition key is turned to the *start* position, through the medium of an engagement fork. As the solenoid reaches the end of its stroke, internal contacts energise the starter motor and the flywheel is rotated. The drive pinion incorporates a one-way roller clutch to prevent damage to the starter motor when the engine fires.

12 Starter motor – removal and refitting

1   Open the bonnet and disconnect the battery negative terminal.
2   Unscrew and remove the starter bracket mounting bolts on the cylinder block (photo).
3   Unscrew and remove the starter mounting bolt on the clutch housing, then remove the starter bracket bolt.
4   Lift the starter motor from the clutch housing and detach the supply wires.
5   Refitting is a reversal of removal, but if difficulty is experienced in locating the upper mounting bolt, bend wire around the bolt head,

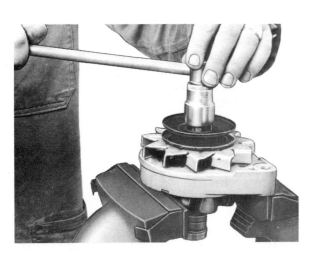

Fig. 8.8 Removing the alternator pulley retaining nut

Fig. 8.9 Withdrawing the alternator rotor end bearing

Fig. 8.10 Starter motor location

Fig. 8.11 Removing the armature location spring and brush holder from the starter

insert it in the hole, then pull the wire free. Always tighten the main mounting bolts before the bracket bolts.

13 Starter motor – overhaul

1   Remove the starter motor as described in Section 12.
2   Unscrew the solenoid switch terminal nut and detach the motor cable.
3   Using a suitable diameter soft metal drift, drive the fork hinge pin from the end housing.
4   Unscrew and remove the starter motor commutator and cover retaining nuts, and the four solenoid switch retaining nuts.
5   Withdraw the end housing from the starter motor and solenoid switch, then lift the solenoid switch and fork assembly from the starter motor housing.
6   Prise the starter motor commutator end cover from the starter motor and push the armature from the motor housing until the brushes are visible.
7   Lift the tension springs and pull the carbon brushes from their holders.
8   Remove the housing and field windings from the armature then mount the armature in a soft jaw vice.
9   Unscrew and remove the retaining bolt and withdraw the brush holder from the end of the armature together with the washers and spring.
10 Clean all components with petrol, but do not dip the armature or field windings in the fuel; use a fuel moistened lint-free cloth to wipe them clean.
11 Inspect the components for wear or damage and renew them as necessary. If the brushes are less than the minimum specified length they must be renewed.
12 Examine the surface of the commutator for scoring and pitting; if slight this can be removed with fine glasspaper. In extreme cases the commutator must be machined on a lathe.
13 Using a suitable width hack saw blade, undercut the segment insulation to a depth of 0.02 in (0.5 mm).
14 Check the armature brushes for wear and if necessary press in new ones using a vice and suitable diameter tubing. Bear in mind that if too many components have to be renewed it will probably be more economical to obtain a reconditioned or good secondhand starter motor. When installing the commutator end bush, the inside edge of the bush must be flush with the inside edge of the brushholder bore. New brushes should be soaked in SAE 80 oil for half an hour prior to fitting them.
15 Check the teeth of the pinion for wear, and renew the drive if necessary by extracting the circlip from the end of the shaft. Lubricate the splines with a little graphite grease before reassembly.
16 If the armature and field windings are suspected of being faulty they can be tested with a 12 volt battery, testlamp and leads. Test the armature for insulation by connecting the negative lead to the armature shaft and the positive lead to each segment in turn. The testlamp will not glow if the insulation is in good order. The windings can be similarly checked for open circuit by connecting the leads to opposite segments of the commutator; the testlamp will glow if the windings are in good order.
17 Reassembly is basically a reversal of dismantling but the following essential procedures should be noted.
18 With the armature assembled to the starter motor housing the distance from the edge of the housing to the further edge of the pinion should be between 2.3 and 2.35 in (58.4 and 59.6 mm). If not, shims must be fitted at the commutator end of the armature until the dimension is correct.
19 Move the pinion drive to the engaged position and check that the distance as checked in paragraph 18 is now between 2.75 and 2.81 in (69.5 and 71.5 mm).
20 With the complete starter motor assembled, check the fork for correct function. To do this, press in the bolt at the end of the solenoid switch as far as possible, and check that the distance from the pinion stop to the nearest pinion edge is between 0.002 and 0.06 in (0.05 and 1.5 mm). If not, adjust the bolt outer sleeve until the dimension is correct.
21 If adjustment is made impossible by a faulty fork, it must be renewed as necessary; refer to Fig. 8.12 for the correct location of the components. Note that where a fibre washer is fitted, the plastic sleeve is not required and vice-versa.

14 Fuses

1   The fusebox is located on the left-hand side of the engine compartment on Daf 55, RHD Daf 66, and Volvo 66 models (photo). On LHD Daf 66 models it is located inside the car beneath the fascia panel. On Volvo 343 models it is located on the right-hand side of the engine compartment, in front of the bulkhead.
2   Eight circuits are protected on Daf 55 and Daf 66 models, twelve circuits on Volvo 66 models, and sixteen circuit on Volvo 343 models. A list of circuits is given below.

Daf 55 and Daf 66

1   Main beam
2   Dipped beam
3   Windscreen wipers
4   Direction indicators, stop lights, heater motor, vacuum valve switch
5   RH parking light, RH tail light, number plate light
6   LH parking light, LH tail light
7   Horn
8   Interior light

Volvo 66

1   Rear window heater
2   Spotlamps
3   Hazard warning lights
4   Horns
5   LH front and RH rear parking lights, bootlight, and two doors on GL models
6   RH front and LH rear parking lights
7   Heater motor
8   Windscreen wipers
9   LH headlamp dipped beam
10 RH headlamp dipped beam
11 LH headlamp main beam
12 RH headlamp main beam

Volvo 343

1   Direction indicators
2   Rear window heater and wiper motor, rear fog lamp and low ratio hold
3   Voltmeter, voltage regulator, heater motor, instrument panel lamps
4   Windscreen wipers, stop lights and declutching mechanism
5   Selector lever and headlamp wash/wipe
6   LH headlamp dipped beam
7   RH headlamp dipped beam
8   LH headlamp main beam and warning lamp
9   RH headlamp main beam
10 LH front and RH rear parking lights
11 RH front and LH rear parking lights, number plate lamp
12 Headlamp flasher, and hazard warning lamps
13 Bootlight, radio and clock
14 Cigar lighter, courtesy light and instrument panel lamps
15 Heated rear window
16 Horns

3   Always renew a fuse with one of a similar rating and never renew it more than once without finding the source of the trouble. The cause of a fuse blowing is usually a short-circuit, which may be the result of broken or deteriorated wiring.

15 Direction indicator flasher system

1   The flasher unit is located beneath the fascia panel on a bracket on Daf 55, Daf 66 and Volvo 66 models. On Volvo 343 models it is located within the fusebox adjacent to the hazard warning flasher unit.
2   Should the flashers become faulty in operation, check the bulbs and make sure the connecting leads are secure. If these are in order and the fuse has not blown, the unit is at fault and should be renewed.

16 Hazard warning flasher system

1   The hazard warning flasher unit is located adjacent to the direction

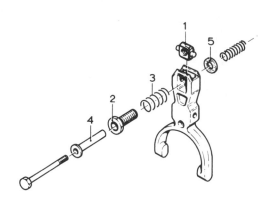

Fig. 8.12 Starter motor engagement fork components

    1 *Nut*   4 *Plastic tube*
    2 *Adjusting sleeve*   5 *Fibre washer*
    3 *Spring*

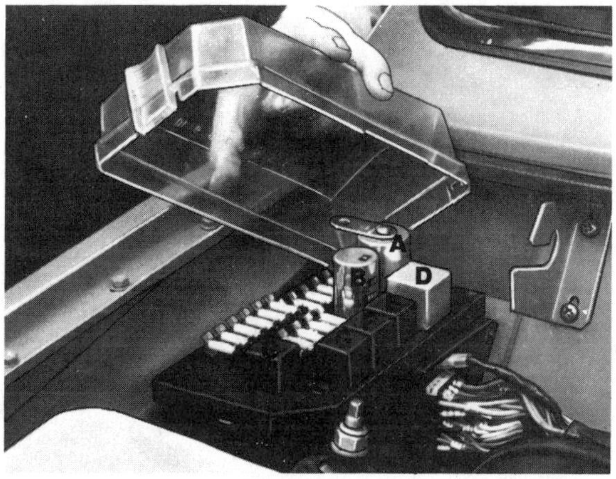

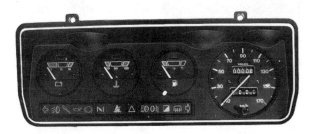

Fig. 8.13 Fusebox location on Volvo 343 models

  A Flasher unit   *E Lighting relay*
  B Hazard warning unit   *F Starter inhibitor relay*
  C Horn relay   *G Heated rear window relay*
  D Main beam relay

Fig. 8.14 The instrument panel (Volvo 343 models)

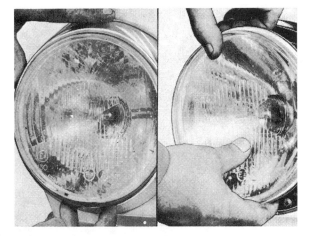

Fig. 8.15 Removing the headlamp rim and reflector on Daf 55 models

Fig. 8.16 Removing the headlamp unit on Volvo 66 models

20.1 Removing the instrument panel (Daf 66 models)

22.2A Releasing the headlamp rim (Daf 66 models)

22.2B Removing the headlamp rim (Daf 66 models)

22.3 Withdrawing the headlamp (Daf 66 models)

22.5A Removing the side and headlamp bulbs (Daf 66 models)

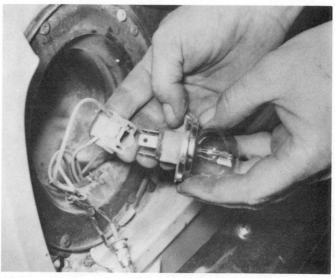

22.5B Multi-plug connector for the headlamp bulb (Daf 66 models)

Fig. 8.17 Removing the headlamp bulb

Fig. 8.18 Removing the parking light bulb

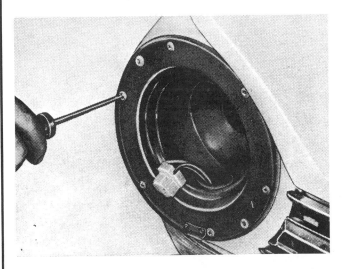

Fig. 8.19 Removing the headlamp baseplate (Daf 55 models)

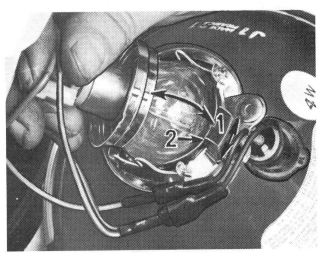

Fig. 8.20 Headlamp bulb location method

1 Recess   2 Slide

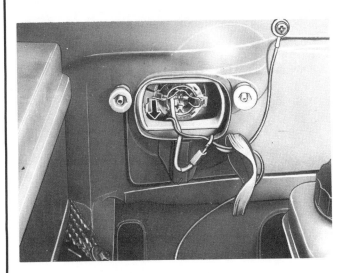

Fig. 8.21 Removing the spotlamp bulb

Fig. 8.22 Location of the headlamp rear cover (Volvo 343 models)

indicator flasher unit.
2   Failure of the system may be due to bulb failure in the flasher lamp units, disconnected wiring, a blown fuse, or faulty switch contacts. If these are in order, renew the flasher unit.

17   Ignition (steering lock switch) – removal and refitting

The procedure is covered in Chapter 9 as it involves work on the steering column.

18   Combination switches – removal and refitting

1   Disconnect the battery negative terminal.
2   On Daf 55 models, unscrew and remove the retaining screws and withdraw the lower steering column cover, then detach the combination switch from the steering column and disconnect the wires noting their locations.
3   On Daf 66, Volvo 66 and Volvo 343 models, unscrew and remove the choke control knob, then unscrew the retaining screws and remove the column lower shroud. Detach the combination switches and disconnect the wires, noting their locations.
4   Refitting is a reversal of removal.

19   Fascia panel switches – removal and refitting

1   Three types of switch are fitted: rocker type, push-push type and turn type.
2   Before removing a switch the battery negative terminal must be disconnected.
3   On early type switches, remove the knob and unscrew the retaining nut, then push the switch through the fascia panel and disconnect the supply wires after noting their location.
4   On the rocker type switch, depress the lugs and push the switch out from the fascia panel, then disconnect the supply wires after noting their location.
5   On the push-push type switch, pull the multi-plug connections from the rear of the switch and press the switch out from the fascia panel.
6   Refitting is a reversal of removal.

20   Instrument panel – removal and refitting

1   The procedure is included in Chapter 10 under the removal and refitting of the fascia panel (photo).

21   Temperature and fuel gauges – testing, removal and refitting

1   If the temperature and fuel gauges are faulty, first check the voltage stabilizer as this component is largely responsible for the correct functioning of the gauges.
2   Remove the instrument panel and locate the voltage stabilizer on the rear of the panel. With a voltmeter connected between the *I* and *E* terminals of the stabilizer, the voltage should oscillate between 0 and 5 volts. If this is not the case the voltage stabilizer is faulty and must be renewed.
3   If the fuel gauge is still faulty remove the fuel tank unit (see Chapter 3) and connect an ohmmeter between the terminal and base; with the float in the empty position the resistance should be 250 Ohms, and with it in the full position the resistance should be 19 Ohms.
4   If the float operates correctly, trace the wiring to the fuel gauge and warning lamp terminals on the rear of the instrument panel. If the wiring is good, renew the gauge by withdrawing the rear of the instrument panel. To do this, unscrew and remove the eight retaining screws.
5   If the temperature gauge is still faulty, check the temperature sender resistance with the engine at operating temperature; this should be between 35 and 45 Ohms. If an ohmmeter is not available, obtain a new sender and observe whether the fault is corrected.
6   If the sender appears to be in good order, trace the wiring to the

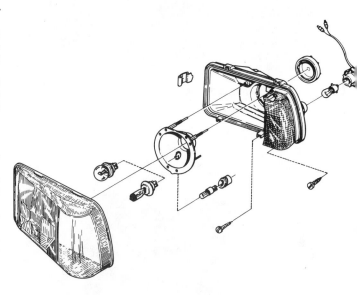

Fig. 8.23 Exploded view of the headlamp and front indicator lamps (Volvo 343 models)

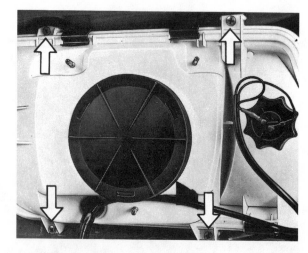

Fig. 8.24 Headlamp unit retaining screws (Volvo 343 models)

Fig. 8.25 Headlamp beam adjustment screws (except Volvo 343 models)

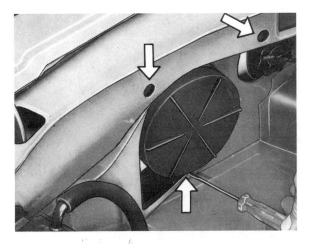

Fig. 8.26 Headlamp beam adjustment screws (Volvo 343 models)

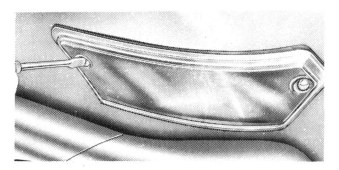

Fig. 8.27 Removing the front parking/direction indicator lens (Daf 55 Marathon models)

temperature gauge terminals on the rear of the instrument panel. If the wiring is good, unscrew and remove the eight retaining screws, withdraw the cover, and renew the gauge.

7   Refitting is a reversal of removal.

22 Headlamps (Daf 55, Daf 66 and Volvo 66 models) — bulb renewal and lamp unit removal and refitting

1   On Daf 55 models, insert two fingers into the openings at the bottom of the headlamp rim, pull the rim forwards, and lift the rim away.

2   On Daf 66 and Volvo 66 models, unscrew the three retaining screws a quarter of a turn, and withdraw the rim forwards (photos).

3   Pull the headlamp reflector from the three retaining studs and hold it face down to expose the supply wires (photo).

4   Pull the multi-plug connector from the headlamp bulb terminals and disconnect the parking light wires.

5   Prise the two retaining spring clips from the headlamp bulb and lift the bulb from the reflector (photos).

6   The parking light bulb can be removed by pulling the fitting from the reflector (except Daf 55 Marathon models).

7   To ensure long life of the bulbs and reflectors, take care not to touch the glass. If the glass is dirty, clean it with methylated spirit before fitting it.

8   If necessary, the base plate and rubber seal can be removed from the front wing by removing the six retaining screws.

9   Refitting is a reversal of removal but make sure that the projection on the bulb fitting engages with the corresponding recess or slide on the edge of the reflector fitting.

23 Spotlamps (Daf 66 and Volvo 66 models) — bulb renewal

1   Open the bonnet and pull back the rubber cover from the rear of the spotlamp.

2   Push the spring clamp aside and withdraw the halogen bulb; take care not to touch the glass of the bulb.

3   Refitting is a reversal of removal.

24 Headlamps (Volvo 343 models) — bulb renewal

1   Open the bonnet and remove the spare wheel if the left-hand bulb is being renewed.

2   Turn the lamp rear cover anti-clockwise and remove it.

3   Pull the multi-plug connector from the bulb terminals.

4   Prise up the two retaining spring clips and withdraw the bulb taking care not to touch the glass.

5   Refitting is a reversal of removal but make sure that the projection on the bulb fitting engages with the recess on the reflector fitting.

25 Headlamps and front indicator lamps (Volvo 343 models) — removal and refitting

1   Open the bonnet and remove the spare wheel and spare wheel bracket. Disconnect the battery negative terminal.

2   Unscrew and remove the inner front panel retaining screws by gaining access through the spare wheel bracket aperture and air filter aperture; turn the air supply pipe to one side to do this.

3   Unscrew and remove the three upper retaining screws.

4   Remove the front grille as described in Chapter 10, then unscrew and remove the two upper retaining screws from within the grille aperture.

5   Unscrew and remove the two side retaining screws located just above the bumper.

6   Withdraw the front panel a little way from the body, then disconnect the wiring from the horn.

7   Remove the headlamp, parking and direction indicator bulbs as described in Sections 24 and 27.

8   Completely withdraw the front panel.

9   Unscrew and remove the four retaining screws and lift the headlamp unit from the front panel.

10   If necessary, the headlamp may be dismantled by prising away the

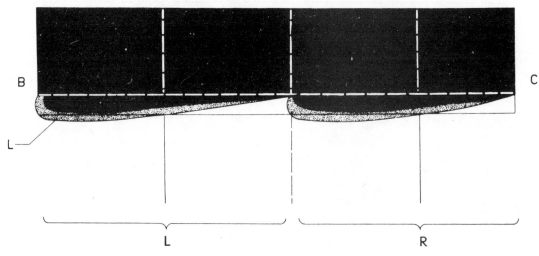

Fig. 8.28 Headlamp beam setting diagram

B-C = height of headlamp centres
L = line drawn 4 in (10 cm) lower than B-C

Fig. 8.29 Removing the rear lamp cluster cover (Volvo 343 models)

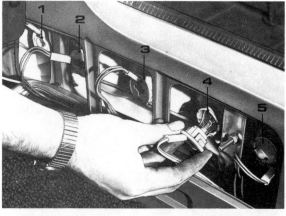

Fig. 8.30 Rear lamp cluster bulbs (Volvo 343 models)

1 Direction indicator   4 Fog lamp
2 Stop/tail lamp   5 Reversing lamp
3 Tail lamp

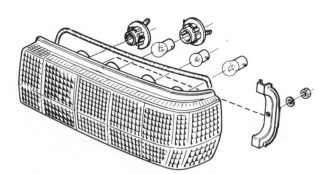

Fig. 8.31 Exploded view of the rear lamp cluster (Volvo 343 models)

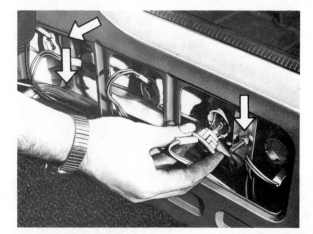

Fig. 8.32 Rear lamp cluster body retaining nuts (Volvo 343 models)

Fig. 8.33 Removing the number plate lamp cover (Volvo 66 models)

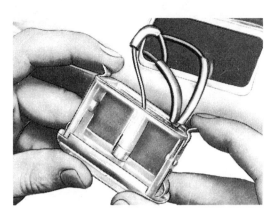

Fig. 8.34 Removing the number plate lamp bulb (Daf 55 models)

spring clamps and removing the glass cover. Unscrew and remove the two retaining screws and withdraw the direction indicator glass.
11 Refitting is a reversal of removal.

26 Headlamps – alignment

1   It is recommended that headlamp alignment is carried out by your dealer using modern beam setting equipment. However in an emergency the following procedure will provide an acceptable light pattern.
2   Position the car on a level surface with tyres correctly inflated, about 33 feet (10 metres) in front of a vertical surface such as a wall or garage door. Make sure that the car is at right angles to the surface.
3   Measure the distance from ground level to the centre of the headlamps (disregard the direction indication on Volvo 343 models), then draw a chalk line on the vertical surface horizontally 4 in (10 cm) lower than the dimension obtained.
4   Mark the line at each side at a point where the distance between the headlamp centres is projected onto the vertical surface, then mark a further point midway between these two marks.
5   Switch on dipped headlamps and observe whether the light pattern is as given in Fig. 8.28. It will help if each headlamp is checked separately while shielding the remaining one.
6   Adjustment on Daf 55, Daf 66 and Volvo 66 models is provided by three adjustment screws. First remove the rim to expose the adjustment screws. Vertical adjustment is made by screwing the two upper screws in or out; horizontal adjustment is made by screwing the two side screws in or out. It will be observed that one of these screws is common to both adjustment movements (photo).
7   On Volvo 343 models adjustment is carried out as described in paragraph 6, but the adjustment screws are located at the rear of the headlamp, access being made from the engine compartment.

27 Lamp bulbs – renewal

1   Lamp bulbs should always be renewed with the same type and rating as listed in Specifications.

Front parking/direction indicator lamps (Daf 55 Marathon models)
2   The double filament bulbs are accessible after removal of the lens (two screws) and have a bayonet type fitting.

Front parking lamps (except Daf 55 Marathon models)
3   The procedure is identical to that for renewal of the headlamp bulb. Pull the parking lamp fitting from the headlamp reflector; the bulb has a bayonet type fitting (photo).

Front direction indicator lamps (except Daf 55 Marathon and Volvo 343 models)
4   The bulbs are accessible after removal of the lens (two screws). The bulbs have a bayonet type fitting except for Daf 55 models where festoon type bulbs are fitted (photo).

Front direction indicator lamps (Volvo 343 models)
5   If the left-hand side bulb is to be renewed, first remove the spare wheel and jack.
6   Locate the bulb fitting behind the front panel and turn it anti-clockwise to remove it. The bulb has a bayonet type fitting.

Side repeater lamps (Daf 66 and Volvo 66 models)
7   Reach under the front wing and pull the bulb fitting from the lamp. The bulb has a bayonet type fitting (photo).

Rear lamp cluster (except Volvo 343 models)
8   The bulbs are accessible after removal of the lens, and have bayonet type fittings (photo).
9   When refitting the lens, do not overtighten the retaining screws otherwise the lens may be fractured.

Rear lamp cluster (Volvo 343 models)
10 Open the tailgate and remove the lamp cover.
11 Pull out the appropriate bulb fitting and remove the bulb; the bulbs have bayonet type fittings.
12 The cluster body is secured by three nuts and spring washers.

Rear number plate lamp
13 On Daf 66 models prise off the lamp cover; on Volvo 66 models squeeze the end of the cover and lift it from the lamps.
14 Press the lamp from the rear bumper using a screwdriver if necessary to depress the retaining spring (photos).
15 Pull back the retaining tag or spring and withdraw the body to expose the bulb which has a bayonet type fitting.
16 When refitting the bulb on Volvo 66 models, make sure that the rubber seal is located correctly.

Interior lamp
17 Using a screwdriver, carefully prise the cover from the lamp taking care not to damage the roof lining. A festoon type bulb is fitted (photo).

Rear compartment lamp (Volvo 343 models)
18 Grip the lamp cover and pull it outwards. A festoon type bulb is fitted, but if it fails to operate, make sure that the tailgate switch is not faulty.

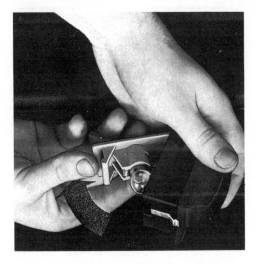

Fig. 8.35 Removing the number plate lamp bulb (Volvo 343 models)

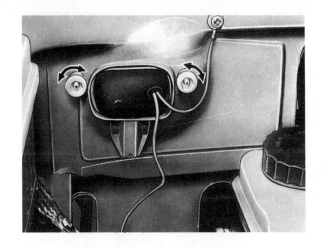

Fig. 8.36 Spotlamp adjustment nut location

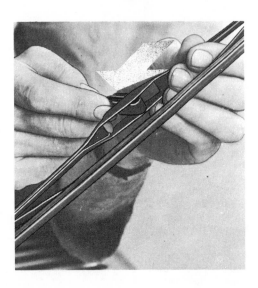

Fig. 8.37 Wiper blade removal (Daf 55 and Daf 66 models)

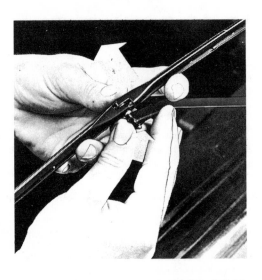

Fig. 8.38 Wiper blade removal (Volvo models)

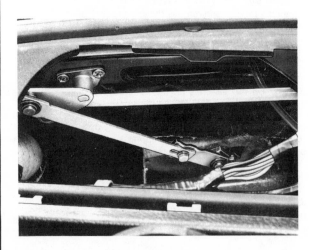

Fig. 8.39 The wiper linkage (except Volvo 343 models)

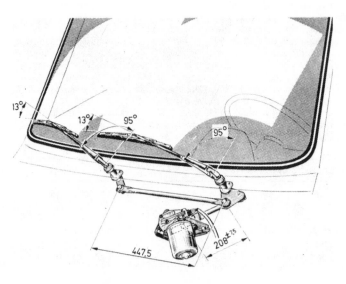

Fig. 8.40 Correct windscreen wiper sweep area

26.6 Adjusting the headlamp beam (Daf 66 models)

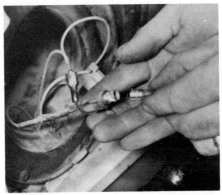

27.3 Removing the parking lamp bulb (Daf 66 models)

27.4 Front direction indicator components (Daf 66 models)

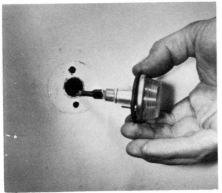

27.7 Side repeater lamp (Daf 66 models)

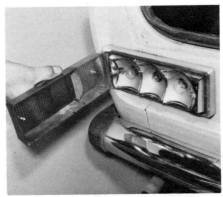

27.8 Rear lamp cluster (Daf 66 models)

27.14A Removing the number plate lamp cover (Daf 66 models)

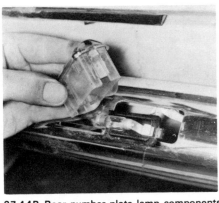

27.14B Rear number plate lamp components (Daf 66 models)

27.17 Interior lamp

29.2 Removing the windscreen wiper blade (Daf 66 models)

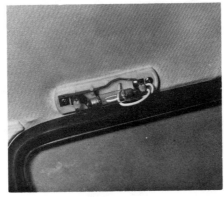

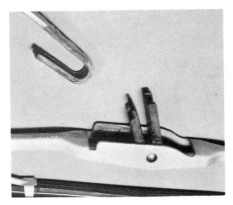

35.3 Horn location (Daf 66 models)

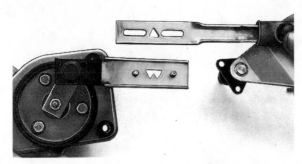

Fig. 8.41 Wiper linkage connecting rod and adjustment (Volvo 343 models)

Fig. 8.42 Location of the windscreen wiper motor (Volvo 343 models)

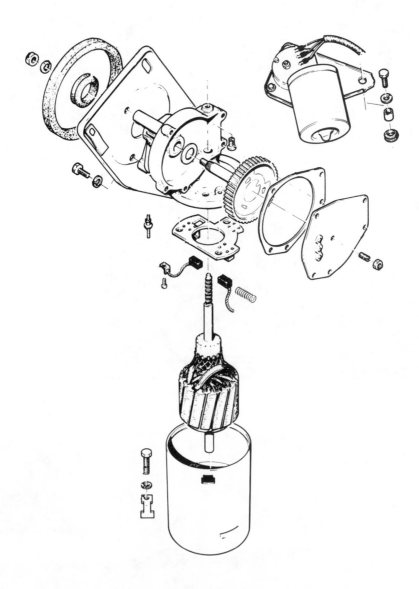

Fig. 8.43 Exploded view of SWF type windscreen wiper motor

28 Spotlamps (Daf 66 and Volvo 66 models) – alignment

1 The procedure is very similar to that for the headlamp alignment in Section 26. However the distance between the lamp centres will be different, and the beam should be adjusted parallel to the ground.
2 To adjust the spotlamps, open the bonnet and locate the two plastic adjustment nuts. Horizontal adjustment is made by screwing the nuts in or out separately, vertical adjustment by screwing the nuts in or out together.

29 Wiper blades – renewal

1 The wiper blades should be renewed whenever they no longer clean the windscreen effectively.
2 To remove the wiper blades on Daf 55 and Daf 66 models, depress the clip on the wiper arm and withdraw the blade (photo). The rear window wiper blade on Volvo models is removed in the same manner, but the front wiper blades are removed by pushing the pivot clip and sliding out the blade complete with the pivot.
3 Refitting is a reversal of removal.

30 Wiper linkage (Daf 55, Daf 66 and Volvo 66 models) – removal and refitting

1 Disconnect the battery negative terminal.
2 Remove the windscreen wiper blades as described in Section 29.
3 Using a wide blade screwdriver, prise the wiper arms off the spindles.
4 Unscrew and remove the retaining nuts and spacers from the two spindles.
5 Working inside the car disconnect the speedometer cable from the rear of the speedometer head.
6 On Daf 55 and Daf 66 models withdraw the instrument panel from the fascia panel as described in Section 20.
7 Unscrew and remove the connecting rod adjustment bolt noting its location in the elongated hole.
8 Unscrew and remove the spindle flange retaining screws.
9 Lower the wiper linkage and remove it from beneath the fascia panel.
10 If necessary the remaining section of the linkage connecting rod can be removed from the motor spindle by unscrewing the retaining nut. Before removing the linkage, mark its position in relation to the spindle.
11 Refitting is a reversal of removal, but the following additional points should be noted:

(a) Make sure that the previously made marks are aligned when fitting the connecting rod to the motor spindle
(b) Lubricate the spindles with a few drops of engine oil
(c) Check the sweep of the wiper blades with reference to Fig. 8.40; if adjustment is necessary, loosen the connecting rod bolt and adjust the length of the connecting rod accordingly

31 Wiper linkage (Volvo 343 models) – removal and refitting

1 Disconnect the battery negative terminal.
2 Remove the windscreen wiper blades as described in Section 29.
3 Using a wide blade screwdriver, prise the wiper arms off the spindles.
4 Unscrew and remove the retaining nuts and spacers from the two spindles.
5 Working inside the car, mark the position of the connecting rod adjustment, and the position of the motor crank relative to the motor spindle.
6 Unscrew and remove the retaining nuts and withdraw the crank and short connecting rod from the motor spindle.
7 Detach the left-hand defroster and defroster hose, then remove the ashtray.
8 Remove the left-hand air supply pipe from the heater unit after releasing the central press stud.
9 Unscrew and remove the spindle flange retaining screws.
10 Lower the wiper linkage and remove it from beneath the fascia panel.

11 Refitting is a reversal of removal but the following additional points should be noted:

(a) Align the previously made marks before tightening the connecting rod nuts
(b) Lubricate the spindles with a few drops of engine oil
(c) If necessary adjust the position of the wiper blades so that they are parallel to the lower edge of the windscreen when parked. To do this loosen the connecting rod nuts and adjust the length of the connecting rod accordingly

32 Windscreen wiper motor – removal and refitting

1 Disconnect the battery negative terminal.
2 On Daf 55, Daf 66 and Volvo 66 models, detach the speedometer cable from the rear of the speedometer head and remove the instrument panel from the fascia; refer to Section 20 if necessary.
3 On all models unscrew and remove the connecting rod retaining/adjustment nuts or bolt as applicable, and mark the location of the motor crank relative to the motor spindle.
4 Unscrew and remove the motor crank retaining nut and withdraw the crank from the spindle.
5 Disconnect the wiper motor supply wires in the engine compartment.
6 Unscrew and remove the windscreen wiper motor mounting nuts and withdraw the motor from the car.
7 Refitting is a reversal of removal.

33 Windscreen wiper motor – overhaul

1 Remove the wiper motor as described in Section 32.
2 Unscrew and remove the gearwheel cover retaining screws and lift the cover away.
3 Extract the circlip and withdraw the gearwheel and washers from the housing; on some models the circlip is omitted.
4 Unscrew and remove the retaining nuts and remove the gearwheel housing from the armature, together with the brushes.
5 Lift out the armature.
6 Inspect all components for wear, and clean them with petrol. If the armature commutator is worn, light scoring may be removed with fine glasspaper. Renew the carbon brushes if they are excessively worn; this will necessitate unsoldering the leads and on some models removing the three rubber suspension pins to release the brush carrier.
7 If the motor bearings, gearwheel, or wormwheel are worn it will probably be more economical to obtain a reconditioned or good secondhand unit.
8 Reassembly is a reveral of dismantling, but the following additional points should be noted:

(a) Grease the gearwheel and wormwheel surfaces sparingly
(b) On Femsa units adjust the armature endfloat by turning the adjustment screw which locates on the ball bearing
(c) On all but Femsa units, adjust the gearwheel endfloat by loosening the locknut and turning the adjustment screw clockwise as far as possible. Then loosen the screw a quarter of a turn and tighten the locknut; where a locknut is not fitted retain the screw by application of a liquid locking agent

34 Windscreen washer – maintenance

1 Periodically check the pipe connections, and where electric washers are fitted check the electrical connections for security.
2 The fluid in the washer reservoir should be kept topped-up at the routine weekly checks. It is recommended that a cleaning solvent is added to the water to aid the cleaning action and reduce the chance of freezing during winter conditions.
3 The washer jets can be adjusted as required by inserting a pin and moving them to the desired angle.

35 Horn – description, removal and refitting

1 On Daf 55 models a single note horn is fitted, but on all other models two horns are fitted having a low and a high pitch note.

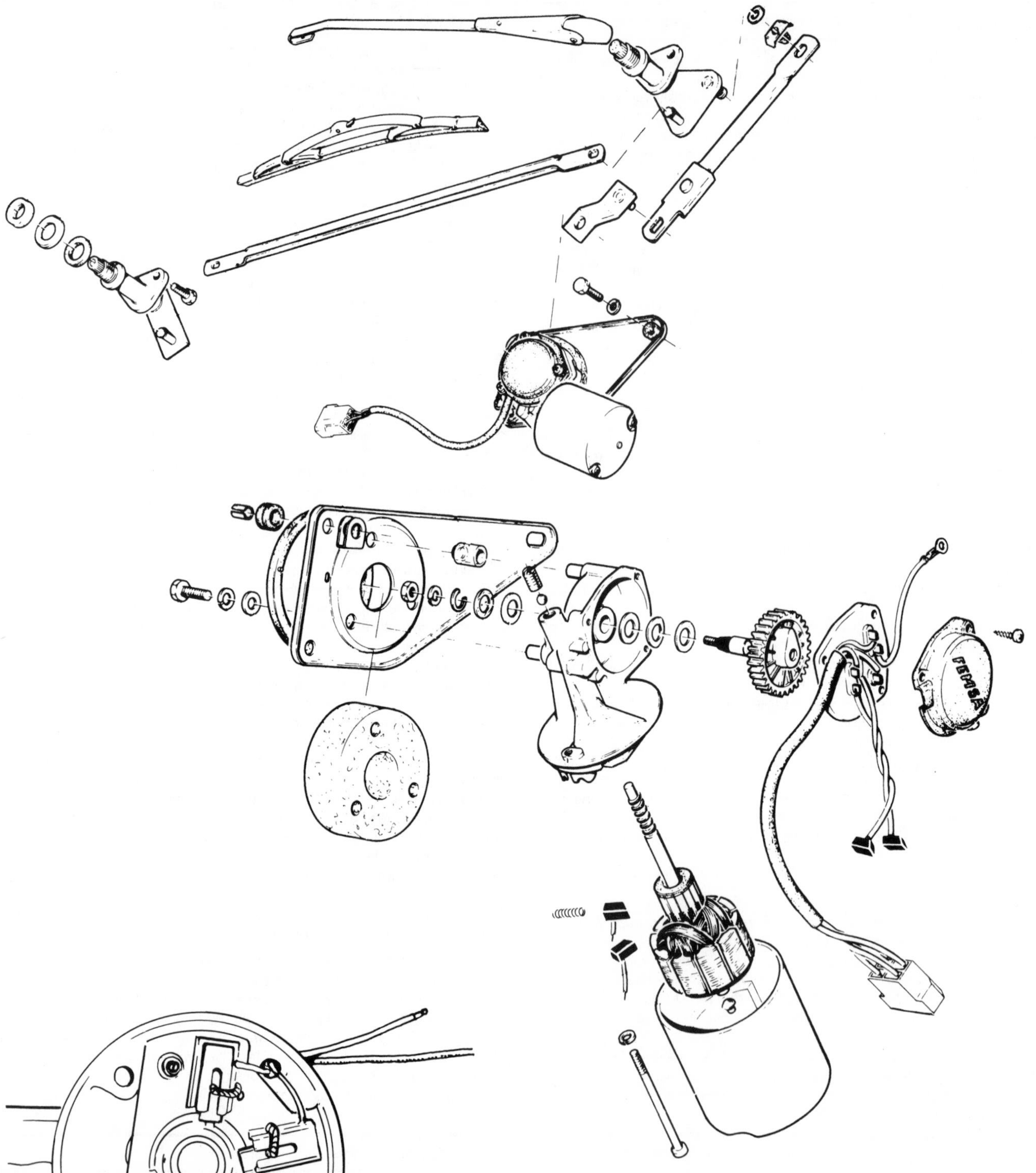

Fig. 8.44 Exploded view of Femsa type windscreen wiper motor

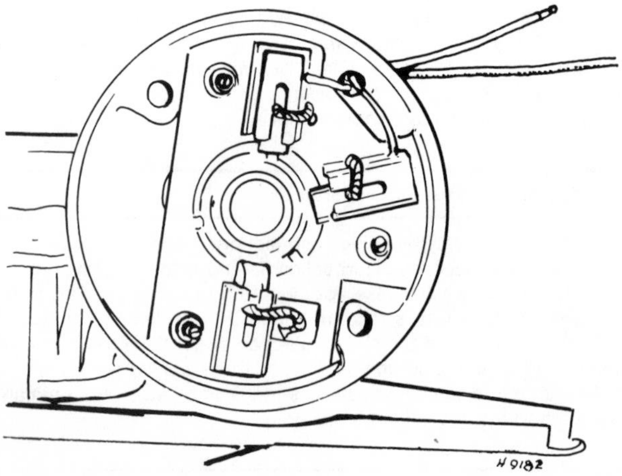

Fig. 8.45 Windscreen wiper motor brush carrier location

2 Twin horn models are fitted with a horn relay.
3 Removal is straightforward but the battery negative terminal should first be disconnected (photo). On Volvo 343 models the bumper extension must also be removed.
4 When refitting the horns, make sure that the wires are fitted securely to the terminals.

36 Fault diagnosis – electrical system

Symptom	Reason/s
Starter motor fails to turn engine: No voltage at starter motor	Battery discharged Battery defective internally Battery terminal leads loose or earth lead not securely attached to body Loose or broken connections in starter motor circuit Starter motor switch or solenoid faulty
Voltage at starter motor	Starter motor pinion jammed in mesh with flywheel ring gear Starter brushes badly worn, sticking or brush wires loose Commutator dirty, worn or burnt Starter motor armature faulty Field coils earthed
Starter motor turns engine very slowly	Battery in discharged condition Starter brushes badly worn, sticking or brush wires loose Loose wires in starter motor circuit
Starter motor operates without turning engine	Pinion or flywheel ring gear teeth broken or worn
Starter motor noisy or rough engagement	Pinion or flywheel ring gear teeth broken or worn Starter motor retaining bolts loose
Battery will not hold charge	Battery defective internally Electrolyte level too low or electrolyte too weak due to leakage Plate separators no longer fully effective Battery plates severely sulphated Generator drivebelt slipping Battery terminal connections loose or corroded Generator not charging properly Short in lighting circuit causing continual battery drain Regulator unit not working correctly
Ignition light fails to go out	Generator drivebelt loose and slipping, or broken Brushes worn, sticking, broken or dirty Brush springs weak or broken Regulator incorrectly set Cut-out incorrectly set Open circuit in wiring of cut-out and regulator unit, or alternator stator and rotor coils
Fuel gauge gives no reading	Fuel tank empty! Electric cable between tank sender unit and gauge earthed or loose Fuel gauge case not earthed Fuel gauge supply cable interrupted Fuel gauge unit broken
Fuse gauge registers full all the time	Electric cable between tank unit and gauge broken or disconnected
Horn fails to operate	Blown fuse Cable connection loose or broken Horn incorrectly adjusted Internal fault
Horn operates all the time	Horn push contacts stuck Short in horn circuit
Lights fail to come on	If engine not running, battery discharged Light bulb filament burnt out or bulbs broken Wire connections loose, disconnected or broken Light switch shorting or otherwise faulty
Lights give poor illumination	Lamp glasses dirty Reflectors tarnished or dirty Lamps out of adjustment

Symptom	Reason/s
Lights work erratically	Battery terminals or earth connections loose Faulty light switch
Wipers fail to operate	Blown fuse Wire connections loose, disconnected or broken Brushes or armature worn
Wipers operate very slowly	Commutator dirty or worn Linkage restriction Seized restriction Seized armature or gearwheel bearings Worn brushes

Fig. 8.46 Key to wiring diagram for 1968 Daf 55 models

1 Headlight, main beam/dipped beam/parking light
2 Direction indicator light
3 Ignition coil
4 Horn
5 Oil pressure warning light switch
6 Generator
7 Starter
8 Battery
9 Distributor
10 Spark plug
11 Windscreen wiper motor
12 Voltage regulator
13 Fuse holder
14 Stop light switch
15 Wire connector, 6-pole
16 Courtesy light switch
17 Courtesy light
18 Ignition switch
19 Flasher unit
20 Direction indicator/horn switch
21 Windscreen wiper switch
22 Parking light/headlight switch
23 Headlight dipped beam/main beam switch
24 Fuel tank element
25 Instruments
    (a) Battery charge warning light (red)
    (b) Oil pressure warning light (amber)
    (c) Instrument lighting
    (d) Direction indicator warning light (blue)

    (e) Main beam warning light (blue)
    (f) Earth
    (g) Fuel gauge
    (h) Temperature gauge
26 Stop/tail/direction indicator light
27 Number plate light
30 Temperature gauge sender unit
31 Heater blower motor
32 Heater blower motor control resistance
33 Transmission low ratio hold switch
34 Electromagnetic vacuum valve
35 Control switch for 34
    (–) Female wire terminal
    (O) Round wire terminal
Wire, 1 mm^2 cross-section ————
Wire, 2,5 mm^2 cross-section ————
Wire, 4 mm^2 cross-section ████
Wire, 6 mm^2 cross-section ████
Cable, 25 mm^2 cross-section ⋙⋙
Cable, anti-interference ⋙⋙

Bl. = blue
Gr. = green
G = grey
R. = red
Br. = brown
Ge. = yellow
W. = white
Z. = black

Fig. 8.47 Key to wiring diagram for 1970 Daf 55 models

1 Headlamp (main beam/dipped beam)
  Parking light (in headlamp)
2 Direction indicator/parking light
3 Ignition coil
4 Horn
5 Oil pressure warning light switch
6 Generator
7 Starter
8 Battery
9 Distributor
10 Spark plug
11 Windscreen wiper motor
12 Voltage regulator
13 Fuse holder
14 Stop light switch
15 Wire connector, 6-pole
16 Courtesy light switch
17 Courtesy light
18 Ignition switch
19 Flasher unit
20 Direction indicator/horn switch
21 Windscreen wiper switch
22 Parking light/headlight switch
23 Headlight dipped beam/main beam switch
24 Fuel tank elements
25 Instruments
    (a) Battery charge warning light (red)
    (b) Oil pressure warning light (amber)
    (c) Instrument lighting
    (d) Direction indicator warning light (green)
    (e) Main beam warning light (blue)

    (f) Earth
    (g) Fuel gauge
    (h) Temperature gauge
26 Stop/tail/direction indicator light
27 Number plate light
30 Temperature gauge sender unit
31 Heater blower unit
32 Heater blower motor control resistance
33 Transmission low ratio hold switch
34 Electromagnetic vacuum valve
35 Control switch for 34
36 Alarm switch
37 Mercury switch (estate car and delivery van only)
    (–) Female wire terminal
    (O) Round wire terminal

Wire, 1 mm^2 cross-section ————
Wire, 2.5 mm^2 cross-section ————
Wire, 4 mm^2 cross-section ████
Wire, 6 mm^2 cross-section ████
Cable, 25 mm^2 cross-section ⋙⋙
Cable, anti-interference ⋙⋙

Bl. = blue
Gr. = green
G. = grey
R. = red
Br. = brown
Ge. = yellow
W. = white
Z. = black

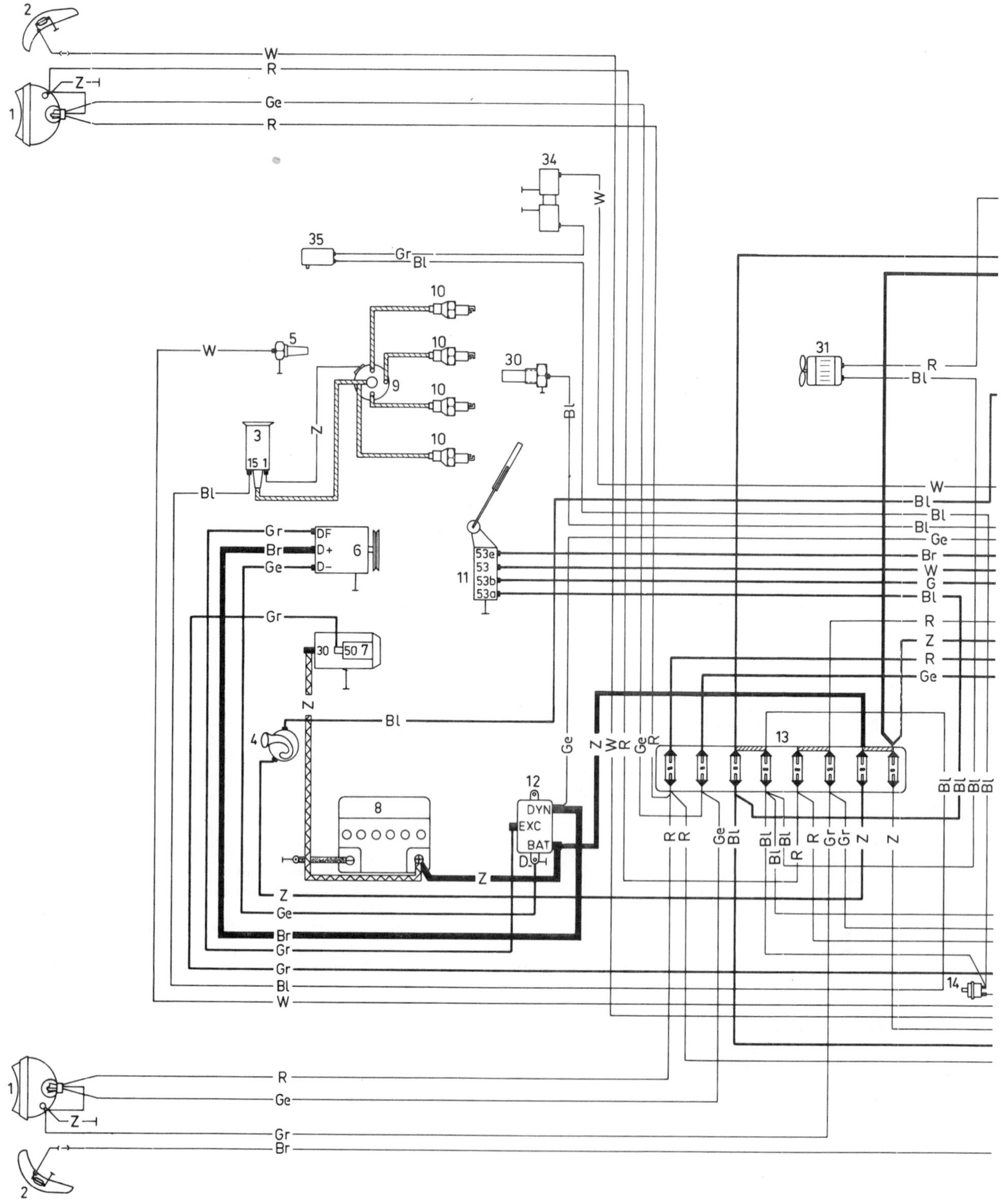

Fig. 8.46 Wiring diagram for 1968 Daf 55 models

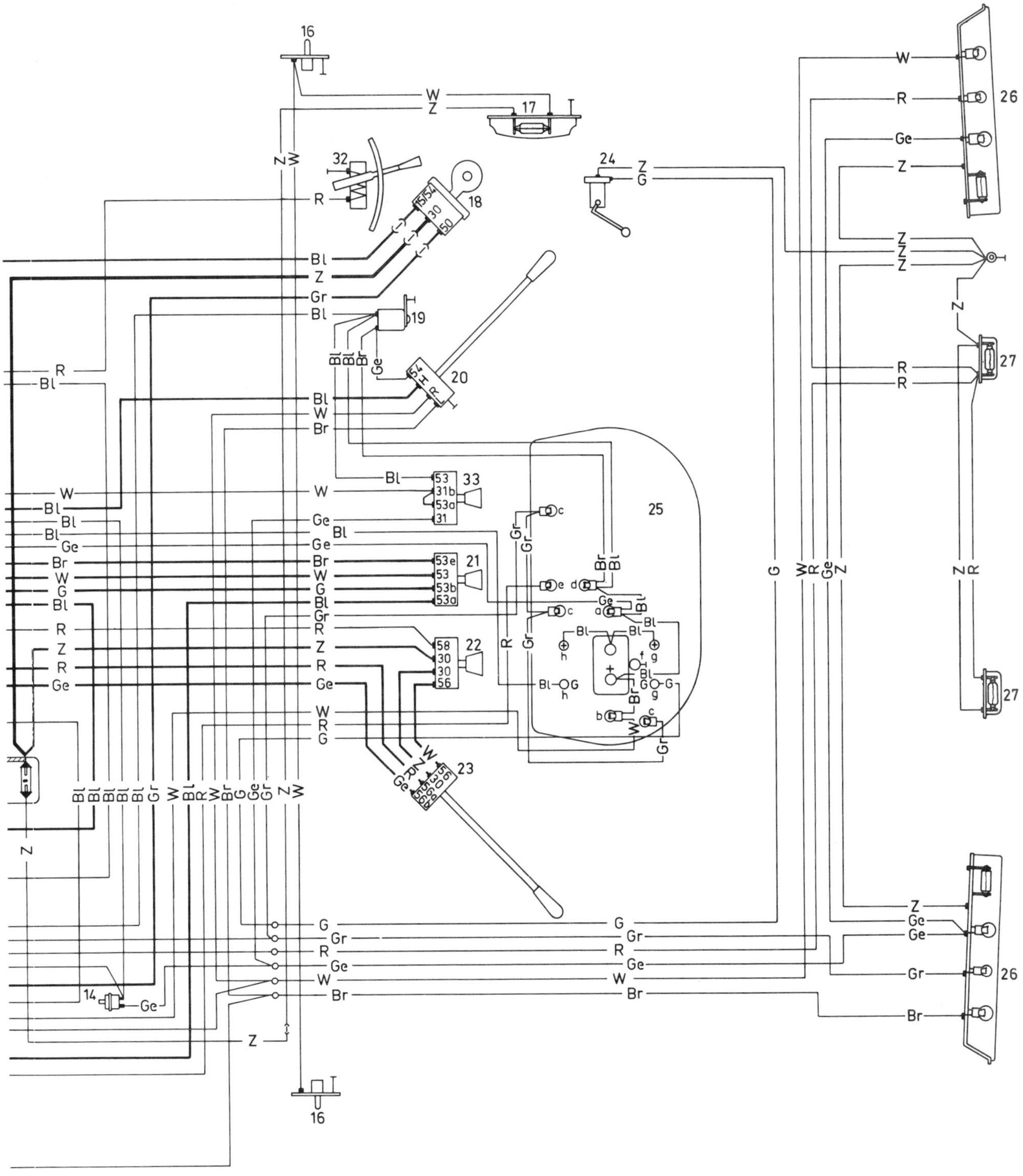

Fig. 8.46 Wiring diagram for 1968 Daf 55 models – continued

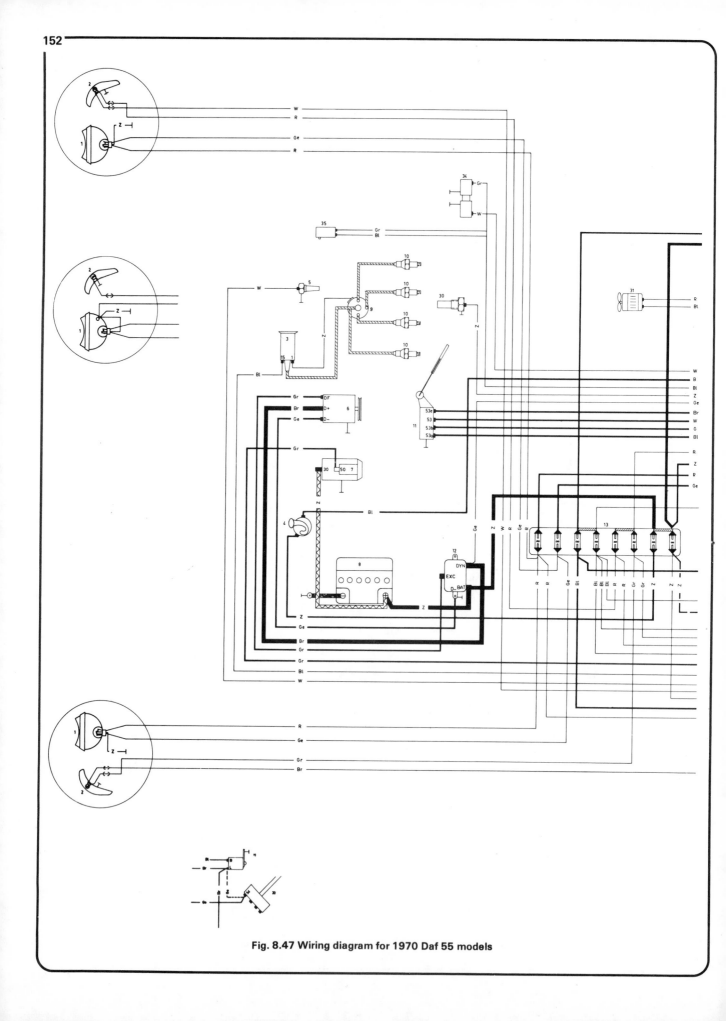

Fig. 8.47 Wiring diagram for 1970 Daf 55 models

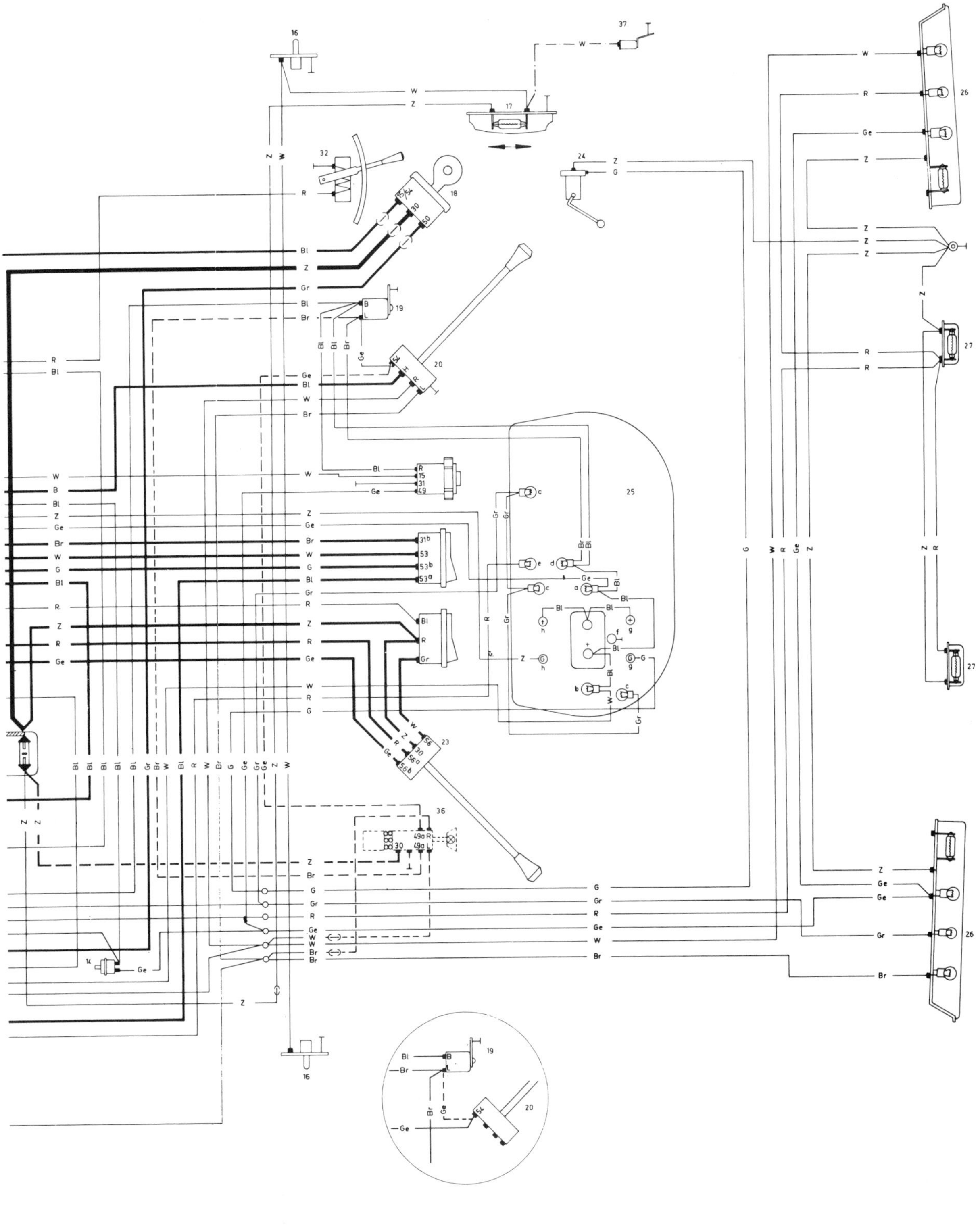

Fig. 8.47 Wiring diagram for 1970 Daf 55 models – continued

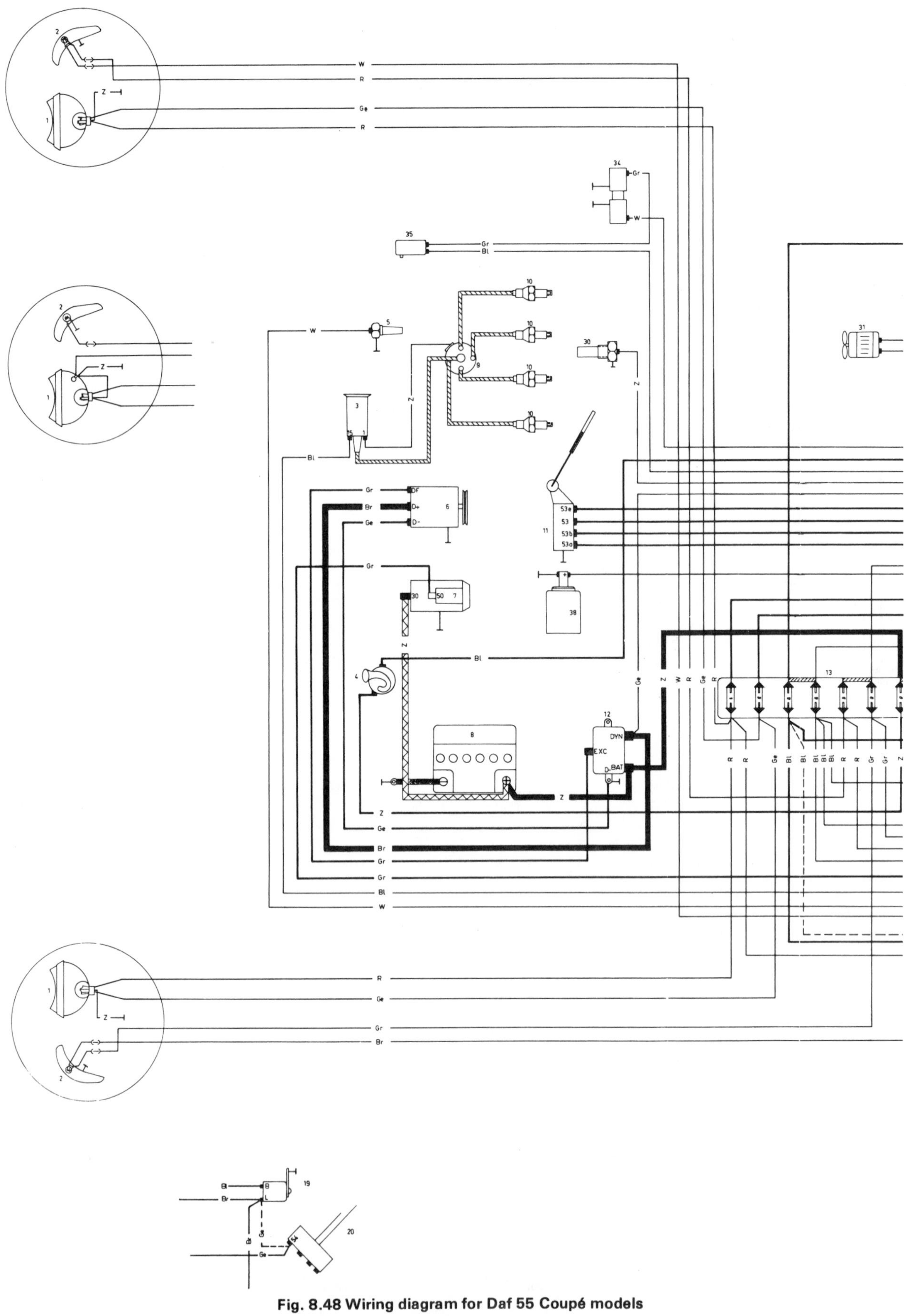

Fig. 8.48 Wiring diagram for Daf 55 Coupé models

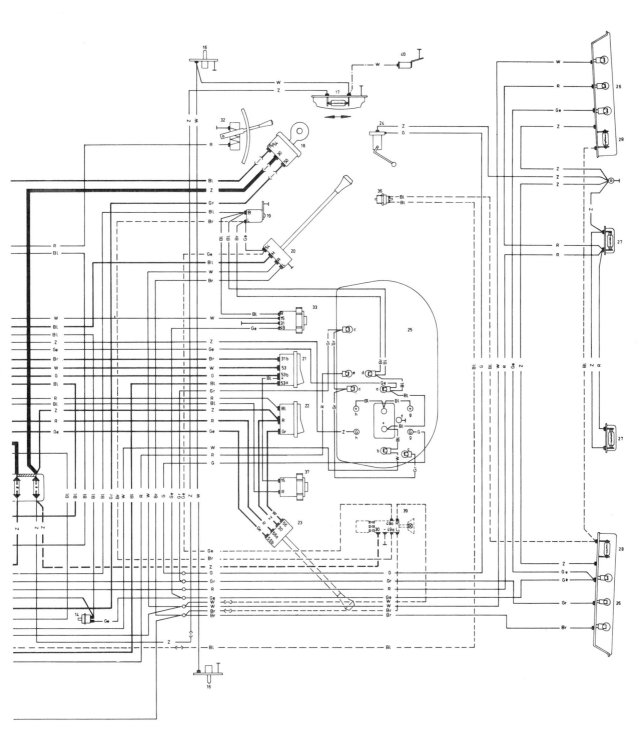

Fig. 8.48 Wiring diagram for Daf 55 Coupé models – continued

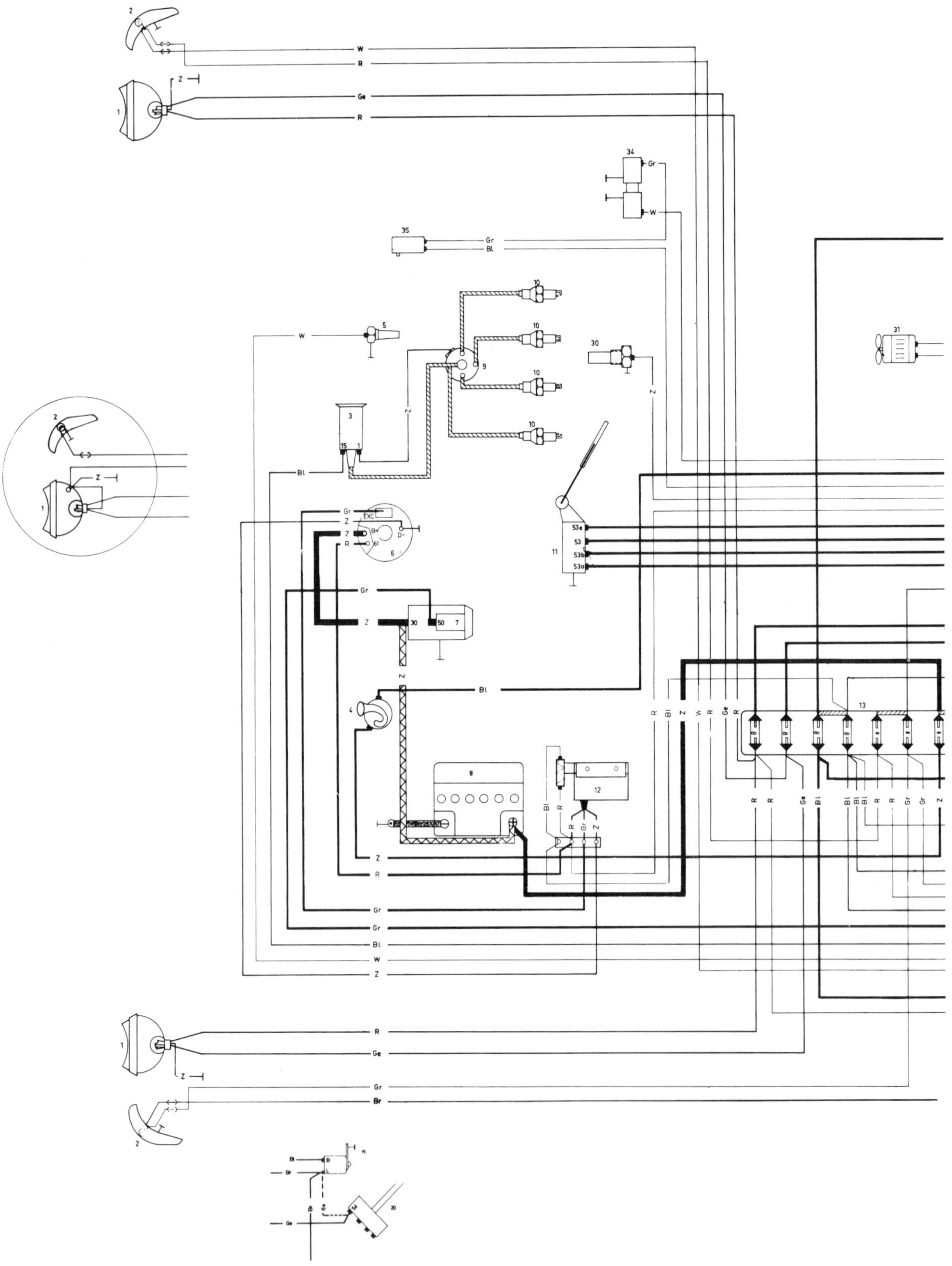

Fig. 8.49 Wiring diagram for Daf 55 models with alternator

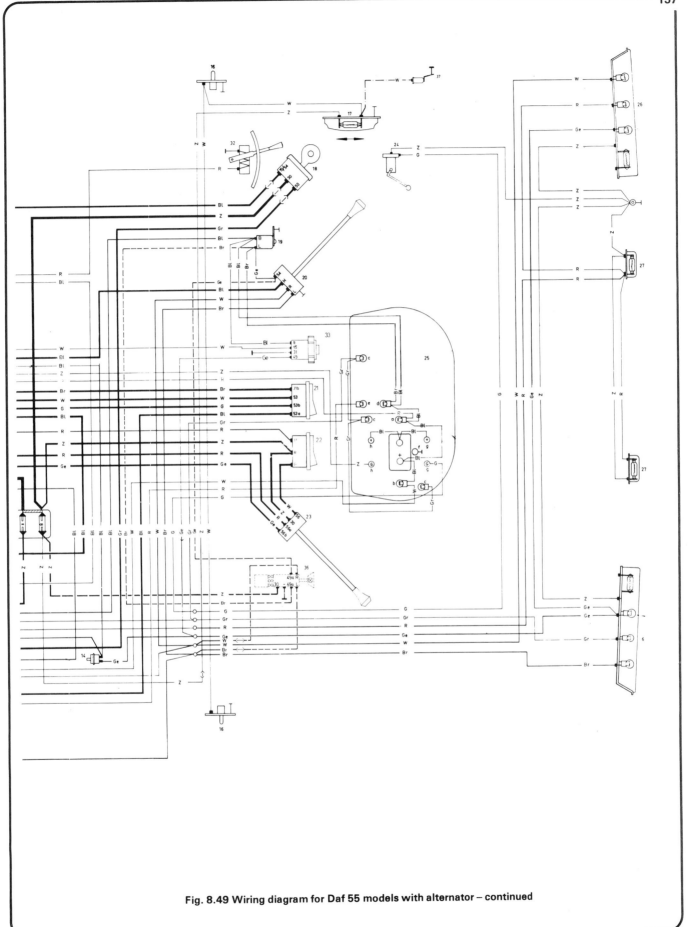

Fig. 8.49 Wiring diagram for Daf 55 models with alternator – continued

Fig. 8.48 Key to wiring diagram for Daf 55 Coupé models

1 Headlamp (main beam/dipped beam)
  Parking light (in headlamp)
2 Direction indicator/parking light
3 Ignition coil
4 Horn
5 Oil pressure warning light switch
6 Generator
7 Starter
8 Battery
9 Distributor
10 Spark plug
11 Windscreen wiper motor
12 Voltage regulator
13 Fuse holder
14 Stop light switch
15 Wire connector, 6-pole
16 Courtesy light switch
17 Courtesy light
18 Ignition switch
19 Flasher unit
20 Direction indicator/horn switch
21 Windscreen wiper switch
22 Parking light/headlight switch
23 Headlight dipped beam/main beam switch
24 Fuel tank element
25 Instruments
    (a) Battery charge warning light (red)
    (b) Oil pressure warning light (amber)
    (c) Instrument lighting
    (d) Direction indicator warning light (green)
    (e) Main beam warning light (blue)

(f) Earth
(g) Fuel gauge
(h) Temperature gauge
26 Stop/tail/direction indicator light
27 Number plate light
28 Reversing lamp
30 Temperature gauge sender unit
31 Heater blower motor
32 Heater blower motor control resistance
33 Transmission low ratio hold switch
34 Electromagnetic vacuum valve
35 Control switch for 34
36 Reversing lamps switch
37 Windscreen washer switch
38 Windscreen washer reservoir and motor
39 Alarm switch
Wire, 1 mm² cross-section ——————
Wire, 2.5 mm² cross-section ══════
Wire, 4 mm² cross-section ━━━━━━
Wire, 6 mm² cross-section ▆▆▆▆▆
Cable, 25 mm² cross-section ⋙⋙⋙⋙
Cable,   anti-interference ⧄⧄⧄⧄

Bl. = blue
Gr. = green
G. = grey
R. = red
Br. = brown
Ge. = yellow
W. = white
Z. = black

Fig. 8.49 Key to wiring diagram for Daf 55 models with alternator

1 Headlamp (main beam/dipped beam)
  Parking light (in headlamp)
2 Direction indicator/parking light
3 Ignition coil
4 Horn
5 Oil pressure warning light
6 Alternator
7 Starter
8 Battery
9 Distributor
10 Spark plug
11 Windscreen wiper motor
12 Voltage regulator with resistance
13 Fuse holder
14 Stop light switch
15 Wire connector, 6-pole
16 Courtesy light switch
17 Courtesy light
18 Ignition switch
19 Flasher unit
20 Direction indicator/horn switch
21 Windscreen wiper switch
22 Parking light/headlight switch
23 Headlight dipped beam/main beam switch
24 Fuel tank element
25 Instruments
    (a) Battery charge warning light (red)
    (b) Oil pressure warning light (amber)
    (c) Instrument lighting
    (d) Direction indicator warning light (green)

(e) Main beam warning light (blue)
(f) Earth
(g) Fuel gauge
(h) Temperature
26 Stop/tail/direction indicator light
27 Number plate light
30 Temperature gauge sender unit
31 Heater blower motor control resistance
33 Transmission low ratio hold switch
34 Electromagnetic vacuum valve
35 Control switch for 34
36 Alarm switch
37 Mercury switch (estate car and delivery van only)
Wire, ½ mm² cross-section ——————
Wire, 1 mm² cross-section ══════
Wire, 1.5mm² cross-section ━━━━━━
Wire, 2.5mm² cross-section ━━━━━━
Wire, 4 mm² cross-section ▆▆▆▆▆
Wire, 6 mm² cross-section ▆▆▆▆▆
Cable, 25 mm² cross-section ⋀⋀⋀⋀
Cable,   anti-interference ⧄⧄⧄⧄

Bl. = blue
Gr. = green
G. = grey
R. = red
Br. = brown
Ge. = yellow
W. = white
Z. = black

Fig. 8.50 Key to wiring diagram for Daf 66/1100 models

1 Headlamp
2 Direction indicator
3 Ignition coil
4 Horn
5 Oil pressure switch
6 Alternator
7 Starter motor
8 Battery
9 Distributor
10 Spark plugs
11 Windscreen wiper motor
12 Voltage regulator
13 Fuse box
14 Stop light switch
15 Cable connector
16 Door switch
17 Courtesy light
18 Contact switch
19 Flasher unit
20 Direction indicator switch/horn switch
21 Windscreen wiper switch
22 Light switch
23 Dipswitch/Main beam switch
24 Fuel tank sender tank
25 Combined instrument
   (a) Coolant warning light (red)
   (b) Oil pressure warning light (red)
   (c) Dial illumination
   (d) Direction indicator warning light (green)
   (e) Main beam warning light (blue)
   (f) Earth connection
   (g) Fuel gauge
   (h) Voltmeter
   (k) Breakdown flasher unit warning light
26 Tail lamp unit
27 Number plate light
30 Coolant temperature sender unit
31 Heater blower motor

32 Blower motor central resistance
33 Exhaust brake switch
34 Electro-magnetic vacuum valve
35 Vacuum control switch
36 Hazard warning switch
37 Mercury switch (estate car and delivery van only)
38 Rear window heating
39 Rear window heating switch
40 Rear window heating relay
41 Windscreen washer water pump (Norway and Sweden only)
42 Switch for 41 (Norway and Sweden only)
43 Reversing lamp switch
44 Hazard warning flasher unit (not for France)
46 Brake fluid float (Norway, Sweden and Switzerland only)
47 Reversing lamp
48 Cover plate (France only)
49 Side direction indicator

Wire $\frac{1}{2}$ mm²
Wire 1 mm²
Wire 1$\frac{1}{2}$ mm²
Wire 2$\frac{1}{2}$ mm²
Wire 4 mm²
Wire 6 mm²
Wire 24 mm²
Wire anti-interference

Bl. = blue
Br. = brown
Gr. = green
Ge. = yellow
G. = grey
R. = red
W. = white
Z. = black

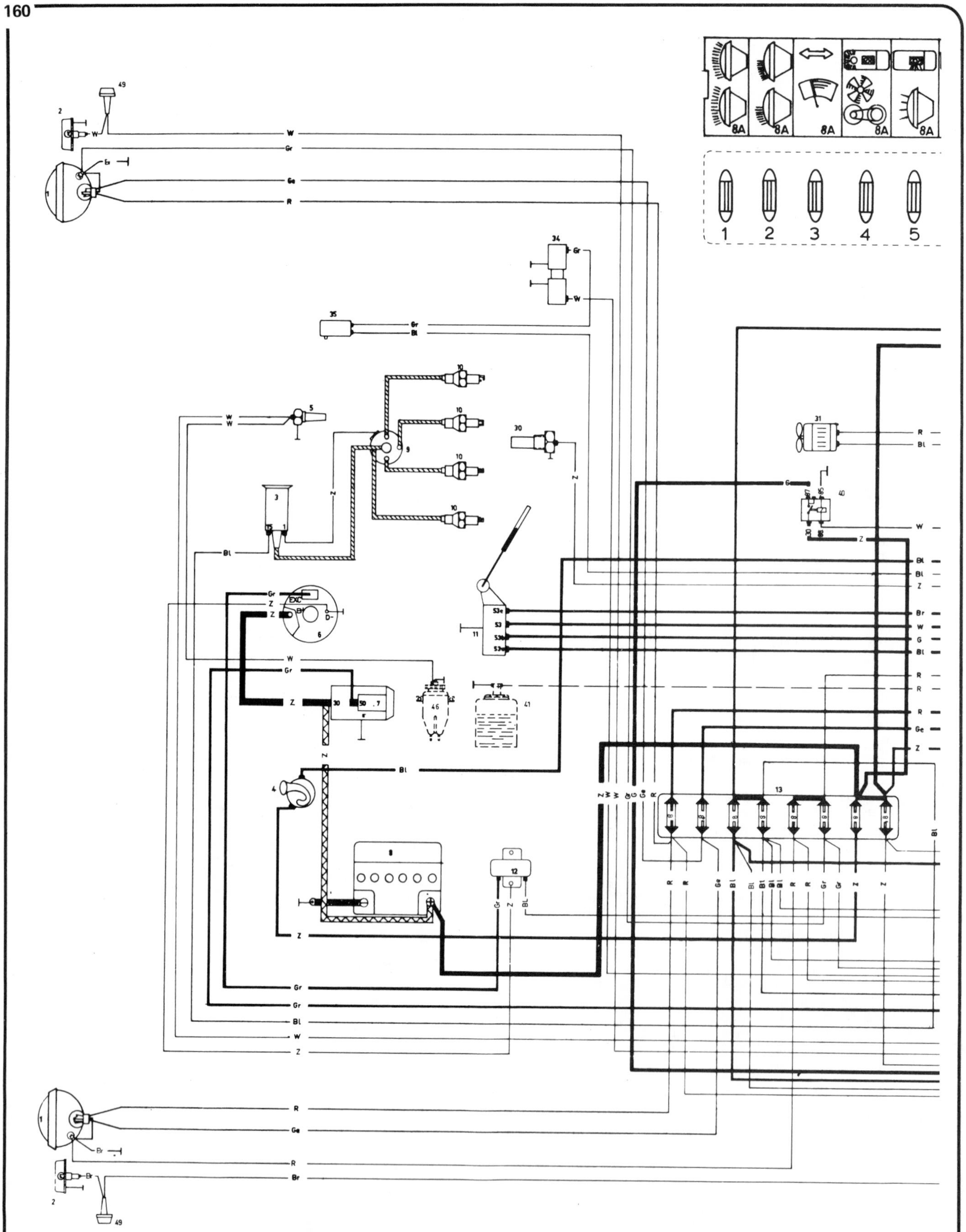

Fig. 8.50 Wiring diagram for Daf 66/1100 models

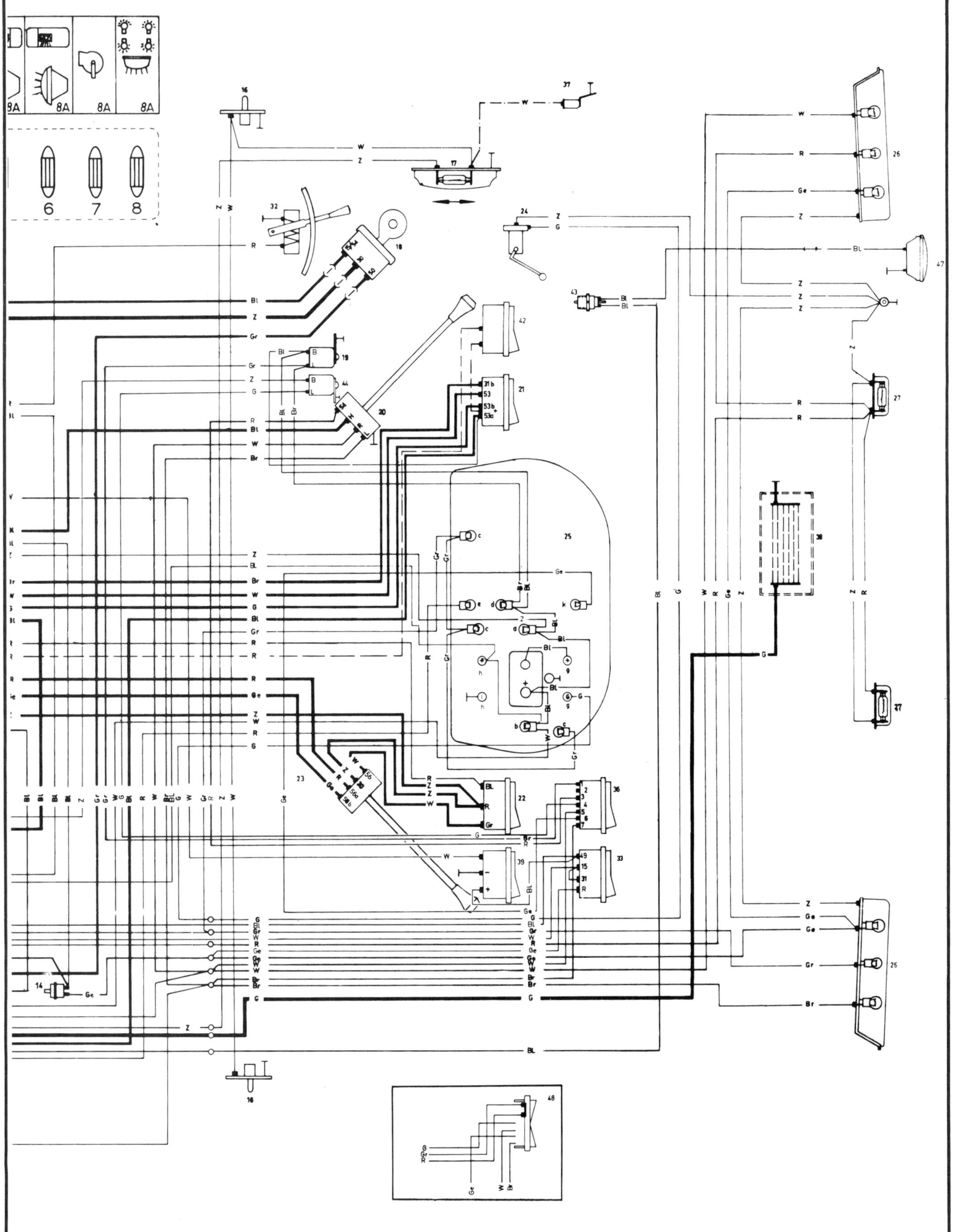

Fig. 8.50 Wiring diagram for Daf 66/1100 models – continued

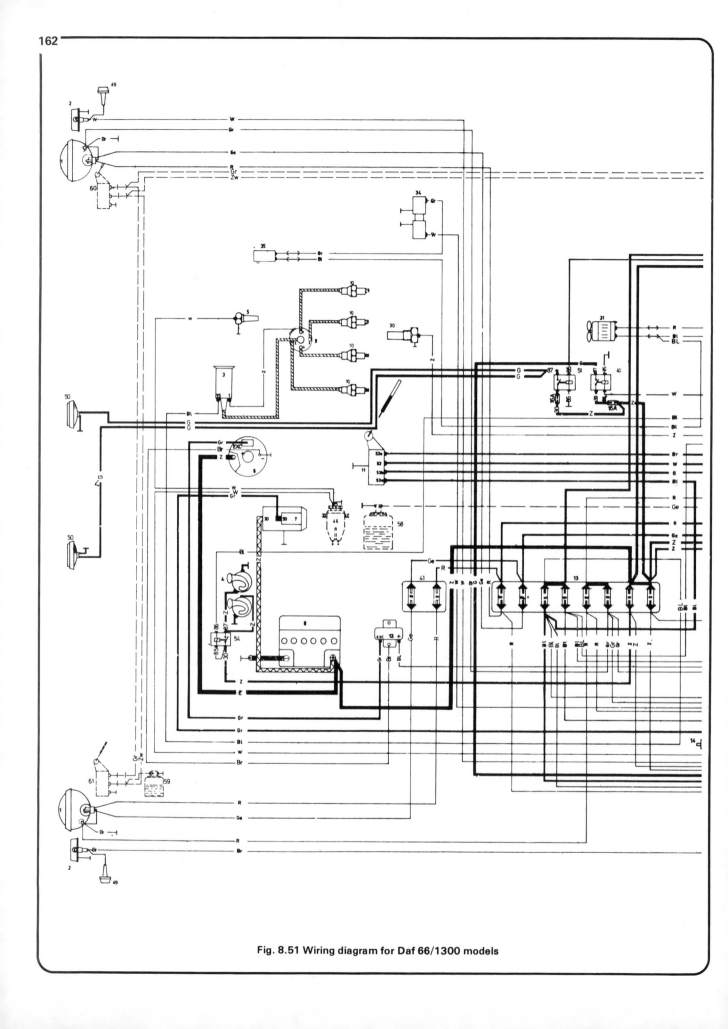

Fig. 8.51 Wiring diagram for Daf 66/1300 models

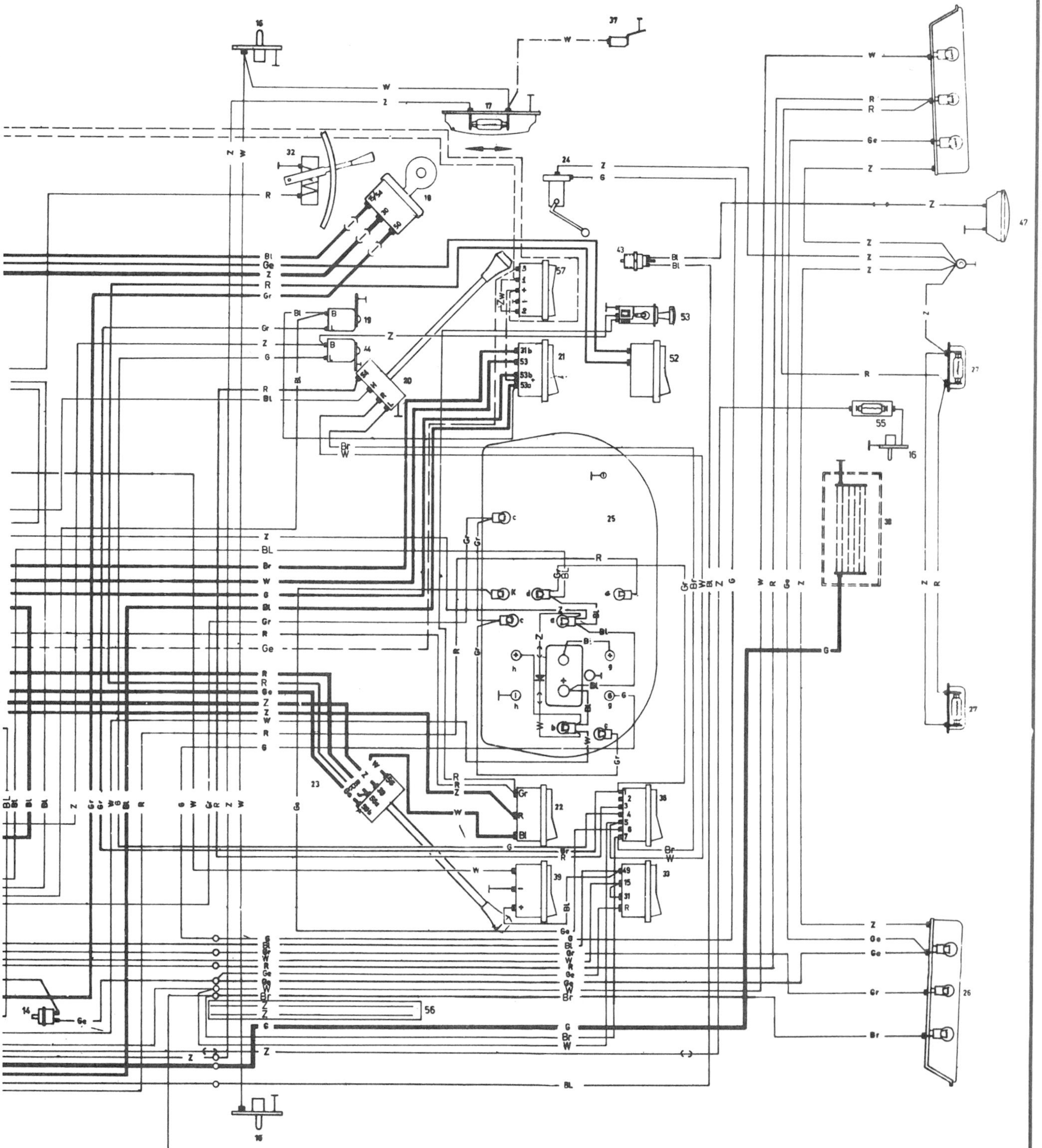

Fig. 8.51 Wiring diagram for Daf 66/1300 models – continued

Fig. 8.51 Key to wiring diagram for Daf 66/1300 models

1 Headlamp
2 Direction indicator
3 Ignition coil
4 Horn
5 Oil pressure switch
6 Alternator
7 Starter motor
8 Battery
9 Distributor
10 Spark plugs
11 Windscreen wiper motor
12 Voltage regulator
13 Fuse box
14 Stop light switch
15 Cable connector
16 Door switch
17 Courtesy light
18 Ignition switch
19 Flasher unit
20 Direction indicator switch/horn switch
21 Windscreen wiper switch
22 Light switch
23 Dipswitch/Main beam switch
24 Fuel tank sender unit
25 Combined instrument
    (a) Coolant temperature warning light (red)
    (b) Oil pressure warning light (red)
    (c) Dial illumination
    (d) Direction indicator warning light (green)
    (e) Main beam warning light (blue)
    (f) Earth connection
    (g) Fuel gauge
    (h) Voltmeter
    (k) Hazard warning unit pilot light
26 Tail lamp unit
27 Number plate light
30 Coolant temperature switch
31 Heater blower unit
32 Blower motor control resistance

33 Exhaust brake switch
34 Electromagnetic vacuum valve
35 Vacuum control switch
36 Hazard warning light switch (not for Italy)
37 Mercury switch (estate car only)
38 Rear window heating
39 Rear window heating switch
40 Rear window heating relay
41 Windscreen washer water pump (Scandinavia only)
42 Switch for 41 (Scandinavia only)
43 Reversing lamp switch
44 Hazard warning light (not for Italy)
46 Brake fluid float (Scandinavia and Switzerland only)
47 Reversing lamp
48 Cover plate (Italy only)
49 Side direction indicator
50 Spot lights
51 Spot light relay
52 Spot light switch
53 Cigar lighter
54 Horn relay
55 Boot light
56 Loudspeaker wiring (not for estate car)

Wire $\frac{1}{2}$ mm^2	
Wire 1 mm^2	
Wire $1\frac{1}{2}$ mm^2	
Wire $2\frac{1}{2}$ mm^2	
Wire 4 mm^2	
Wire 6 mm^2	
Wire 25 mm^2	
Anit-interference wire	

Bl = blue
Br = brown
Gr = green
Ge = yellow
G = grey
R = red
W = white
Z = black

Fig. 8.52 Key to wiring diagram for Volvo 66 models

1   Headlamp
2   Direction indicator
3   Ignition coil
4   Horn
5   Oil pressure warning lamp switch
6   Alternator
7   Starter motor
8   Battery
9   Distributor
10 Spark plug
11 Windscreen wiper motor
12 Voltage regulator
13 Fuse box
14 Brake light switch
15 Cable connector
16 Courtesy light door switch
17 Courtesy light
18 Ignition switch
19 Flasher unit
20 Windscreen and headlamp wipe/wash switch **
21 Brake fluid level/handbrake and choke warning lamps
22 Main light switch
23 Direction indicator stalk with main beam/low beam/horn
24 Fuel tank float
25 Instrument binnacle
    (a) Coolant temperature warning lamp red
    (b) Oil pressure warning lamp red
    (c) Panel lighting (3x) white
    (d) Direction indicator (2x) green
    (e) Main beam blue
    (f) Earth
    (g) Fuel gauge
    (h) Voltmeter
    (k) Hazard warning light
26 Tail light cluster
27 Number plate light
30 Coolant temperature sender

31 Blower motor
32 Blower motor control resistance
33 Transmission low ratio hold switch
34 Electromagnetic vacuum valve
35 Microswitch
36 Hazard warning switch
37 Tailgate switch
38 Heated rear window
39 Heated rear window switch*
40 Relay for heated rear window*
43 Reversing light switch
44 Hazard warning unit (not for Italy)
46 Brake fluid level indicator float
47 Reversing light
49 Side direction indicator
50 Spotlight*
51 Spotlight relay
52 Spotlight switch*
53 Cigar lighter*
54 Horn relay
55 Boot light*
56 Loudspeaker wiring (only estate cars)
57 Interlock relay
58 Water reservoir and pump **
60 Electrical declutching valve
62 Light relay
63 Choke switch
64 Handbrake switch
    only for ⎫
    Nordic ⎬
    version ⎭
65 Rev. counter switch**
66 Three-way valve**
67 Kick-down switch
*   GL version
** Nordic version

cable 25 mm²
cable, interference suppressed
Bl = cable blue
Br = cable brown
Gr = cable green
Ge = cable yellow
G   = cable grey
R   = cable red
W   = cable white
Z   = cable black

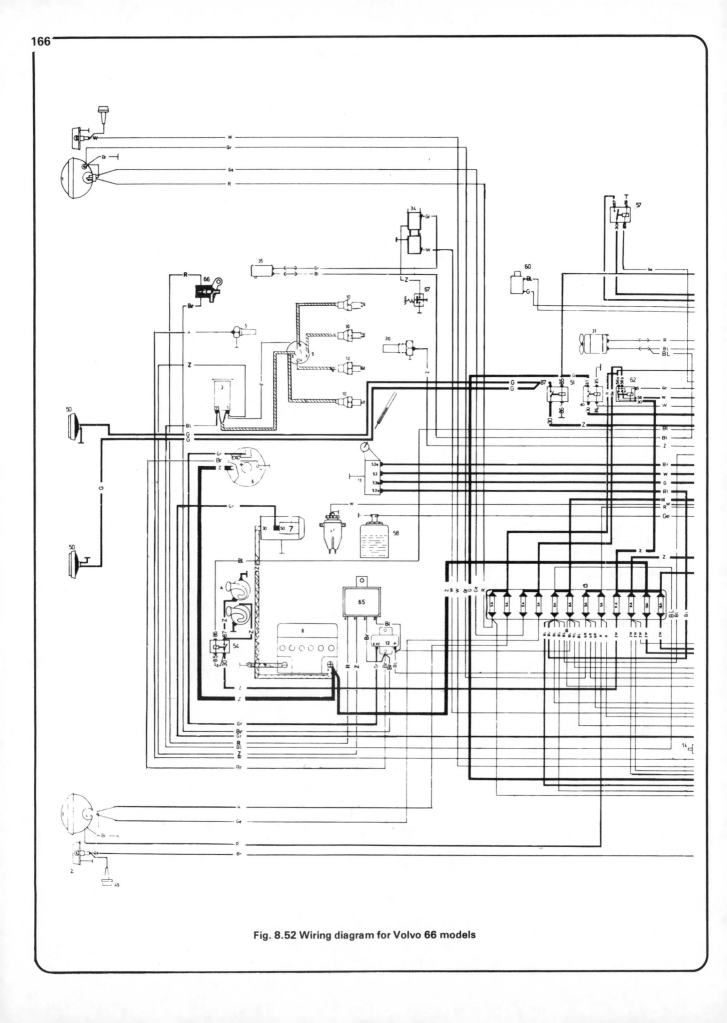

Fig. 8.52 Wiring diagram for Volvo 66 models

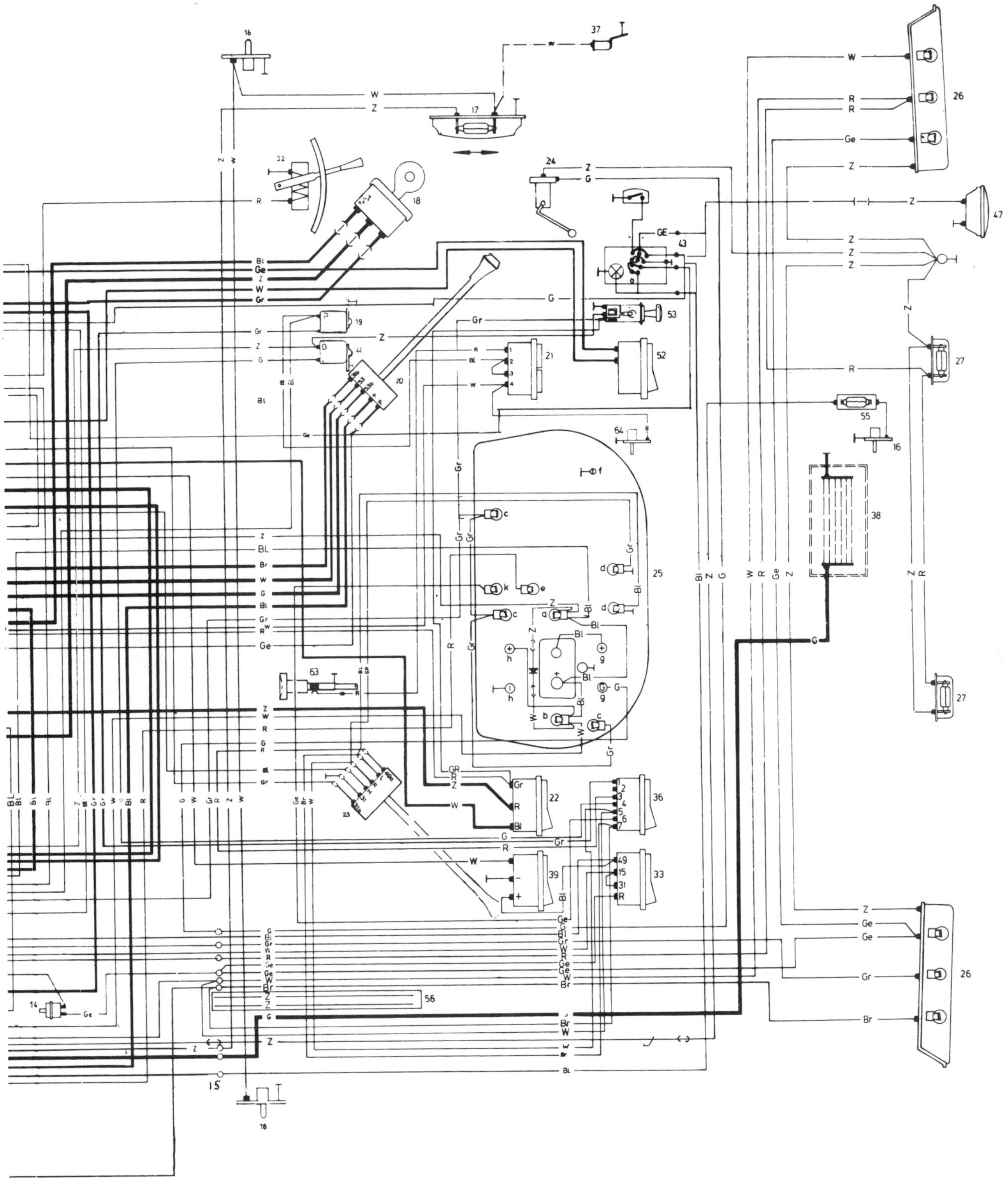

Fig. 8.52 Wiring diagram for Volvo 66 models – continued

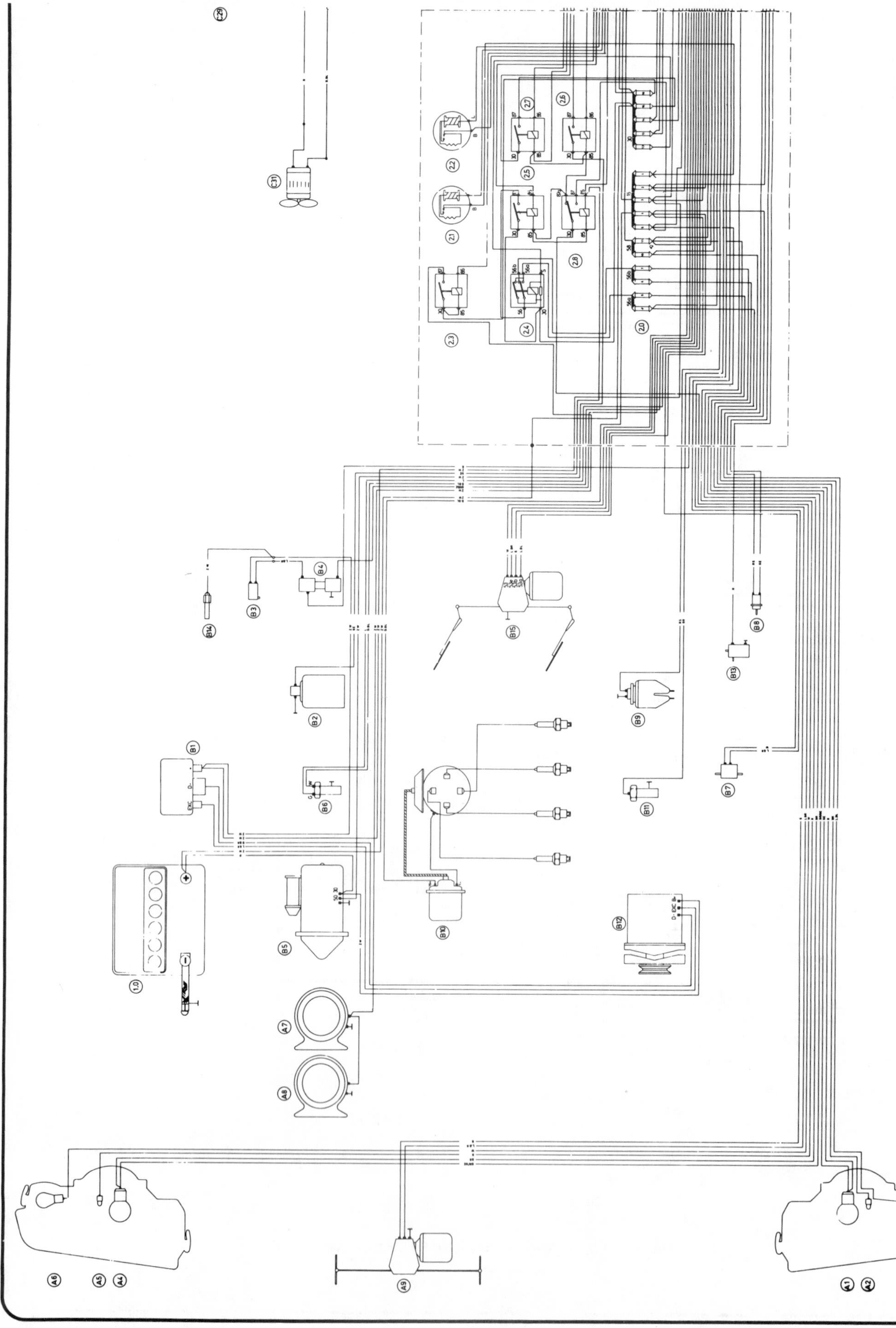

Fig. 8.53 Wiring diagram for Volvo 343 models

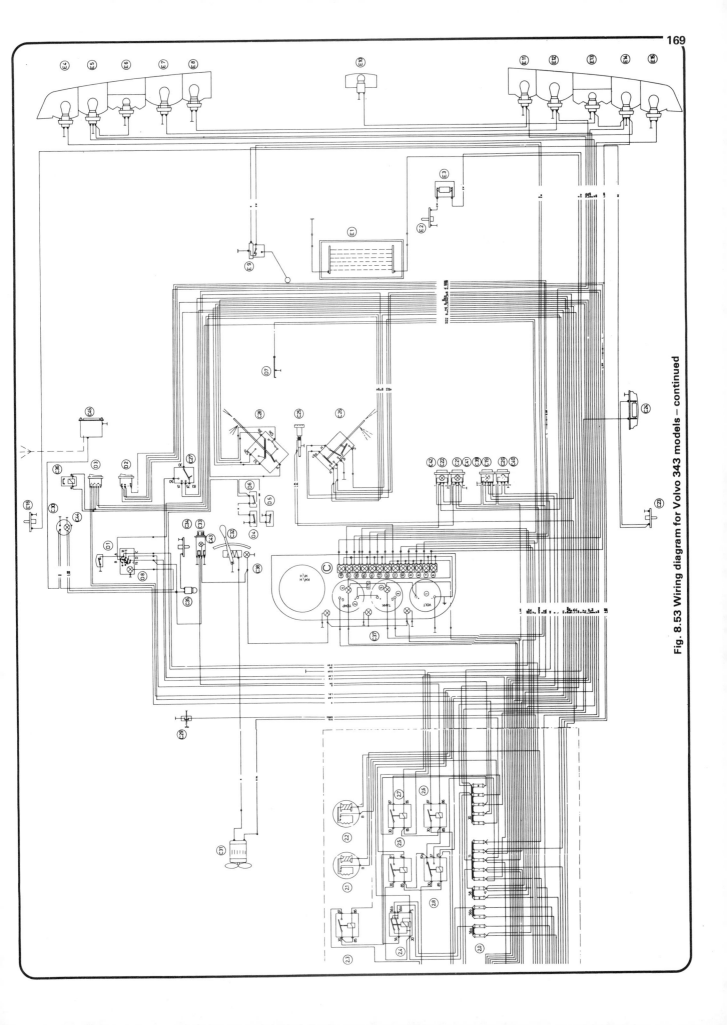

Fig. 8.53 Wiring diagram for Volvo 343 models – continued

Fig. 8.53 Key to wiring diagram for Volvo 343 models

A1 Headlamp main beam/dipped beam
A2 Parking light
A3 Direction indicator
A4 Headlamp main beam/dipped beam
A5 Parking lights
A6 Direction indicator
A7 Horn high-tone
A8 Horn low-tone
A9 Headlamp wiper motor (Nordic)

B1 Voltage regulator
B2 Water pump
B3 Microswitch
B4 4-way valve
B5 Starter motor
B6 Coolant temperature sender/switch
B7 Declutching valve
B8 Brake light switch
B9 Brake fluid level float
B10 Ignition coil
B11 Oil pressure sender
B12 Alternator
B13 3-way valve (Sweden)
B14 Pilot jet (Sweden)
B15 Windscreen wiper motor

C1 Voltmeter
C2 Temperature gauge
C3 Fuel gauge
C4 Coolant temperature warning lamp
C5 Fuel reserve indicating lamp
C6 Direction indicating lamp, left
C7 Parking light indicating lamp
C8 Handbrake warning lamp
C9 Oil pressure warning lamp
C10 Brake fluid level warning lamp
C11 Choke indicating lamp
C12 Seat belt indicating lamp
C13 Hazard warning installation, indicating lamp
C14 Main beam indicating lamp
C15 Rear-warning fog lamp, indicating lamp
C16 Low ratio hold indicating lamp
C17 Heated rear window indicating lamp
C18 Direction indicating lamp, right
C19 Switch for main beam/dipped beam
C20 Switch for parking lights
C21 Switch for heated rear window
C22 Switch for rear-warning fog lamp
C23 Courtesy light door switch, left
C24 Courtesy light, car interior
C25 Choke
C26 Direction indicator switch
C27 Ignition switch
C28 Windscreen wiper switch
C29 Kick-down switch
C30 Clock
C31 Blower
C32 Blower rheostat
C33 Cigar lighter
C34 Switch for glove compartment light
C35 Lamp for glove compartment
C36 Direction indicator

C37 Lamp for instrument lighting
C38 Lamp for illumination of heater controls
C39 Lamp for illumination of main/dipped beam switch
C40 Lamp for illumination of parking lights switch
C41 Lamp for illumination of heated rear window switch
C42 Lamp for illumination of rear warning fog lamp switch
C43 Lamp for illumination of cigar lighter
C44 Lamp for clock illumination (DL)
C45 Radio (optional)

D1 Selector lever switch
D2 Low ratio hold switch
D3 Switch for hazard warning installation
D4 Seat belt contact, left front
D4 Seat belt contact, right front
D6 Seat cushion contact, rear seat
D7 Handbrake switch
D8 Selector scale switch

E1 Heated rear window
E2 Boot light switch
E3 Boot light
E4 Direction indicator
E5 Tail light/brake light
E6 Tail light
E7 Rear-warning fog lamp
E8 Reversing light
E9 Float
E10 Number plate light
E11 Reversing light
E12 Rear-warning fog lamp
E13 Tail light
E14 Tail light/brake light
E15 Direction indicator
E16 Courtesy light door switch, right
W White
R Red
OR Orange
RS Pink
D BR Dark brown
L BR Light brown
D BL Dark blue
L BL Light blue
D GR Dark green
L GR Light green
GR/GE Green/Yellow
GE Yellow
L Lilac
G Grey
ZW Black

1.0 Battery
2.0 Fuse box
2.1 Direction indicator
2.2 Hazard warning installation
2.3 Horn relay
2.4 Main beam/dipped beam relay
2.5 Vehicle lighting relay
2.6 Interlock (start inhibitor) relay
2.7 Heated rear window relay (DL)
2.8 Headlamp wash/wipe installation relay (Nordic)

Chapter 9 Suspension and steering

Contents

Specifications

Front suspension
Type:

Daf 55, Daf 66 and Volvo 66	Torsion bars, lower suspension arms and hydraulic shock absorbers integral with struts, anti-roll bar
Volvo 343	Lower suspension arms, coil springs and hydraulic shock absorbers integral with struts, anti-roll bar

Steering angles:

Camber (Daf 55, Daf 66, Volvo 66) – unladen	1° 21' ± 30'
Camber (Volvo 343) – full load	0°
Castor (Daf 55) – unladen	4° 50' ± 30'
Castor (Daf 66) – unladen	4° 30' ± 30'
Castor (Volvo 66) – full load	22 mm at strut top
Castor (Volvo 343) – full load	24.5 mm at strut top
Kingpin inclination (Daf 55, Daf 66) – full load	8° 30' ± 30'
Kingpin inclination (Volvo 66) – unladen	9° 20' ± 30'
Kingpin inclination (Volvo 343) – full load	10° 5'
Toe-in (all models) – unladen	0.08 to 0.16 in (2 to 4 mm)
Torsion bar adjustment dimension	New: 3.66 in (93 mm) Used: 3.27 in (83 mm)

Rear suspension

Type:

Daf 55 . . . .   Lower wishbones, coil springs, telescopic shock absorbers
Daf 66, Volvo 66, Volvo 343 . . . .   De Dion axle, frictionless parabolic leaf springs, telescopic shock absorbers
Rear wheel driveshaft endplay (Daf 55 models) . . . .   0 to 0.003 in (0 to 0.076 mm)

Steering

Type . . . .   Rack-and-pinion
Number of turns (lock-to-lock):
Daf 55, Daf 66, Volvo 66 . . . .   3.34
Volvo 343 . . . .   4.13
Steering gear lubricant . . . .   Lithium grease NLG 1

Wheels and tyres

Roadwheels . . . .   Pressed steel
Roadwheel size:
Daf 55, Daf 66 standard, Volvo 66 DL . . . .   4B x 14 in
Daf 66 Marathon, Volvo 66 GL . . . . $4\frac{1}{2}$JJ x 13 in
Volvo 343 . . . .   5J x 13 in
Tyre size:
Daf 55, Daf 66 standard . . . .   Radial 135 SR – 14
Volvo 66 DL . . . .   Radial 145 SR – 14
Daf 66 Marathon, Volvo 66 GL, Volvo 343 . . . .   Radial 155 SR – 13
Tyre pressures:
Daf 55, Daf 66 standard, Volvo 66 DL . . . .   Front 23 lbf in² (1.6 kg/sq cm) Rear 26 lbf in² (1.8 kg/sq cm)
Daf 66 Marathon, Volvo 66 GL . . . .   Front 20 lbf in² (1.4 kg/sq cm) Rear 23 lbf in² (1.6 kg/sq cm)
Volvo 343 . . . .   Front 24 lbf in² (1.7 kg/sq cm) Rear 28 lbf in² (2.0 kg/sq cm)
Note . . . .   Add 3 lbf in² (0.2 kg/sq cm) for full load conditions

Torque wrench settings

	lbf ft	Nm
Rear wheel hub (Daf 55)	152 to 210	209 to 290
Rear frame mounting (Daf 55)	62 to 70	86 to 96
Wishbone pivot (Daf 55)	72 to 87	99 to 120
Steering swivel joint	40 to 47	55 to 65
Track-rod ends	20 to 22	27 to 30
Steering housing cover	13 to 14	18 to 20
Steering gear mounting	5.2	7.0
Steering wheel (except Volvo 343)	58 to 65	80 to 90
Shock absorber mounting (Front)	40 to 47	55 to 65
Shock absorber mounting (Rear)	16 to 18	22 to 25
Shock absorber retaining (Front)	87 to 100	120 to 140
Spring bolt	36 to 40	50 to 55
Spring plate	36 to 40	50 to 55
Wheel nuts	58 to 65	80 to 90
Steering flexible coupling	18.1	25
Thrust block retaining screws	11	15
Steering wheel (Volvo 343)	36 to 44	50 to 60
Radius rod front (Volvo 343)	40 to 47	55 to 65
Radius rod rear (Volvo 343)	12 to 13	16 to 18
Suspension arm (Volvo 343)	36 to 40	50 to 55
Rear axleshaft (except Daf 55)	130 to 145	180 to 200
Rear driveshaft (except Daf 55)	23 to 26	32 to 36

1 General description

The independent front suspension is of the Macpherson strut type incorporating torsion bars on all but Volvo 343 models, which are fitted with coil springs. Shock absorbers are an integral part of the suspension struts and an anti-roll bar is fitted.

The independent rear suspension on Daf 55 models is of the low pivot swing axle type, using single coil wishbones, springs and double acting telescopic shock absorbers. The secondary variomatic units are incorporated in the axleshafts and form part of the unsprung weight of the car. On all other models the rear suspension incorporates a De Dion axle with leaf springs and double-acting telescopic shock absorbers.

The steering gear is of the rack-and-pinion type and is mounted forward of the wheels on Volvo 343 models but behind the wheels on all other models. A collapsible steering column is fitted to most models.

2 Front torsion bar – removal and refitting

1   Jack up the front of the car and support it adequately with axle-stands positioned under the body channel sections.

2   Unscrew and remove the anti-roll bar mountings at both wheels and swivel it down out of the way.

3   Unscrew and remove the two retaining nuts from the bottom of the suspension strut and the radius arm mounting nut on the body, then withdraw the radius arm.

4   A suspension arm tension clamp (Daf tool No 7-99-535568/Volvo tool No 5876-535568) must now be obtained from a tool agent or garage. Hook the ends of the tool in the holes located either side of the conical rubber stop and tighten the clamp onto the lower suspension arm.

5   Extract the two bolts from the bottom of the strut and push the wheel outwards away from the lower suspension arm.

6   Unscrew the clamping tool and remove it.

7   Prise the dust cover away from the rear end of the torsion bar and extract the circlip with a pair of circlip pliers.

8   Unscrew and remove the nut from the front of the torsion bar then, using a suitable punch, carefully drive the torsion bar rearwards through the suspension arm and rear support. Be careful not to damage the splines during this operation.

9   Remove the adjustment arm from the rear of the torsion bar.

10   Examine the torsion bar for deterioration, wear and fractures. If

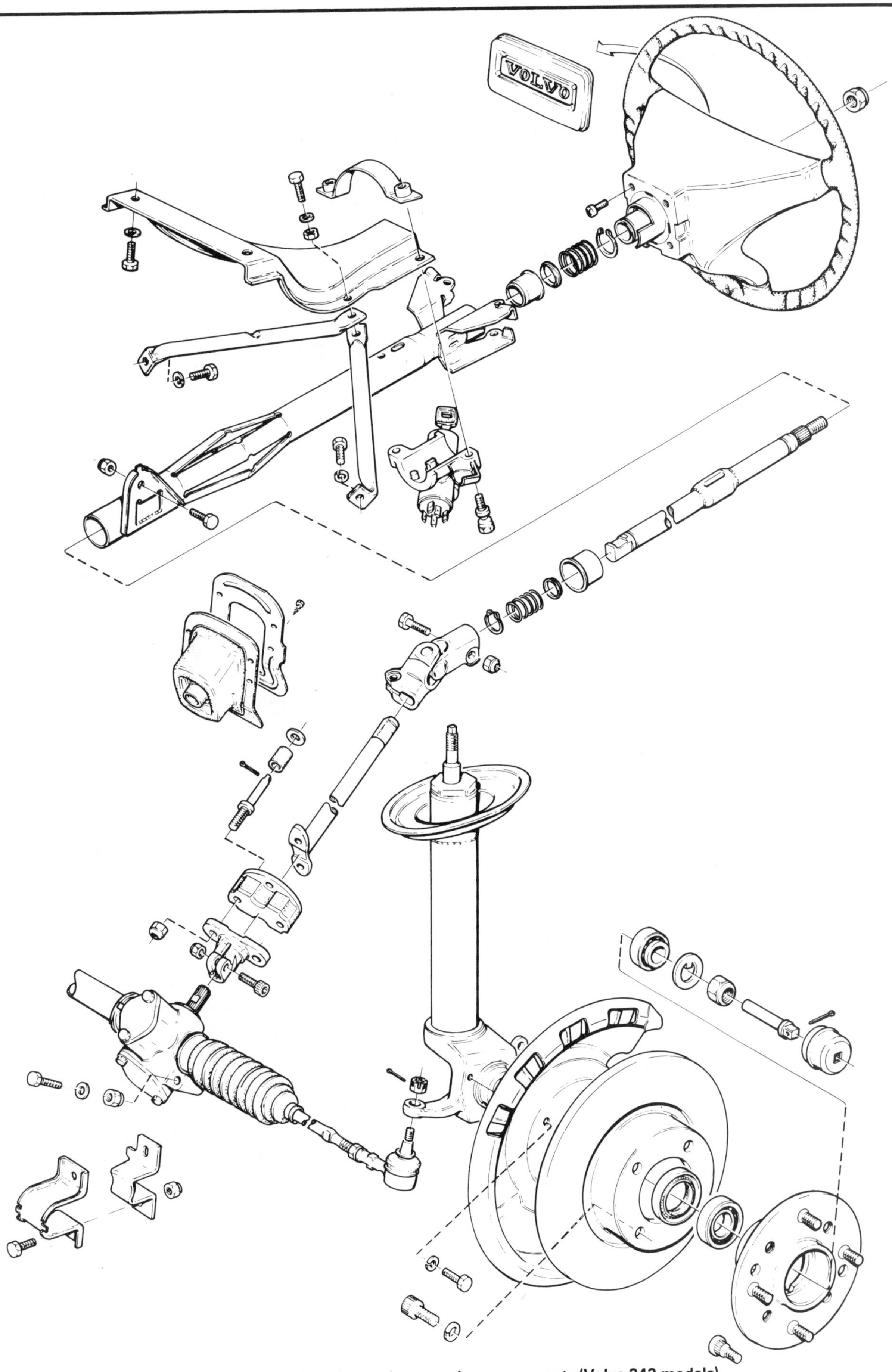

Fig. 9.1 Steering and suspension components (Volvo 343 models)

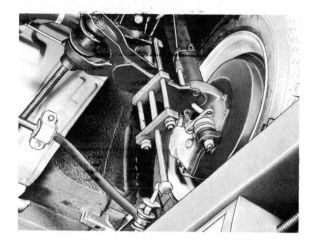

Fig. 9.2 Torsion bar tensioning tool in use

Fig. 9.3 Removing the rear torsion bar circlip

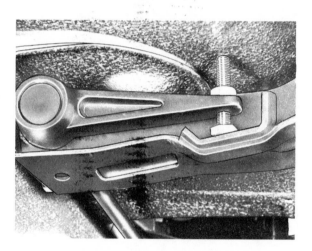

Fig. 9.4 The torsion bar rear adjustment arm

Fig. 9.5 Front steering swivel balljoint (Daf 55/66 and Volvo 66 models)

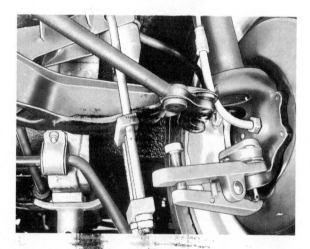

Fig. 9.6 Using a balljoint remover (Daf 55/66 and Volvo 66 models)

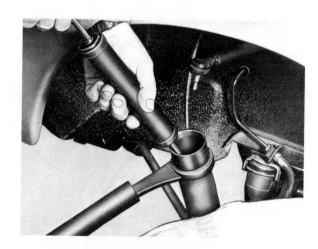

Fig. 9.7 Removing the front shock absorber (Daf 55/66 and Volvo 66 models)

faults are evident, both front torsion bars should be renewed.

11 Refitting is basically a reversal of removal but the following additional points should be noted:

(a) The torsion bars are not interchangeable side for side and are marked L (left) or R (right) on their ends to distinguish them. Make sure that they are fitted on the correct side. As a further precaution the bars are coloured at the centre; green for left and red for right

(b) Grease the splines before fitting the bar and also loosen the adjustment bolt fully

(c) Fit new self-locking nuts but only tighten the nut on the suspension arm and when the weight of the car is on all four wheels

(d) Adjust the torsion bars at the adjustment bolts so that with the car unloaded, the distance betweem the top of the shock absorber and the dust cap plate is as given in Specifications and is identical on both sides of the car. To simplify this operation, make a gauge out of 1.77 in (45 mm) inside diameter tube sawn through lengthwise and cut out to the applicable length. If the correct adjustment cannot be achieved it will be necessary to reposition the adjusting arm or suspension arm by one notch on the torsion bar and the adjustment procedure started again (photo)

3 Front torsion bar crossmember – removal and refitting

1 Remove both torsion bars as described in Section 2.
2 Unscrew and remove both crossmember retaining bolts and withdraw the crossmember pulling the exhaust pipe to one side a little to facilitate its removal (photo).
3 Remove the insulating rubbers from the crossmember.
4 Refitting is a reversal of removal but it will be necessary to adjust the torsion bar as described in Section 2.
5 If it is only required to renew the insulating rubbers, there is no need to remove the torsion bars. In this case, unscrew and remove the two crossmember retaining bolts and insert a 1 in (25 mm) thick block of wood between the crossmember and the car floor. It is then a simple matter to remove the spacer bushes and insulating rubbers.

4 Front lower suspension arm (Daf 55/66 and Volvo 66 models) – removal and refitting

1 The procedure is identical to that for the removal and refitting of the front torsion bar as described in Section 2.

5 Steering swivel balljoint (Daf 55/66 and Volvo 66 models) – removal and refitting

1 Jack up the front of the car and support it adequately on axle-stands placed beneath the body.
2 Detach the front strut from the lower suspension arm by following the procedure given in Section 2 paragraphs 1 to 5 inclusive.
3 Straighten and extract the split-pin from the castellated balljoint retaining nut and then unscrew and remove the nut.
4 Using a balljoint remover separate the balljoint from the strut and withdraw it.
5 Examine the balljoint for wear and if the end clearance is in excess of 0.04 in (1 mm) the complete balljoint must be renewed.
6 Refitting is a reversal of removal but the following additional points should be noted:

(a) Tighten all nuts to the correct specified torque wrench setting

(b) Fit a new split-pin

6 Front shock absorber and strut assembly (Daf 55/66 and Volvo 66 models) – removal, servicing and refitting

1 Jack up the front of the car and remove the roadwheel. Support the car on axle-stands placed beneath the body.
2 Extract the split-pin from the track-rod end and unscrew and remove the castellated nut.
3 Using a balljoint remover, separate the track-rod end from the steering arm.
4 Disconnect the speedometer cable when removing the left-hand side assembly (photo).
5 Obtain a suspension arm clamping tool (Daf tool No 7-9-535568/Volvo tool No 5876-535568) from a tool agent or garage, hook the ends of the tool in the holes located either side of the conical rubber stop, and tighten the clamp until the lower suspension arm is slightly lifted.
6 Open the bonnet and disconnect the upper bearing by unscrewing and removing the retaining nut while restraining the centre piston rod with an open ended spanner (photo).
7 Unscrew and remove the two mounting rubber bolts to facilitate the refitting procedure.
8 Remove the brake caliper when fitted (see Chapter 7). On drum brake models disconnect the brake hose from the wheel cylinder and plug the end of the hose. Suspend the caliper with wire taking care not to strain the hose.
9 Extract the split-pin then unscrew and remove the switch balljoint retaining nut.
10 Unscrew and remove one suspension arm to strut bolt to allow a balljoint remover to be inserted, then separate the balljoint and withdraw it.
11 Withdraw the complete front shock absorber and strut assembly from the cover.
12 If a new assembly is being fitted it will be necessary to remove the wheel hub and fit it to the new assembly, refer to Section 13 as

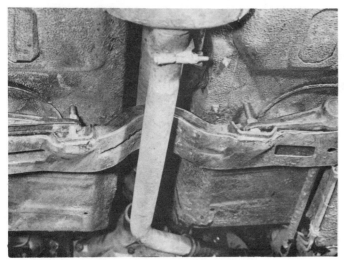

2.11 Front torsion bar adjustment bolt location (Daf 66 models)

3.2 Front torsion bar crossmember retaining bolt (Daf 66 models)

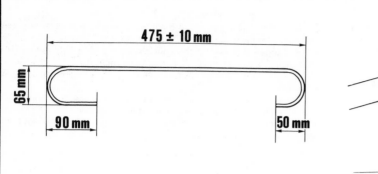

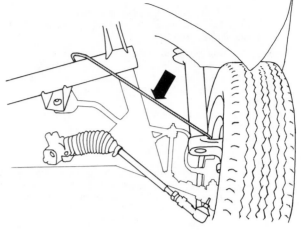

Fig. 9.8 Strut restraining hook dimension (Volvo 343 models)

Fig. 9.9 Strut hook in position (Volvo 343 models)

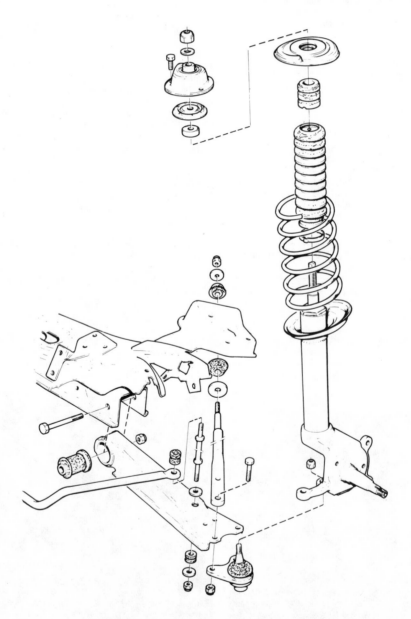

Fig. 9.10 Front suspension components (Volvo 343 models)

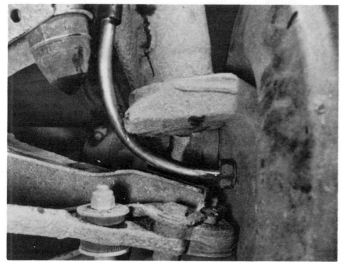

6.4 Speedometer cable connection (Daf 66 models)

6.6 Front strut upper mounting (Daf 66 models)

necessary. On drum brake models it will be necessary to transfer the brake shoes and the backplate (See Chapter 7).

13 If it is decided to recondition the shock absorber unit first obtain a repair kit, and tool No 7-99-535637 (Boge units) or tool No 0-99-535160 (Koni units).

14 Remove the dust cap and, using the special tool, unscrew the locknut or gland nut as applicable. Fit a steel pipe extension over the steering arm during this operation for extra leverage.

15 Extract the shock absorber components using water pump pliers to remove the guide bush.

16 Pour the fluid from the shock absorber body, and clean the tube with methylated spirit, drying it with a lint-free cloth. Thoroughly check the tube for damage and signs of leakage, if evident, the shock absorber will have to be renewed.

17 Clean the piston rod and examine it for scoring and damage, then check it for distortion by rolling it on a flat surface. If distortion exceeds 0.004 in (0.1 mm) it must be renewed and in this case a large repair kit must be obtained.

18 Reassembly of the shock absorber is a reversal of dismantling although it will be necessary to fill the inner tube with 250 cc of fluid (supplied with the repair kit). When fitting the piston rod, make sure that the plunger valve spring is correctly located. Tighten the locknut to the correct torque wrench setting.

19 Refitting the front shock absorber and strut assembly is a reversal of removal but the following points should be noted:

(a) Tighten all nuts to the correct torque wrench setting and fit new split-pins where necessary

(b) Bleed the hydraulic system on drum brake models referring to Chapter 7 as necessary

7 Front coil spring (Volvo 343 models) – removal and refitting

1 Open the bonnet and loosen the upper suspension nut one or two turns.

2 Loosen the three upper strut retaining bolts, but do not remove them.

3 Jack up the front of the car and support it adequately on axle-stands.

4 Extract the split-pin from the track-rod end and remove the nut. Using a balljoint remover separate the track-rod end from the steering arm.

5 Where the left-hand spring is being removed, disconnect the speedometer cable by pulling it out of the rubber bush.

6 Loosen the radius arm rear nut one or two turns then unscrew and remove the anti-roll bar retaining nut from the lower suspension arm.

7 Make up a steel wire hook out of 0.24 in (6 mm) diameter wire to the dimensions shown in Fig. 9.8. Hook it around the lower part of the strut and the engine bearer; this will prevent damage to the brake hoses and steering balljoints.

8 Support the strut with a trolley jack, then unscrew and remove the

upper strut retaining bolts. Lower the jack and at the same time guide the strut down until it can be moved outside the front wing.

9 Obtain a coil spring compressor from a tool agent or garage, and fit the two sections of the coil spring opposite each other and with four coils between the hooks.

10 Compress the spring, then unscrew and remove the shock absorber retaining nut.

11 Loosen the clips retaining the rubber protector and withdraw the mounting, seal, and bearing.

12 Lift off the spring cover, protector, spring and rubber pad.

13 Remove the spring compressor from the spring.

14 Examine the rubber protector for damage and renew it as necessary.

15 Refitting is a reversal of removal but the following additional points should be noted:

(a) Install the rubber stops with their flat sides uppermost

(b) When new protector clamps are fitted, use a pair of pliers to tighten them

(c) If the original upper mounting bolts are used again, a liquid locking agent must be applied

(d) Where necessary remove the left-hand wheel cap and hub cap and relocate the speedometer drive cable

(e) Tighten all nuts to the correct torque wrench setting, but delay tightening the shock absorber retaining nut until the weight of the car is on the wheels

(f) Install new split-pins where necessary

8 Front shock absorber (Volvo 343 models) – removal, servicing and refitting

1 Remove the coil spring as described in Section 7, paragraphs 1 to 12 inclusive.

2 Using the special tool (Volvo tool No 5862) unscrew and remove the shock absorber retaining nut. On the right-hand side it will be necessary to support the strut with a length of wood inserted between the lower end of the strut and the wheel rim.

3 Withdraw the seal and holder.

4 Slowly withdraw the piston rod and inner tube, and then remove the fluid from the tube with a syringe.

5 Thoroughly clean the interior of the tube with lint-free cloth saturated with methylated spirit.

6 Clean the piston rod and check it for distortion; if it is more than 0.004 in (0.1 mm) out of alignment or if it is worn, it must be renewed.

7 Obtain a repair kit and reassemble the shock absorber using a reversal of the removal procedure. Fill the inner tube with the fluid supplied in the kit.

8 Make sure that the piston rod seal is installed with the spring facing downwards, and tighten all nuts to the correct torque wrench setting. When tightening the left-hand shock absorber, support the

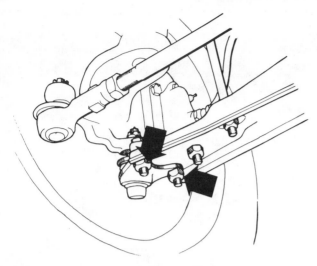

Fig. 9.11 Nuts securing the steering swivel balljoint to the lower suspension arm

Fig. 9.12 Correct fitted position of the anti-roll bar (crank arrowed)

Fig. 9.13 Front radius arm retaining nut locations – arrowed (except Volvo 343 models)

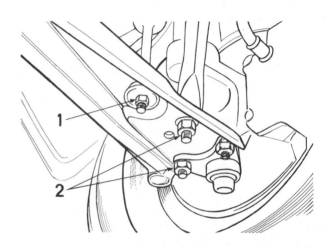

Fig. 9.14 Location of the anti-roll bar (1) and radius arm (2) retaining nuts (Volvo 343 models)

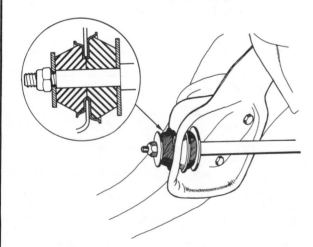

Fig. 9.15 Radius arm rear mounting (Volvo 343 models)

Fig. 9.16 Checking the front hub bearing adjustment

strut with a length of wood inserted between the lower end of the strut and the wheel.

9 Front lower suspension arm (Volvo 343 models) – removal and refitting

1 Jack up the front of the car and support it adequately on axle-stands. Remove the guard shield.
2 Unscrew and remove the anti-roll bar retaining nut and withdraw it from the suspension arm.
3 Loosen the rear radius arm retaining nut a few turns and remove the front retaining bolts from the suspension arm.
4 Unscrew and remove the remaining bolt from the outer end of the suspension arm.
5 Unscrew and remove the nut from the inner pivot of the suspension arm and remove the bolt; the suspension arm can now be lowered and withdrawn.
6 Prise the rubber bush which separates the anti-roll bar from the suspension arm.
7 Examine the pivot bush and, if it requires renewing, press it from the arm using suitable diameter washers, tubing and a long bolt. To assist the fitting of the new bush, dip it in brake fluid or soapy water.
8 Refitting is a reversal of removal, but delay final tightening of the nuts until the weight of the car is on the wheels.

10 Steering swivel balljoint (Volvo 343 models) – removal and refitting

1 Jack up the front of the car and support it adequately on axle-stands placed beneath the body.
2 When working on the left-hand balljoint it will be necessary to remove the speedometer cable by pulling it from its rubber bush.
3 Unscrew and remove the two nuts and bolts securing the balljoint to the suspension arm.
4 Extract the split-pin and unscrew and remove the castellated nut from the balljoint.
5 Using a balljoint remover, separate the balljoint and withdraw it from the strut. Should there not be enough room to accommodate the tool in use, it will be necessary to obtain the special tool (Volvo No 5866).
6 Refitting is a reversal of removal, but delay tightening the nuts to the correct torque wrench setting until the weight of the car is on the wheels. When refitting the left-hand unit, remove the wheel cap and hub cap in order to relocate the speedometer cable. Use new split-pins where necessary.

11 Front anti-roll bar – removal and refitting

1 Jack up the front of the car and support it adequately on axle-stands. Remove the guard shield on Volvo 343 models.
2 Unscrew and remove the underframe bearing mounting bolts and clamps from both mountings.
3 On all but Volvo 343 models unscrew and remove the retaining nuts and withdraw the anti-roll bar links from the radius arms (photo).
4 On Volvo 343 models, hold the front links with a pair of pliers and unscrew and remove the upper retaining nuts and washers.
5 On all models, withdraw the anti-roll bar from the car. As the arms of the bar are cranked, mark each side to facilitate refitting.
6 Remove all bushes from the bar and renew them if they show any signs of wear or deterioration. Where necessary lubricate the bushes with soapy water to facilitate refitting.
7 Refitting is a reversal of removal.

12 Front radius arm – removal and refitting

1 Jack up the front of the car and support it adequately on axle-stands.
2 On all but Volvo 343 models, unscrew and remove the anti-roll bar link retaining nuts from both sides and swivel the bar down from the radius arm. Loosen the lower suspension arm nut one or two turns, then unscrew and remove the three radius arm retaining nuts and withdraw the radius arm (photo).

3 On Volvo 343 models, unscrew and remove the rear mounting nut, washer, and rubber bush. Then unscrew and remove the bolts securing the radius arm to the lower suspension arm and withdraw the radius arm.
4 On all models examine the rubber bushes for wear and deterioration and renew them as necessary.
5 Refitting is a reversal of removal but the following additional points should be noted:

   (a) Renew all self locking nuts
   (b) On all but Volvo 343 models, use water pump pliers to clamp the suspension arm and balljoint surfaces together to erase fitting of the radius arm
   (c) On Volvo 343 models make sure that the large washer and rubber bush are located on the radius arm before fitting it (see Fig. 9.15)
   (d) Tighten all nuts to the correct torque wrench setting with the weight of the car on the wheels

13 Front hub bearings and seal – removal and refitting

1 Jack up the front of the car, remove the roadwheel, and support the car adequately with axle-stands.
2 Using a screwdriver, carefully tap the grease cap from the centre of the hub; the left-hand cap contains the speedometer drive cable (photo).
3 On disc brake models, remove the brake caliper as described in Chapter 7 and suspend it with wire out of the way.
4 On all models, unscrew and remove the hub nut and withdraw the hub assembly, taking care to collect the roller bearings as the hub is removed from the stub axle.
5 Prise the oil seal from the inner end of the hub then, using a suitable soft metal drift, drive the outer wheel bearing track from the hub.
6 Remove the inner bearing track from the hub.
7 Check the wheel bearings for wear by spinning them with the fingers. If they sound noisy or are rough-running, or have grooves or chips in the rollers they must be renewed.
8 Clean the hub of all grease with paraffin, and wipe dry with a lint-free cloth.
9 Pack fresh wheel bearing grease into the hub until it is one third full, then pack grease into the wheel bearings.
10 Drive in the outer wheel bearing followed by the inner wheel bearing track, using a suitable diameter tube. Ensure that they enter squarely. Place the roller races in their respective tracks.
11 Clean the oil seal location then carefully tap it into position with the sealing lip facing into the hub.
12 The remaining refitting procedure is a reversal of removal but it will be necessary to adjust the bearings as follows.
13 Tighten the hub nut as far as it will go, then progressively loosen it until the flat washer or circlip (as applicable) beneath the nut can just be moved to and fro with a screwdriver. When the adjustment is correct, lock the nut onto the stub axle using a screwdriver or similar tool.
14 Pack fresh grease into the grease cap and tap it onto the hub.

14 Rear coil spring (Daf 55 models – removal and refitting

1 Jack up the rear of the car and support it adequately with axle-stands placed under the body.
2 Remove the variomatic reduction gear unit and drivebelt as described in Chapter 6.
3 Unscrew and remove the suspension arm stop screw, lower the suspension arm, and withdraw the coil spring.
4 Refitting is a reversal of removal.

15 Rear suspension arm (Daf 55 models) – removal and refitting

1 Remove the rear coil spring as described in Section 14.
2 Unscrew and remove the suspension arm pivot bolt, using a soft metal drift to drive it out. Note which way round it is fitted.
3 Remove the spacer washers, taper-roller bearings, spacer ring and sleeve from the pivot tube on the underframe.
4 Using a suitable drift, drive the bearing tracks from the tube and

11.3 Front anti-roll bar mountings (Daf 66 models)

12.2A Front radius arm front mounting (Daf 66 models)

12.2B Front radius arm location (Daf 66 models)

13.2 Removing the left-hand grease cap

17.6 Rear spring rear mounting

19.2 Rear radius arm location (Daf 66 models)

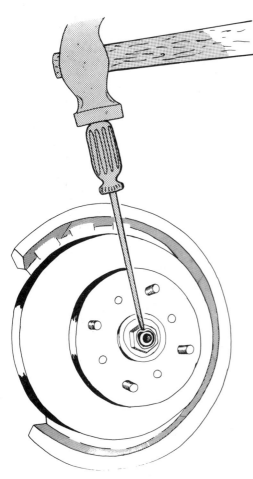

Fig. 9.17 Locking the front hub nut

remove the plastic grease retainers; make sure that the position of each component is noted to facilitate refitting.

5   Clean each component with paraffin and dry with lint-free cloth. Examine the bearings for wear and pitting, and where evident renew them.

6   Assemble the bearings in the reverse order to dismantling; drive the plastic grease seals into the tube with a suitable diameter length of tubing. Make sure their sealing lips face outwards.

7   The bearing preload must be adjusted by altering the spacer ring thickness as necessary. First assemble the bearing with the thickest washers available (obtain them from your Volvo agent) and using suitable tubing tighten the mounting bolt onto the bearings to a torque wrench setting of 72 to 87 lbf ft (99 to 120 Nm). Use a dial gauge to check the endplay then select a spacer ring which will accommodate the endplay plus an extra 0.008 in (0.2 mm) to provide the preload.

8   Before installing the correct spacer ring, pack the bearings with grease. If available, check the tension required to rotate the assembled pivot bolt, this should be 1 to 10 cm kg.

9   Refitting the suspension arm is a reversal of removal, but, if the spacer washers are renewed, make sure that they are both of the same thickness so that the distance between the discs of the variomatic drive unit and the reduction gear unit is the same on each side.

16 Rear suspension frame mounting (Daf 55 models) – removal and refitting

1   Jack up the rear of the car and support it adequately on axle-stands placed beneath the body.

2   Unscrew and remove the bolt securing the brake line T-connection to the rear floor.

3   Place two trolley jacks beneath the suspension frame.

4   Unscrew and remove the nuts securing the suspension frame to the mounting, and lower the trolley jacks until the frame is clear of the mounting.

5   Unscrew and remove the retaining bolts and withdraw the mounting(s).

6   Drive the bolt out of the mounting.

7   Refitting is a reversal of removal.

17 Rear spring (Daf 66, Volvo 66 and Volvo 343 models) – removal and refitting

1   Jack up the rear of the car and support it adequately on axle-stands placed beneath the body. To facilitate the removal procedure, it is advisable to arrange the height of the supports so that the wheels are just touching the ground.

2   Loosen the rear upper shackle nut one or two turns.

3   Unscrew and remove the front and rear nuts from the spring eye mounting bolts.

4   Unscrew and remove the spring anchor plate retaining nuts and bolts.

5   Jack up the spring a little to enable the anchor plate to be moved to one side and on later models remove the plastic locking plates.

6   Drive out the spring eye bolts and lower the spring to the ground (photo).

7   Refitting is a reversal of removal but the following points should be noted:

   (a)   Grease the plastic locking plates before assembly
   (b)   Where the part number is stamped on the lower side of the spring, this must be facing towards the front
   (c)   Estate car model springs are colour coded in red
   (d)   Before tightening the nuts to the correct torque wrench setting, the full weight of the car plus a 110 lb (50 kg) weight in the luggage compartment should be on the wheels
   (e)   The radius arm mounting nuts should be loosened and retightened to settle the mountings

18 Rear spring bushes (Daf 66, Volvo 66 and Volvo 343 models) – removal and refitting

1   Remove the spring as described in Section 17.

2   Using a long bolt, tubing and spacers, press the bushes from the

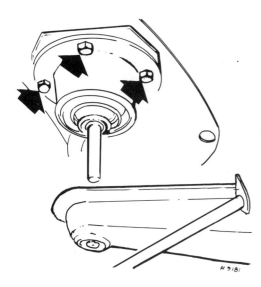

Fig. 9.18 Rear suspension frame mounting – securing bolts (Daf 55 models)

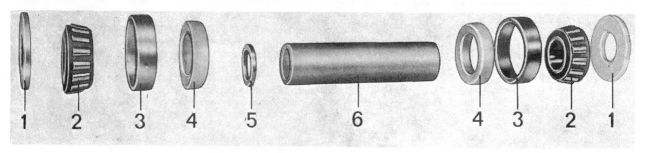

Fig. 9.19 Rear suspension arm bearing components (Daf 55 models)

1 Spacer washer
2 Taper roller bearings
3 Bearing outer tracks
4 Plastic grease retainer
5 Spacer ring
6 Spacer sleeve

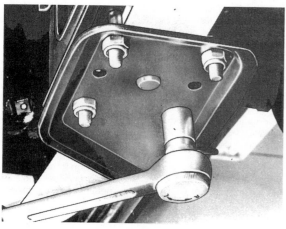

Fig. 9.20 Removing the rear spring anchor plate (except Daf 55 models)

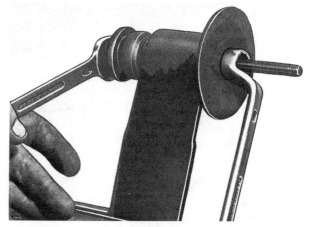

Fig. 9.21 Removing the rear spring bush (except Daf 55 models)

Fig. 9.22 Rear shock absorber (Daf 55 models)

Fig. 9.23 Rear shock absorber (except Daf 55 models)

spring and shackle.

3   Before installing the new bushes, lubricate them with soapy water or Vaseline.

4   The remaining refitting procedure is a reversal of removal, referring to Section 17 as necessary.

19 Rear radius arm (Daf 66, Volvo 66 and Volvo 343 models) – removal and refitting

1   Jack up the rear of the car and support it adequately on axle-stands.

2   Unscrew and remove the two mounting bolts, noting the location of any shims fitted to the rear mounting (photo).

3   Withdraw the radius arm.

4   Using a long bolt, tubing and spacers, press the bushes from the arm.

5   Lubricate the new bushes with soapy water or Vaseline and press them into the radius arm.

6   Refitting is a reversal of removal but the nuts should only be tightened to their correct torque wrench setting when full weight of the car plus a 110 lb (50 kg) weight in the luggage compartment is on the wheels.

20 De Dion axle (Daf 66, Volvo 66 and Volvo 343 models) – removal and refitting

1   Jack up the rear of the car and support it adequately with axle-stands placed beneath the body.

2   Remove the rear wheels.

3   Using a brake hose clamp, pinch the right-hand brake hose and unscrew the brake line union. Alternatively remove the brake fluid reservoir cap and tighten it down onto a sheet of polythene.

4   Detach the two driveshafts from their outer flanges by unscrewing and removing the retaining bolts. An Allen key will be required and the flanges should be marked in relation to each other to ensure correct refitting.

5   Use welding wire or string to suspend the driveshafts out of the way.

6   Remove the brake drums and shoes as described in Chapter 7.

7   Remove the outer short axleshafts as described in Section 23.

8   Disconnect the handbrake cable from the brake backplates.

9   Disconnect the brake lines from the axle but not from the wheel cylinders.

10   Unscrew and remove the backplate retaining bolts and withdraw the backplates.

11   Unscrew and remove the eccentric retaining bolts from the radius arm mountings.

12   Unscrew and remove the nuts and bolts and swivel the anchor plates to one side.

13   Remove the spring plastic locking plates.

14   Withdraw the De Dion axle from the car.

15   Refitting is a reversal of removal but the following additional points should be noted:

　(a)   Grease the plastic locking plates before assembly
　(b)   Fit new gaskets to the driveshaft flanges
　(c)   Refer to Section 23 and Chapter 7 as necessary
　(d)   Tighten the nuts to the correct torque wrench setting only when the full weight of the car plus a 110 lb (50 kg) weight in the luggage compartment is on the wheels
　(e)   Bleed the brake hydraulic system (see Chapter 7).

21 Rear shock absorber – removal and refitting

1   Locate the rear shock absorber upper mounting within the rear of the car. On Volvo 343 models this necessitates removing the parcel shelf and folding the seat forwards. On all other models the mounting is within the boot.

2   Unscrew and remove the two mounting nuts and washer.

3   Jack up the rear of the car and support it adequately on axle-stands.

4   Unscrew and remove the lower mounting nut(s) and withdraw the shock absorber, bushes and washers (photo).

5   To test the shock absorber for serviceability, grip the lower mounting in a soft jaw vice with the shock absorber vertical. Fully extend and retract the unit ten or twelve times; the unit should give an even resistance when extending with a somewhat less resistance when retracting. Any jerkiness or lack of resistance indicates that the unit is faulty and should be renewed.

6   Examine the mounting rubbers and renew them as necessary.

7   Refitting is a reversal of removal. Tighten the mounting nuts to the correct torque wrench setting.

22 Rear hub bearing and seal (Daf 55 models) – removal and refitting

1   Jack up the rear of the car and support it adequately on axle-stands.

2   Remove the roadwheel then remove the brake drum referring to Chapter 7 as necessary.

3   Remove the variomatic guard panels and drain the oil from the secondary gear-case.

4   Unscrew and remove the brake backplate retaining bolts, detach the brake line from the retaining clip, and tie the backplate to one side.

5   Using Daf tool No 8-9-535538 (obtainable from a tool agent or Daf garage) pull the driveshaft complete with bearing from the secondary gearcase.

6   Drive the bearing from the shaft, then clean all components in paraffin and check them for wear. Spin the bearing by hand and

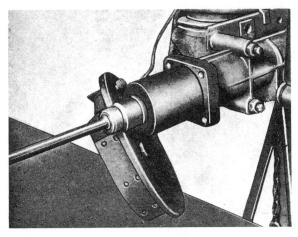

Fig. 9.24 Removing the rear hub bearing (Daf 55 models)

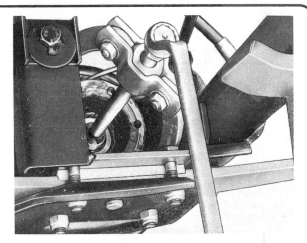

Fig. 9.25 Withdrawing the rear wheel drive flange (except Daf 55 models)

attempt to rock it laterally to check for excessive wear or any roughness.

7   Remove the oil seal from the bearing retainer and discard it.
8   Smear the axle tube bore and outer bearing race with a liquid sealing agent, then drive it into the axle using the special tool.
9   Fit a new oil seal to the bearing retainer, making sure that the sealing lip faces inwards.
10 Check the driveshaft endplay with a dial gauge (see Specifications) and if incorrect, adjust it with shims fitted to the bearing retainer.
11 The remaining refitting procedure is a reversal of removal but the following additional points should be noted:

   (a) *Tighten all nuts to the correct torque wrench setting*
   (b) *Make sure that the brake line is positioned so that it does not foul the coil spring*
   (c) *Refer to Chapter 7 as necessary when refitting the brake components*
   (d) *Refill the secondary gear case with oil (refer to Chapter 6)*

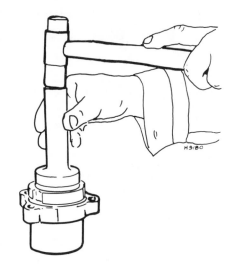

Fig. 9.26 Installing rear hub oil seals (except Daf 55 models)

23 Rear hub bearings and seal (Daf 66, Volvo 66 and Volvo 343 models) – removal and refitting

1   Jack up the rear of the car and support it adequately on axle-stands, then remove the guard panels.
2   Remove the wheel then remove the brake drum (see Chapter 7).
3   Unscrew and remove the driveshaft flange retaining bolts after marking the flanges in relation to each other, then suspend the driveshaft outer end with wire or string so that it is out of the way.
4   Unscrew and remove the flange nut; to do this, temporarily refit the wheel and use this to restrain the shaft while the nut is being loosened.
5   Using a two or three leg puller, withdraw the drive flange from the shaft.
6   Drive the shaft out of the bearings from inside using a soft metal drift.
7   Unscrew and remove the four backplate retaining bolts, move the backplate forwards and withdraw the bearing housing; detach the brake line from the axle if necessary.
8   Using a screwdriver, extract the inner and outer oil seals.
9   Heat the bearing housing with a blowlamp, and then immediately drive the bearings out from either side with a soft metal drift.
10 Clean the housing with paraffin and wash all grease from the bearings. Examine the bearings for wear by spinning them and attempting to rock them laterally. Any worn or damaged bearings must be renewed.
11 Refitting is a reversal of removal but the following additional points should be noted:

   (a) *Pack the bearings with a lithium based grease*
   (b) *Install the oil seals with their sealing lips facing inwards towards the bearings*
   (c) *Apply a liquid locking agent to the inner threads of the driveshaft*
   (d) *Tighten all nuts to the correct torque wrench setting*

Fig. 9.27 Location of the steering shaft coupling (LHD shown)

24 Steering wheel – removal and refitting

1   Set the front roadwheels in the straight-ahead position.
2   Prise the motif from the centre of the steering wheel.
3   Using a socket and extension bar, unscrew and remove the steering wheel retaining nut (and washer when fitted).
4   Mark the relative position of the wheel to the steering shaft by dot punching the end faces.
5   Using both hands, pull the steering wheel from the shaft; if necessary use the palms of the hands to thump the steering wheel free.
6   Refitting is a reversal of removal. Tighten the retaining nut to the correct torque wrench setting.

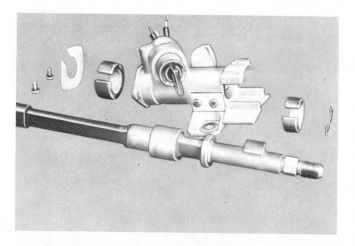

Fig. 9.28 Steering column components (Daf 66 and Volvo 66 models)

25 Ignition/steering lock – removal and refitting

1   Disconnect the battery negative terminal.
2   Remove the steering wheel as described in Section 24.

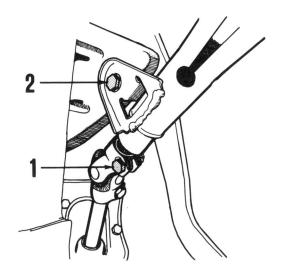

Fig. 9.29 Location of lower clamp bolt (1) and column mounting bolt (2) on Volvo 343 models

Fig. 9.30 Steering gear eccentric bush and nylon bushes (except Volvo 343 models)

Fig. 9.31 Steering gear locating bush and sealing rings (except Volvo 343 models)

3   Unscrew and remove the screws retaining the two steering column shrouds and lift the lower shroud away from the column. On all but very early models it will be necessary to unscrew the choke control knob in order to remove the lower shroud.

4   Remove and place the two switches to one side, then disconnect the ignition switch wires from beneath the dash panel.

5   On all but Volvo 343 models, set the steering lock to *O*.

6   On Daf 55 models use a 0.118 in (3 mm) Allen key to remove the retaining bolt then withdraw the ignition and steering lock from the steering column. With the key inserted and turned to the *OFF* position, push in the locating pin and withdraw the ignition switch.

7   On Daf 66 and Volvo 66 models use a 0.118 in (3 mm) drill to drill a hole in the lock safety bolt, then use an easy-out or left-hand tap to unscrew and remove it. Detach the switch holder and unscrew the two mounting bolts, then remove the upper shroud and turn the steering column slightly clockwise. The steering lock and ignition switch can now be removed. If the switch holder only requires removing, it is not necessary to remove the safety bolt.

8   On Volvo 343 models drill through the steering lock retaining bolts with a 0.35 in (9 mm) drill. Remove the lock and extract the bolts with a pair of pliers.

9   Refitting is basically a reversal of removal but the following additional points should be noted:

(a)   *On Daf 55 models make sure that the locating pin enters the hole correctly by turning the ignition key anti-clockwise, then centralising the steering column before finally tightening the retaining bolts*

(b)   *On Daf 66, Volvo 66 and Volvo 343 models insert the new safety bolt, check that the switch functions correctly, then tighten the bolt until its head breaks off. Before tightening the column mounting bolts, remove the ignition key and operate the steering lock, then centralise the column before tightening the mounting bolts*

26 Steering column (Daf 55 models) – removal, servicing and refitting

1   Disconnect the battery negative terminal.

2   Unscrew and remove the retaining screws and withdraw the lower steering column cover.

3   With the front wheels in the straight-ahead position, detach the steering shaft from the flexible coupling by unscrewing the two retaining nuts visible from above.

4   Remove the steering wheel as described in Section 24.

5   Unscrew and remove the steering column mounting bolts and withdraw the upper shroud.

6   Unscrew and remove the combination switch from the column but do not disconnect the wires.

7   Remove the ignition switch as described in Section 15.

8   Remove the driver's seat and withdraw the complete steering column from the car.

9   Withdraw the shaft key and extract the bearing bushes.

10   Clean all components in paraffin and wipe with a lint free cloth. Examine the bushes for wear and renew them if necessary.

11   Refitting is a reversal of removal but the following points should be noted:

(a)   *Lubricate the bushes with grease before fitting them*

(b)   *In order to refit the steering wheel in the correct position the key must face upwards*

(c)   *Refer to Section 35 paragraph 9 before tightening the mounting bolts*

27 Steering column (Daf 66 and Volvo 66 models) – removal, servicing and refitting

1   Disconnect the battery negative terminal.

2   Remove the driver's seat.

3   Unscrew and remove two opposing retaining nuts from the flexible coupling at the bottom of the column.

4   Unscrew and remove the choke control knob.

5   Unscrew the retaining screws and remove the column lower shroud.

6   Remove the steering wheel as described in Section 24.

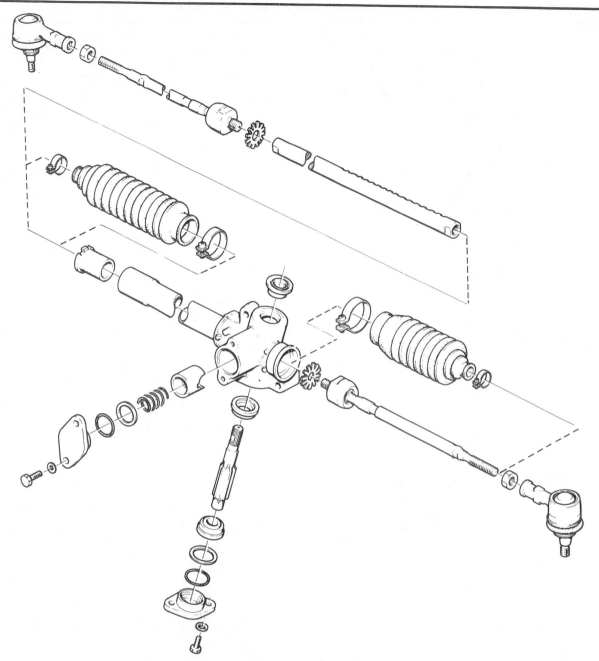

Fig. 9.32 Steering gear components (Volvo 343 models)

21.4 Rear shock absorber lower mounting (Daf 66 models)

30.4 Steering gear location (Daf 66 models)

33.1 Track-rod end location (Daf 66 models)

7   Disconnect the ignition switch wires and detach both switches.
8   Unscrew and remove the choke cable nuts and the steering column bolts.
9   Withdraw the steering column and shaft from the car.
10 Detach the retaining plate after unscrewing the two bolts.
11 Extract the lockring from the top and prise the rubber bearing from both sides of the column which can then be removed from the shaft.
12 Clean all the components as necessary in paraffin and renew the bearings if they are excessively worn or damaged. If the car has been in a collision, check that the length of the shaft is still 22.36 ± 0.04 in (568 ± 1mm). If not it must be renewed; the shaft must *NOT* be reset to this dimension if incorrect.
13 Refitting is a reversal of removal but the following additional points should be noted:

   (a)   *Do not use grease on the bearings as this may cause the felt sealing ring to sag*
   (b)   *Fit new self-locking nuts as a safety precaution*

28 Steering column (Volvo 343 models) – removal, servicing and refitting

1   Remove the ignition/steering lock as described in Section 25.
2   Unscrew the retaining screws and remove the direction indicator and windscreen wiper switches from the steering column, letting them hang to one side.
3   Unscrew and remove the lower clamp bolt and column mounting bolt and withdraw the steering column from the car.
4   Carefully clamp the steering column in a vice and, using a two leg puller, press the shaft through the column a little way so that the circlip at the other end can be removed. At the same time remove the spring and seat.
5   Extract the circlip, spring, and seat from the upper end of the column.
6   Heat each end of the column with a blowlamp and remove the bearings using the steering shaft as a puller.
7   Clean all components with paraffin and examine the bearings for wear; if evident, they must be renewed.
8   Refitting is a reversal of removal but the following additional points should be noted:

   (a)   *Drive the bearings into the column until they are flush with the end of the column*
   (b)   *Refer to Section 25 when refitting the ignition/steering lock*

29 Steering shaft vibration damper (Volvo 343 models) – removal and refitting

1   Jack up the front of the car and support it adequately with axle-stands.
2   Set the front wheels to the straight-ahead position.
3   Remove the guard panels from under the engine.
4   Unscrew and remove the bolts securing the steering shaft to the lower steering flange.
5   Unscrew and remove the clamp bolt and withdraw the flange and vibration damper.
6   Mount the damper in a vice and unscrew the two flange nuts; the flange and damper can now be removed.
7   Refitting is a reversal of removal but the following additional points should be noted:

   (a)   *Make sure that the flange stud washers are retained by a split-pin in good order*
   (b)   *Tighten the steering shaft bolts before the clamp bolt*

30 Steering gear – removal and refitting

1   Jack up the front of the car and support it adequately on axle-stands.
2   Set the front wheels to the straight-ahead position and remove the engine guard panels where fitted.
3   Extract the split-pins from the two track-rod ends and unscrew the castellated nuts.
4   Using a balljoint remover, separate the track-rod ends from the

steering arms. Where track-rod ends are fitted at the steering gear end of the track-rods, remove these rather than the outer ones (photo).

Daf 55, Daf 66 and Volvo 66 models

5   Mark the position of the steering shaft to the flexible coupling then unscrew and remove the two lower retaining nuts from the coupling.
6   Where fitted, cut the locking wire from the pinion cover retaining screws, unscrew and remove the screws (bolts on later models) and withdraw the cover.
7   Withdraw the steering rack from the housing at the same time turning and releasing the eccentric bush.
8   Unscrew and remove the steering gear retaining bolts and, with the eccentric bush pushed down, withdraw the steering gear from the car.

Volvo 343 models

9   Mark the position of the lower steering shaft in relation to the vibration damper, then unscrew and remove the two retaining bolts.
10 Unscrew and remove the steering gear retaining nuts and lower the steering gear from the car.
11 Refitting is a reversal of removal but the following additional points should be noted.

Daf 55, Daf 66 and Volvo 66 models

12 Where fitted, renew all self-locking nuts or fit new split-pins.
13 When installing the steering rack, turn the steering wheel 20° clockwise from the straight ahead position. Move the rack in until it protrudes 6.5 in (165 mm) then turn the eccentric bush to give the minimum running clearance between the pinion and rack. The rack should protrude 6.38 in (162 mm) with the steering wheel straight ahead; operate the steering lock if fitted.
14 Fit the cover and tighten the retaining nuts hand tight, then turn the eccentric bush to give the minimum rack clearance at both extreme right and left positions. Tighten the cover retaining bolts or screws evenly to the correct torque wrench setting and lock them with locking wire where necessary.
15 On Daf 55 models check that if the eccentric bush does not have a limiting cam, a limiting spring is fitted behind the left-hand retaining screw.
16 Renew the rubber boots and nylon washers on the track-rod ends if necessary.
17 Adjust the track as described in Section 34.

Volvo 343 models

18 Renew all self-locking nuts and split-pins.
19 Before installing the steering gear, turn the pinion clockwise as far as possible, then two turns anti-clockwise.
20 The inner clamp of the right-hand retaining bolt must be located with the curve facing the wheel.
21 Delay tightening the retaining bolt until the steering gear is fully fitted.
22 Adjust the track as described in Section 34.

31 Steering gear (Daf 55, Daf 66 and Volvo 66 models) – overhaul

1   Clean the exterior of the steering gear with paraffin and wipe dry (removal is described in Section 30).
2   Mount the steering gear in a vice, press the pinion and eccentric bush together and remove the locking disc and gasket when fitted.
3   Withdraw the pinion and eccentric bush followed by the locating bush and washers.
4   Carefully drive the nylon bushes from the eccentric bush.
5   Clean all components with paraffin and examine them for wear. Renew all bushes and seals. New rack leather sealing rings must be soaked in oil for a minimum of 30 minutes before reassembly.
6   Start reassembly by driving the nylon bushes into the eccentric bush with their grooves facing outwards.
7   Install the leather sealing rings with the rough sides facing the O-ring, followed by the locating bush.
8   Apply a lithium based grease to the eccentric bush and pinion.
9   Install the busy and pinion in the housing, clamp them together in a vice, and fit the locking disc.
Note: *When fitting an eccentric bush without locating pegs, a gasket must be fitted on both sides of the locking disc, also that there are two*

types of disc (see Fig 9.33).

10 Refill the steering gear with approximately 40 cc of a lithium based grease (see Specifications).

32 Steering gear (Volvo 343 models) – overhaul

1 Clean the exterior of the steering gear with paraffin and wipe dry (removal is described in Section 30).

2 Mount the steering gear in a vice and turn the pinion fully clockwise.

3 Mark the housing directly below the damper flange clamp split to faciliate refitting, then unscrew and remove the clamp bolt and withdraw the vibration damper and flange.

4 Check the steering rod inner balljoints for excessive play and note where this is evident.

5 Loosen the locknuts then unscrew the track-rod ends from the steering rods noting how many turns are required to remove them.

6 Loosen the clips and remove the rubber bellows from the housing and steering rods.

7 Using a screwdriver, prise the locktabs from the steering rod inner ends, then, using an open ended spanner to stop the rack turning, unscrew the rods from the rack.

8 Unscrew and remove the steering bolts and withdraw the thrust block cover, spring, shims, and thrust block.

9 Unscrew and remove the retaining bolts and withdraw the pinion cover, bearing cup and shims. Tap the pinion if necessary to release the cup.

10 Remove the rack from the steering gear.

11 Withdraw the pinion and seal, then using a soft metal drift, drive out the pinion bearing outer race.

12 Depress the two locking pins and extract the rack locating bush with a pair of pliers.

13 Thoroughly clean all components with paraffin and wipe dry with a lint-free cloth. Examine all components for damage and excessive wear, and renew them as necessary. Obtain all new seals for the steering gear.

14 Before starting reassembly grease all moving parts and surfaces with a lithium based grease.

15 Using suitable diameter tubing drive the inner bearing race onto the pinion shaft, then similarly drive the outer race of the upper pinion bearing into the steering gear housing.

16 Install the pinion and bearings and drive in the outer race of the lower bearing.

17 Fit the pinion cover and tighten the retaining bolts.

18 With the pinion uppermost, lightly tap the shaft to settle the bearings then measure the endfloat with a dial gauge. The bearings must be preloaded and to do this, make up a pack of shims equalling the endfloat plus a further 0.00 to 0.002 in (0.00 to 0.05 mm). Remove the pinion cover, pinion and bearings.

19 Press the rack locating bush into the housing so that the two locking pins engage the housing recesses.

20 Insert the rack into the housing from the pinion end until it protrudes 2.8 ± 0.02 in (71 ± 0.5 mm) from the opposite end.

21 Grease the bearings and fit them together with the pinion shaft without moving the rack.

22 Fit the previously assembled shims to the outer bearing cup followed by the pinion cover, and tighten the retaining bolts.

23 Fit the thrust block and use a micrometer to measure the distance from the block to the housing face whilst keeping the block firmly in contact with the rack. Similarly measure the distance from the cover inside face to the outer contact face.

24 Select a shim that will allow a clearance of 0.006 to 0.014 in (0.15 to 0.35 mm) between the adjacent surfaces of the cover and block.

25 Install the shim, spring, O-ring and cover and tighten the retaining bolts evenly.

26 Using a torque wrench, turn the rack from the extreme left to the extreme right and check that the torque is between 0.58 and 1.09 lbf ft (0.8 and 1.5 Nm). If too high in any position, have the rack in this position and recalculate the shim thickness as described in paragraph 24. Should it be impossible to obtain the correct torque or the rack moves unevenly with the thrust block removed, the rack is distorted and must be renewed.

27 Install the pinion seal.

28 Tighten the steering rods into position using two open ended spanners and lock them by bending the tabs onto the rack and balljoints.

29 Refit the two bellows and tighten the clips, making sure that the right-hand bellows locates over the locking pins.

30 Install the track-rod ends to their original positions and tighten the locknuts.

31 Position the flange on the pinion shaft in alignment with the previously made mark, but leave the clamp nut loose until the steering gear is installed in the car.

32 Temporarily remove the thrust block cover, spring, shim and block and fill the cavity with a lithium based grease, then press the thrust block into position and refit the shim, spring and cover.

33 Track-rod end balljoints – testing and renewal

1 Periodically check the condition of the track-rod end balljoints. If there is any free movement in a vertical direction when the track-rod is moved up and down, the balljoint must be renewed (photo).

2 To remove the balljoint first extract the split-pin and unscrew the retaining nut.

3 Using a balljoint remover separate the balljoint from the steering arm or rack as applicable.

4 On Daf 55, Daf 66 and Volvo 66 models, separate both balljoints and remove the track-rod from the car. Loosen the locknut and unscrew the balljoint.

5 On Volvo 343 models, loosen the locknut and unscrew the balljoint if the outer balljoint only is being renewed. Removal of the track-rod and inner balljoint is carried out by loosening the clips, withdrawing the bellows, releasing the locktabs and unscrewing the balljoint from the rack using two open ended spanners.

6 On all models refitting is a reversal of removal, but the following additional points should be noted:

(a)   The balljoints must be screwed onto the track-rods equally on either side of the car and either end of the rod as applicable

(b)   On Volvo 343 models apply a lithium based grease to the balljoints before assembly

(c)   Clean the balljoint taper pin before fitting it, and always fit new split-pins

(d)   Adjust the track as described in Section 34.

34 Steering angles and front wheel alignment

1 Accurate front wheel alignment is essential for good steering and even tyre wear.

2 Before making any check, note that wear in the steering balljoints, incorrect tyre pressures, worn or incorrectly adjusted front wheel bearings, loose suspension mountings and buckled wheels can give incorrect readings.

3 There are four factors to consider:

Camber, is the angle at which the front wheels are set from the vertical when viewed from the front; when the top of the wheel tilts outwards it is said to have positive camber.

Castor, is the angle at which the steering axis is set from the vertical when viewed from the side of the car; when the top of the axis tilts towards the rear of the car it is said to have positive castor.

King-pin inclination, is the angle between the vertical and an imaginary line down through the steering axis when viewed from the front. This angle is also not adjustable.

Toe-in, is the amount by which the distance between the front inside edges of the front wheels is less than the distance between the rear inside edges of the front wheels measured at hub height.

4 Accurate checking of the steering angles is only possible with specialised equipment and is therefore best left to a competent garage. Neither *camber* or *castor angles* are adjustable and if shown to be incorrect the steering and suspension components and mountings must be checked for damage or distortion.

5 *To adjust the toe-in,* first place the car on level ground with the front wheels in the straight-ahead position.

6 Make up a gauge which can be adjusted between the inner or outer wheel rims at hub height.

7 Adjust the gauge between the rear rims of the front wheels and mark the contact points with chalk on the tyres.

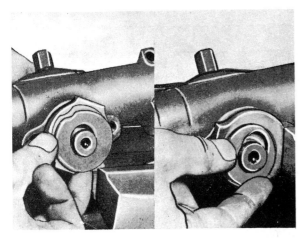

Fig. 9.33 Alternative types of pinion locking disc (except Volvo 343 models)

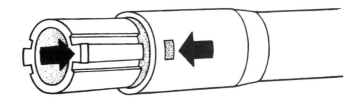

Fig. 9.34 Locating bush locking pins and recess – arrowed (Volvo 343 models)

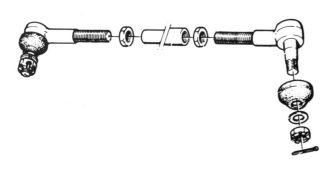

Fig. 9.35 Track-rod end components (except Volvo 343 models)

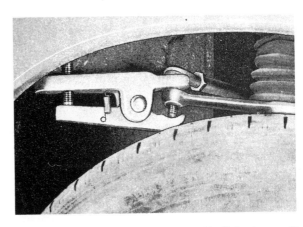

Fig. 9.36 Removing the outer track-rod end balljoint (except Volvo 343 models)

8   Remove the gauge and roll the car forwards so that the chalk marks are now at the front.

9   Place the gauge between the front rims of the front wheels by the chalk marks; the resulting gap should equal the toe-in setting (see Specifications).

10 If adjustment is required, loosen the track-rod end locknuts and bellows outer clip where necessary.

11 Turn the track-rods equal amounts on either side until the adjustment is correct, then tighten the locknuts. The position of the track-rod ends on the track-rods must not vary more than 0.08 in (2 mm) when compared side for side.

35 Roadwheels and tyres

1   Whenever the roadwheels are removed, it is a good idea to clean them especially on the insides to remove the accumulation of mud and dirt.

2   Check the condition of the wheel and repaint it if it is deteriorating.

3   Examine the wheel stud holes and if they have become elongated, renew the wheel.

4   Take the opportunity to remove any stones from the tyre tread and check the tyre for splits and damage; if damage is evident or if the depth of the tread is less than 1 mm, the tyre must be renewed.

5   Regular repositioning of the roadwheels is worthwhile in order to even out wear, and the spare should be included in the sequence.

6   Balancing of the wheels may become essential when the tyre treads are half worn, in which case they all should be removed from the car and rebalanced. Where wheels are balanced on the car they must be kept with the same hub, and both wheel and wheel stud must be marked to ensure that the balance is retained.

7   Regularly check the pressures of the tyres, preferably when they are cold, and always refit the dust caps onto the valves.

Fault diagnosis overleaf

36 Fault diagnosis

Symptom	Reason/s
Excessive play at steering wheel	Worn rack-and-pinion Worn steering balljoint Loose steering gear mounting bolts
Steering wander	Incorrect front wheel alignment Incorrectly adjusted or worn wheel bearings Worn suspension balljoints
Heavy or stiff steering	Low tyre pressures Seized balljoint Dry rack assembly Distorted steering shaft or rack
Wheel wobble and vibration	Wheels out of balance Buckled wheel Faulty shock absorber Faulty tyre
Excessive pitching or rolling on corners and when braking	Faulty shock absorber Weak or broken spring

Chapter 10 Bodywork and fittings

Contents

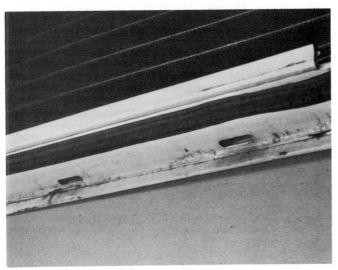

2.4 Door drain hole locations

1 General description

The main bodyshell and underframe is of all-steel unitary construction and incorporates many safety features.

On Volvo 343 models, the main passenger compartment is in the
form of a safety cage, and impact energy on collision is absorbedby the
front and rear body panels, the passenger compartment remaining
intact.

Also on Volvo 343 models, the front wings and front panel are
bolted to the main bodyframe, and renewal of these items is therefore
straightforward.

2 Maintenance – bodywork and underframe

1   The general condition of a car's bodywork is the one thing that
significantly affects its value. Maintenance is easy but needs to be
regular and particular. Neglect, particularly after minor damage, can
lead quickly to further deterioration and costly repair bills. It is
important also to keep watch on those parts of the car not immediately
visible, for instance, the underside, inside all the wheel arches and the
engine compartment.

2   The basic maintenance routine for the bodywork is washing – pre-

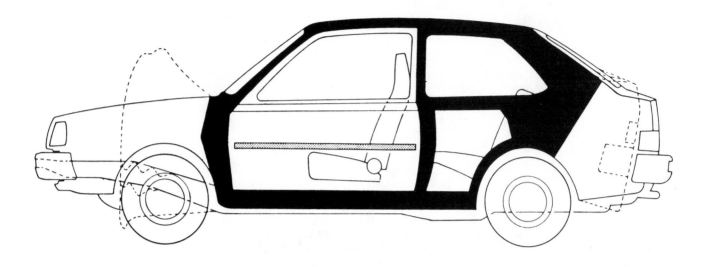

Fig. 10.1 Volvo 343 safety cage construction

ferably with a lot of water, from a hose. This will remove all the solids which may have stuck to the car. It is important to flush these off in such a way as to prevent grit from scratching the finish. The wheel arches and underbody need washing in the same way to remove any accumulated mud which will retain moisture and tend to encourage rust. Paradoxically enough, the best time to clean the underbody and wheel arches is in wet weather when the mud is thoroughly wet and soft. In very wet weather the underbody is usually cleaned of large accumulations automatically and this is a good time for inspection.

3   Periodically it is a good idea to have the whole of the underside of the car steam cleaned, engine compartment included, so that a thorough inspection can be carried out to see what minor repairs and renovations are necessary. Steam cleaning is available at many garages and is necessary for removal of accumulations of oily grime which sometimes cakes thick in certain areas near the engine and transmission. The facilities are usually available at commercial vehicle garages but if not there are one or two excellent grease solvents available which can be brush applied. The dirt can then be hosed off.

4   After washing paintwork, wipe it with a chamois leather to give an unspotted clear finish. A coat of clear protective wax polish will give added protection against chemical pollutants in the air. If the paintwork sheen has dulled or oxidised, use a cleaner/polisher combination to restore the brilliance of the shine. This requires a little more effort, but is usually caused because regular washing has been neglected. Always check that door drain holes are completely clear so that water can drain out (photo). Bright work should be treated the same way as paintwork. Windscreen and windows can be kept clear of the smeary film which often appears if a little ammonia is added to the water. If they are scratched, a good b with a proprietary metal polish will often clear them. Never use any form of wax or chromium polish on glass.

3   Maintenance – upholstery and carpets

1   Mats and carpets should be brushed or vacuum cleaned regularly to keep them free of grit. If they are badly stained remove them from the car for scrubbing or sponging and make quite sure they are dry before replacement. Seats and interior trim panels can be kept clean by a wipe over with a damp cloth. If they do become stained (which

can be more apparent on light coloured upholstery) use a little liquid detergent and a soft nailbrush to scour the grime out of the grain of the material. Do not forget to keep the head lining clean in the same way as the upholstery. When using liquid cleaners inside the car do not over-wet the surfaces being cleaned. Excessive damp could get into the seams and padded interior causing stains, offensive odours or even rot. If the inside of the car gets very wet accidentally, it is worthwhile taking some trouble to dry it out properly, particularly where the carpets are involved. Do *NOT* leave oil or electric heaters inside the car for this purpose.

4   Minor body damage – repair

The photo sequences on pages 198 and 199 illustrate the operations detailed in the following sub-sections.

Repair of minor scratches in the car's bodywork

If the scratch is very superficial, and does not penetrate to the metal of the bodywork, repair is very simple. Lightly rub the area of the scratch with a paintwork renovator, or a very fine cutting paste, to remove loose paint from the scratch and to clear the surrounding bodywork of wax polish. Rinse the area with clean water.

Apply touch-up paint to the scratch using a thin paint brush; continue to apply thin layers of paint until the surface of the paint in the scratch is level with the surrounding paintwork. Allow the new paint at least two weeks to harden, then blend it into the surrounding paintwork by rubbing the paintwork, in the scratch area, with a paintwork renovator or a very fine cutting paste. Finally, apply wax polish.

An alternative to painting over the scratch is to use a paint transfer. Use the same preparation for the affected area, then simply pick a patch of a suitable size to cover the scratch completely. Hold the patch against the scratch and burnish its backing paper; the patch will adhere to the paintwork, freeing itself from the backing paper at the same time. Polish the affected area to blend the patch into the surrounding paintwork.

Where the scratch has penetrated right through to the metal of the bodywork, causing the metal to rust, a different repair technique is required. Remove any loose rust from the bottom of the scratch with a penknife, then apply rust inhibiting paint to prevent the formation of rust in the future. Using a rubber or nylon applicator fill the scratch with bodystopper paste. If required, this paste can be mixed with cellulose thinners to provide a very thin paste which is ideal for filling narrow scratches. Before the stopper paste in the scratch hardens, wrap a piece of smooth cotton rag around the top of a finger. Dip the finger in cellulose thinners and then quickly sweep it across the surface of the stopper paste in the scratch; this will ensure that the surface of the stopper paste is slightly hollowed. The scratch can now be painted over as described earlier in this Section.

Repair of dents in the car's bodywork

When deep denting of the car's bodywork has taken place, the first task is to pull the dent out, until the affected bodywork almost attains its original shape. There is little point in trying to restore the original shape completely, as the metal in the damaged area will have stretched on impact and cannot be reshaped fully to its original contour. It is better to bring the level of the dent up to a point which is about $\frac{1}{8}$ inch (3 mm) below the level of the surrounding bodywork. In cases where the dent is very shallow anyway, it is not worth trying to pull it out at all.

If the underside of the dent is accessible, it can be hammered out gently from behind, using a mallet with a wooden or plastic head. Whilst doing this, hold a suitable block of wood firmly against the impact from the mallet blows and thus prevent a large area of the bodywork from being 'belled-out'.

Should the dent be in a section of the bodywork which has double skin or some other factor making it inaccessible from behind, a different technique is called for. Drill several small holes through the metal inside the dent area – particularly in the deeper sections. Then screw long self-tapping screws into the holes just sufficiently for them to gain a good purchase in the metal. Now the dent can be pulled out by pulling on the protruding heads of the screws with a pair of pliers.

The next stage of the repair is the removal of the paint from the damaged area, and from an inch (25.4 mm) or so of the surrounding 'sound' bodywork. This is accomplished most easily by using a wire brush or abrasive pad on a power drill, although it can be done just as effectively by hand using sheets of abrasive paper. To complete the preparation for filling, score the surface of the bare metal with a screwdriver or the tang of a file, or alternatively, drill small holes in the affected area. This will provide a really good key for the filler paste.

To complete the repair see the Section on filling and respraying.

Repair of rust holes or gashes in the car's bodywork

Remove all paint from the affected area and from an inch or so of the surrounding sound bodywork, using an abrasive pad or a wire brush on a power drill. If these are not available a few sheets of abrasive paper will do the job just as effectively. With the paint removed you will be able to judge the severity of the corrosion and therefore decide whether to renew the whole panel (if this is possible) or to repair the affected area. New body panels are not as expensive as most people think and it is often quicker and more satisfactory to fit a new panel than to attempt to repair large areas of corrosion.

Remove all fittings from the affected area except those which will act as a guide to the original shape of the damaged bodywork (eg headlamp shells etc). Then, using tin snips or a hacksaw blade, remove all loose metal and any other metal badly affected by corrosion. Hammer the edges of the hole inwards in order to create a slight depression for the filler paste.

Wire brush the affected area to remove the powdery rust from the surface of the remaining metal. Paint the affected area with rust inhibiting paint; if the back of the rusted area is accessible treat this also.

Before filling can take place it will be necessary to block the hole in some way. This can be achieved by the use of one of the following materials: Zinc gauze, Aluminium tape or Polyurethane foam.

Zinc gauze is probably the best material to use for a large hole. Cut a piece to the approximate size and shape of the hole to be filled, then position it in the hole so that its edges are below the level of the surrounding bodywork. It can be retained in position by several blobs of filler paste around its periphery.

Aluminium tape should be used for small or very narrow holes. Pull a piece off the roll and trim it to the approximate size and shape required, then pull off the backing paper (if used) and stick the tape over the hole; it can be overlapped if the thickness of one piece is insufficient. Burnish down the edges of the tape with the handle of a

screwdriver or similar, to ensure that the tape is securely attached to the metal underneath.

Polyurethane foam is best used where the hole is situated in a section of bodywork of complex shape, backed by a small box section (eg where the sill panel meets the rear fender arch – most cars). The usual mixing procedure for this foam is to put equal amounts of fluid from each of the two cans provided in the kit, into one container. Stir until the mixture begins to thicken, then quickly pour this mixture into the hole, and hold a piece of cardboard over the larger apertures. Almost immediately the polyurethane will begin to expand, gushing out of any small holes left unblocked. When the foam hardens it can be cut back to just below the level of the surrounding bodywork with a hacksaw blade.

Bodywork repairs – filling and respraying

Before using this Section, see the Sections on dent, deep scratch, rust hole and gash repairs.

Many types of bodyfiller are available, but generally speaking those proprietary kits which contain a tin of filler paste and a tube of resin hardener are best for this type of repair. A wide, flexible plastic or nylon applicator will be found invaluable for imparting a smooth and well contoured finish to the surface of the filler.

Mix up a little filler on a clean piece of card or board – use the hardener sparingly (follow the maker's instructions on the pack) otherwise the filler will set very rapidly.

Using the applicator, apply the filler paste to the prepared area; draw the applicator across the surface of the filler to achieve the correct contour and to level the filler surface. As soon as a contour that approximates the correct one is achieved, stop working the paste – if you carry on too long the paste will become sticky and begin to pick-up on the applicator.

Continue to add thin layers of filler paste at twenty-minute intervals until the level of the filler is just proud of the surrounding bodywork.

Once the filler has hardened, excess can be removed using a Surform plane or Dreadnought file. From then on, progressively finer grades of abrasive paper should be used, starting with a 40 grade wet and dry paper. Always wrap the abrasive paper around a flat rubber, cork, or wooden block – otherwise the surface of the filler will not be completely flat. During the smoothing of the filler surface the wet-and-dry paper should be periodically rinsed in water – this will ensure that a very smooth finish is imparted to the filler at the final stage.

At this stage the dent should be surrounded by a ring of bare metal, which in turn should be encircled by the finely 'feathered' edge of the good paintwork. Rinse the repair area with clean water, until all of the dust produced by the rubbing-down operation is gone.

Spray the whole repair area with a light coat of primer; this will show up any imperfections in the surface of the filler. Repair these imperfections with fresh filler paste or bodystopper, and once more smooth the surface with abrasive paper. If bodystopper is used, it can be mixed with cellulose thinners to form a really thin paste which is ideal for filling small holes. Repeat this spray-and-repair procedure until you are satisfied that the surface of the filler and the feathered edge of the paintwork are perfect. Clean the repair area with clean water and allow to dry fully.

The repair area is now ready for final spraying. Paint spraying must be carried out in a warm, dry, windless and dust-free atmosphere. This condition can only be created satisfactorily if you have access to a large indoor working area, but if you are forced to work in the open, you will have to pick your day very carefully. If you are working indoors, dousing the floor in the work area with water will lay the dust which would otherwise be in the atmosphere. If the repair area is confined to one body panel, mask off the surrounding panels; this will help to minimise the effects of a slight mis-match in paint colours. Bodywork fittings (eg; chrome strips, door handles etc) will also need to be removed or masked off. Use genuine masking tape and several thicknesses of newspaper for the masking operations.

Before commencing to spray, agitate the aerosol can thoroughly, then spray a test area (an old tin, or similar) until the technique is mastered. Cover the repair area with a thick coat of primer; the thickness should be built up using several thin layers of paint rather than one thick one. Using 400 grade wet-and-dry paper, rub down the surface of the primer until it is really smooth. While doing this, the work area should be thoroughly doused with water, and the 'wet-and-dry' paper periodically rinsed in water. Allow to dry before spraying on more paint.

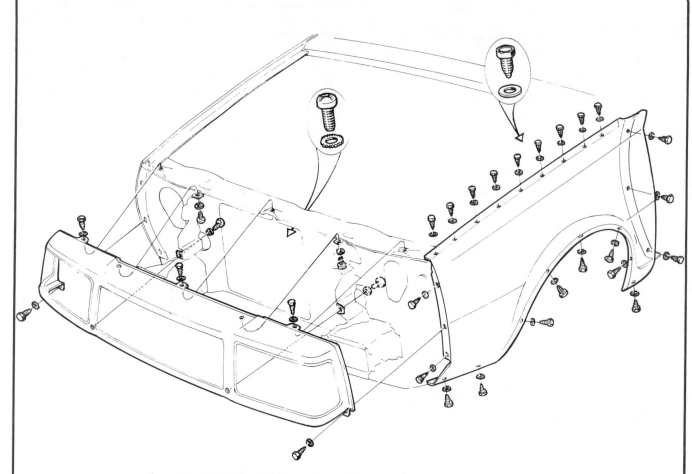

Fig. 10.2 Volvo 343 front wing and front panel retaining bolt location

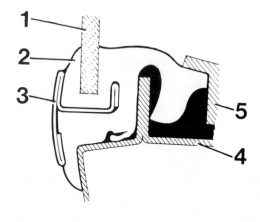

Fig. 10.3 Windscreen weatherstrip location on Volvo 343 models

1 Windscreen   4 Body
2 Weatherstrip   5 Fascia
3 Moulding

Fig. 10.4 Removing the windscreen

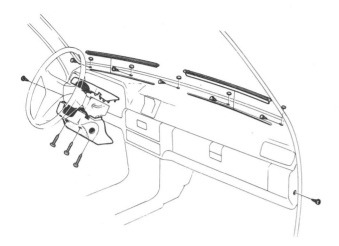

Fig. 10.5 Location of the fascia panel retaining screws (Volvo 343 models)

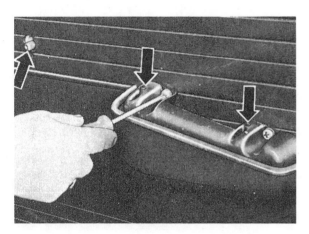

Fig. 10.6 Removing the arm rest (Daf 55 models)

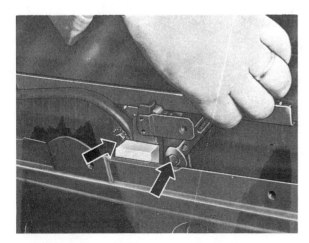

Fig. 10.7 Removing the door window (Daf 55 models)

Spray on the top coat, again building up the thickness by using several thin layers of paint. Start spraying in the centre of the repair area and then using a circular motion, work outwards until the whole repair area and about 2 inches (50 mm) of the surrounding original paintwork is covered. Remove all masking material 10 to 15 minutes after spraying on the final coat of paint. Allow the new paint at least two weeks to harden fully; then, using a paintwork renovator or a very fine cutting paste, blend the edges of the new paint into the existing paintwork. Finally, apply wax polish.

5 Bodywork repairs – major damage

Where serious damage has occurred or large areas need renewal due to neglect, it means certainly that completely new sections or panels will need welding in and this is best left to professionals. If the damage is due to impact it will also be necessary to completely check the alignment of the bodyshell structure. Due to the principle of construction the strength and shape of the whole can be affected by damage to a part. In such instances the services of a Daf/Volvo agent with specialist checking jigs are essential. If a body is left misaligned it is first of all dangerous as the car will not handle properly and secondly uneven stresses will be imposed on the steering, engine and transmission, causing abnormal wear or complete failure. Tyre wear may also be excessive.

6 Maintenance – hinges and locks

1   Oil the hinges of the bonnet, boot and doors with a drop or two of light oil periodically. A good time is after the car has been washed.
2   Oil the hood release catch pivot pin and the safety catch pivot pin periodically.
3   Do not over-lubricate door latches and strikers. Normally a little oil on the rotary cam spindle alone is sufficient.

7 Doors – tracing rattles and their rectification

1   Check first that the door is not loose at the hinges and that the latch is holding the door firmly in position. Check also that the door lines up with the aperture in the body.
2   If the hinges are loose or the door is out of alignment it will be necessary to renew the hinge pins or hinges.
3   If the latch is holding the door properly it should hold the door tightly when fully latched and the door should line up with the body. If it is out of alignment it needs adjustment. If loose, some part of the lock mechanism must be worn out and require renewal.
4   Other rattles from the door would be caused by wear or looseness in the window winder, the glass channels and sill strips or the door interior latch release mechanism (photo).

8 Front wings and front panel (Volvo 343 models) – removal and refitting

1   On Volvo 343 models only, the front wings and front panel are bolted to the main bodyframe, and it is therefore a simple matter for the home mechanic to renew either of these items.
2   Refer to Fig. 10.2 for the location of the retaining bolts, also to Chapter 8 for the removal of the headlamps.
3   Refitting is a reversal of removal but renew any mastic sealing compound, and apply a protective coating to the under surface. The outer surface can be resprayed to match the body colour.

9 Windscreen glass – removal and refitting

1   If the windscreen has been shattered, the fascia air vents should be covered with masking tape to prevent any glass from entering them. It is also helpful to stick adhesive sheeting to the outside of the windscreen then remove as much of the glass as possible.
2   Remove the windscreen wipers and interior mirror.
3   On Volvo 343 models it will be necessary to move the fascia back a little in order to release the windscreen weatherstrip. To do this, first

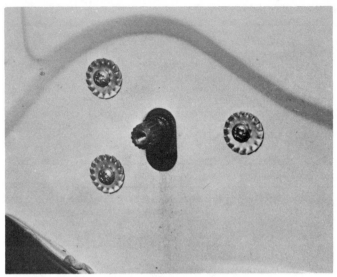

7.4 Window regulator retaining screw locations

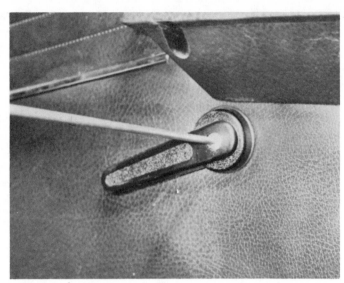

10.1A Removing the interior door handle

10.1B Removing the arm rest from the door

10.1C Removing the window winder handle

10.2 Removing the door cover plate (Daf 66 models)

10.4 Door glass retaining screw location (Daf 66 models)

disconnect the battery negative lead, then remove the two steering column upper shrouds (see Chapter 9). Prise the defroster vents from the fascia, and unscrew and remove the fascia retaining bolts (see Fig. 10.5). Unscrew and remove the two retaining bolts in the glove compartment and the two screws beneath the heater control panel. The fascia can now be released from the weatherstrip.

4 If the windscreen is being removed intact, an assistant will be required. Place a wad of cloth on the inside of the windscreen by a top corner and, whilst sitting in a front seat, use the feet to carefully push the glass from the aperture. Extreme care should be taken to avoid over stressing the windscreen in any direction otherwise it will shatter.

5 Where a shattered windscreen has been removed, pull the weatherstrip from the aperture; where the windscreen is intact remove the weatherstrip from the windscreen.

6 Remove the ornamental moulding from the weatherstrip.

7 Before fitting a windscreen, thoroughly clean the weatherstrip, windscreen and body aperture with methylated spirit, and check the aperture for distortion. If evident the aperture must be corrected using metal filler as necessary.

8 Fit the ornamental moulding to the weatherstrip and the weatherstrip to the windscreen.

9 Insert a length of strong cord into the weatherstrip channel with the ends overlapping at the bottom of the windscreen.

10 Offer the windscreen to the body aperture with the cord inside, then, while the assistant presses on the outside, pull the cord so that the weatherstrip engages over the body flange.

11 Using a rubber block, gently tap around the windscreen edge to settle the weatherstrip.

12 Apply a bead of sealant both between the windscreen and body aperture to weatherstrip outer sealing surfaces, making sure that the scuttle drainage slots are not obstructed.

13 On Volvo 343 models refit the fascia using a reversal of the removal procedure.

10 Door window – removal and refitting

Daf 55 and Daf 66 models

1 Detach the window regulator, door interior handle, and arm rest from the trim panel (photos).

2 Remove the trim panel and cover plate (photo).

3 Place a 1 in (25 mm) thick wooden block between the inner door plate and window regulator controls.

4 Unscrew and remove the two retaining bolts and withdraw the door glass (photo).

5 Refitting is a reversal n val, but if a new channel is fitted it must be positioned so that the distance from the rear of the channel to the rear edge of the window is 14.7 in (372.5 mm). Use a rubber mallet to tap it onto the glass.

Volvo 66 models

6 Detach the window regulator, door interior handle, and arm rest from the trim panel.

7 Remove the trim panel and cover plate.

8 Remove the door glass channel, weatherstrip, and quarter light glass.

9 Unscrew and remove the lower channel retaining crosshead screws and withdraw the door glass.

10 Refitting is a reversal of removal, but if a new channel is fitted it must be positioned so that the distance from the rear mounting hole of the channel to the rear edge of the window is 12.4 in (314.5 mm).

Volvo 343 models

11 Fully lower the window and detach the window regulator and arm rest.

12 Push the door latch surround rearwards and remove it from the trim panel.

13 Using a screwdriver carefully prise the trim panel from the door.

14 Remove the front window channel by unscrewing and removing the four retaining screws and lifting it out.

15 Detach the lower cover plate from the door.

16 Unscrew and remove the window regulator retaining screws, then detach the arm from the lifting channel by pulling it forwards, and withdraw the regulator.

17 Lift out the window and remove the weatherstrip.

18 Refitting is a reversal of removal, but if a new channel is fitted it must be positioned so that the distance from the rear of the channel to the rear edge of the window is 7.1 in (180 mm). Delay tightening the channel and regulator retaining screws until the window is fully fitted.

11 Rear window – removal and refitting

1 The procedure is identical to that described in Section 9 for the removal and refitting of the windscreen.

12 Quarter light window (Volvo 343 models) – removal and refitting

1 Fully lower the window and detach the window regulator and arm rest.

2 Push the door latch surround rearwards and remove it from the trim panel.

3 Using a screwdriver, carefully prise the trim panel from the door.

4 Remove the front window channel by unscrewing and removing the four retaining screws and lifting it out.

5 Lift out the quarter light window.

6 If the weatherstrips have deteriorated, remove them and fit replacements.

Fig. 10.8 Location of the door cover plate and window channel retaining screws (except Volvo 343 models)

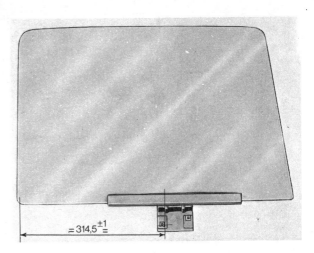

Fig. 10.9 Door window channel setting (Volvo 66 models)

This sequence of photographs deals with the repair of the dent and paintwork damage shown in this photo. The procedure will be similar for the repair of a hole. It should be noted that the procedures given here are simplified — more explicit instructions will be found in the text

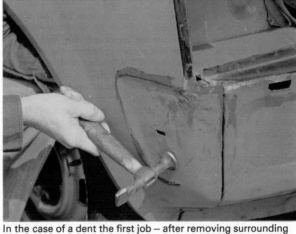

In the case of a dent the first job — after removing surrounding trim — is to hammer out the dent where access is possible. This will minimise filling. Here, the large dent having been hammered out, the damaged area is being made slightly concave

Now all paint must be removed from the damaged area, by rubbing with coarse abrasive paper. Alternatively, a wire brush or abrasive pad can be used in a power drill. Where the repair area meets good paintwork, the edge of the paintwork should be 'feathered', using a finer grade of abrasive paper

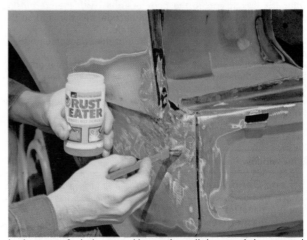

In the case of a hole caused by rusting, all damaged sheet-metal should be cut away before proceeding to this stage. Here, the damaged area is being treated with rust remover and inhibitor before being filled

Mix the body filler according to its manufacturer's instructions. In the case of corrosion damage, it will be necessary to block off any large holes before filling — this can be done with zinc gauze or aluminium tape. Make sure the area is absolutely clean before...

...applying the filler. Filler should be applied with a flexible applicator, as shown, for best results; the wooden spatula being used for confined areas. Apply thin layers of filler at 20-minute intervals, until the surface of the filler is slightly proud of the surrounding bodywork

Initial shaping can be done with a Surform plane or Dreadnought file. Then, using progressively finer grades of wet-and-dry paper, wrapped around a sanding block, and copious amounts of clean water, rub down the filler until really smooth and flat. Again, feather the edges of adjoining paintwork

The whole repair area can now be sprayed or brush-painted with primer. If spraying, ensure adjoining areas are protected from over-spray. Note that at least one inch of the surrounding sound paintwork should be coated with primer. Primer has a 'thick' consistency, so will fill small imperfections

Again, using plenty of water, rub down the primer with a fine grade of wet-and-dry paper (400 grade is probably best) until it is really smooth and well blended into the surrounding paintwork. Any remaining imperfections can now be filled by carefully applied knifing stopper paste

When the stopper has hardened, rub down the repair area again before applying the final coat of primer. Before rubbing down this last coat of primer, ensure the repair area is blemish-free – use more stopper if necessary. To ensure that the surface of the primer is really smooth use some finishing compound

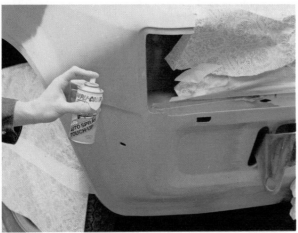

The top coat can now be applied. When working out of doors, pick a dry, warm and wind-free day. Ensure surrounding areas are protected from over-spray. Agitate the aerosol thoroughly, then spray the centre of the repair area, working outwards with a circular motion. Apply the paint as several thin coats

After a period of about two weeks, which the paint needs to harden fully, the surface of the repaired area can be 'cut' with a mild cutting compound prior to wax polishing. When carrying out bodywork repairs, remember that the quality of the finished job is proportional to the time and effort expended

7   Refitting is a reversal of removal, but make sure that the weather-strip is fitted to the rear edge of the quarter light with its widest edge on the outside, and delay tightening the channel retaining screws until the window has been operated several times.

13 Door – removal and refitting

1   Fully open the front door and remove the check arm clevis pin using a suitable metal drift from beneath the pin (photo).
2   Remove the plastic plugs from the hinges, where fitted, and drive out the lower hinge followed by the upper hinge pin. The lower hinge pin must be tapped up through the hinge; the upper pin down through the hinge.
3   Lift the door away from the car.
4   If a new door is being fitted, the window, regulator, door lock and handles must be transferred to the new door by referring to the applicable Sections of this Chapter.
5   Refitting is a reversal of removal, but it will be necessary to adjust the striker plate. Loosen the two striker plate retaining screws, and adjust the plate so that its upper edge is horizontal, and so that when the door is shut it is neither lifted up or pressed down to engage the striker. Check that the lock engages its second position when the door is fully shut and that the door panel aligns with the rear wing panel.

14 Door lock (Daf 55, Daf 66 and Volvo 66 models) – removal and refitting

1   Unscrew and remove the screws retaining the window winder, arm rest and door handle and withdraw each item.
2   Lift and remove the door inside trim panel.
3   Remove the window as described in Section 10.
4   Unscrew and remove the two crosshead retaining screws and detach the door handle remote control (photo).
5   Using a screwdriver, extract the clamping plate and plastic ring and withdraw the cylinder lock. If necessary extract the further clamping plate and withdraw the exterior door handle.
6   Unscrew and remove the lock retaining screws and withdraw the lock from inside the door (photo).
7   Refitting is a reversal of removal.

15 Door lock (Volvo 343 models) – removal and refitting

1   Close the window and remove the door trim panel as described in Section 12, paragraphs 1,2 and 3.
2   Unscrew and remove the retaining screws and detach the rear cover plate from the door.
3   Disconnect the four rods from the door lock.
4   Unscrew and remove the lock retaining bolts and remove the lock.
5   Refitting is a reversal of removal.

16 Door outside handle (Volvo 343 models) – removal and refitting

1   Close the window and remove the door trim panel as described in Section 12, paragraphs 1,2 and 3.
2   Unscrew and remove the retaining screws and detach the rear cover plate from the door.
3   Disconnect the two handle connecting rods at the lock.
4   Unscrew and remove the retaining bolt and withdraw the handle.
5   Remove the rubber sealing ring.
6   Refitting is a reversal of removal.

17 Boot lid lock (Daf 55, Daf 66 and Volvo 66 models) – removal and refitting

1   Open the boot lid and unscrew the lock retaining crosshead screws, then remove the lock.
2   Slide the lock retainer to one side and withdraw the lock cylinder, after removing the retaining screw.
3   Refitting is a reversal of removal.

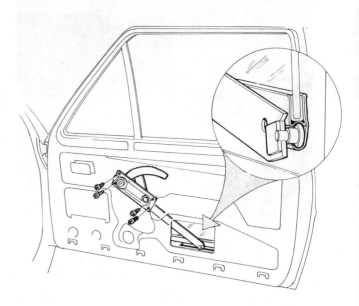

Fig. 10.10 Window regulator location (Volvo 343 models)

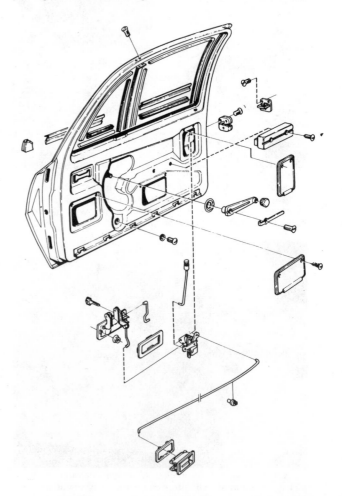

Fig. 10.11 Door lock and handle components (Volvo 343 models)

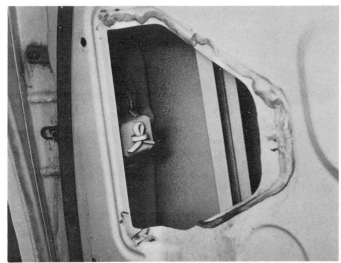

13.1 Door check arm inner retaining pin

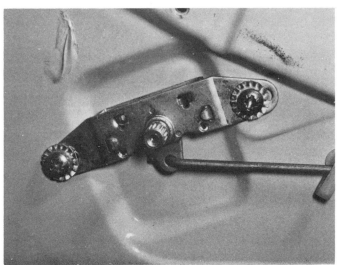

14.4 Door handle remote control

14.6 Door lock location and retaining screws

18 Tailgate lock (Volvo 343 models) – removal and refitting

1 Detach the cover from the tailgate interior.
2 Disconnect and remove the handle and lock connecting rod.
3 Unscrew and remove the retaining bolts, and withdraw the lock. If necessary the handle may be removed by unscrewing the retaining nut.
4 Refitting is a reversal of removal.

19 Boot lid (Daf 55, Daf 66 and Volvo 66 models) – removal and refitting

1 Unhook the boot lid tension springs.
2 Mark the position of the hinges on the boot lid, then unscrew and remove the retaining bolts and lift off the boot lid.
3 Refitting is a reversal of removal, but use a length of wire to reconnect the tension springs at the same time keeping the protecting sleeve away from the end of the spring with a pair of pliers. Adjust the spring tension as necessary by bending the retaining lug. The latch on the body may be adjusted if necessary by loosening the retaining bolts and moving it up or down.

20 Tailgate (Volvo 343 models) – removal and refitting

1 Open the tailgate and detach the telescopic tubes from each side of the tailgate.
2 Prise the two covers from the rear of the headlining and unscrew and remove one hinge retaining bolt from each side.
3 While an assistant holds the tailgate, unscrew and remove the remaining bolts, then lift off the tailgate.
4 Refitting is a reversal of removal.

21 Bonnet (Daf 55, Daf 66 and Volvo 66 models) – removal and refitting

1 Fully open the bonnet and on Daf 55 models remove the front grille upper ornamental mouldings.
2 Where fitted, unscrew and remove the check spring retaining bolt and withdraw it.
3 Mark the position of the hinges on the bonnet then, while an assistant holds the bonnet, unscrew and remove the hinge retaining bolts.
4 Lift the bonnet away from the car.
5 Refitting is a reversal of removal, but if adjustment of the bonnet position is necessary proceed as follows.
6 If the bonnet front height needs adjustment on Daf 55 and Daf 66 models, it will be necessary to make up metal strips to fit between the hinge and bonnet. On Volvo 66 models, remove the plastic front grille and loosen the lower hinge bolts; adjustment is then possible within the limits of the elongated holes.
7 If the bonnet rear height needs adjustment, loosen the lock retaining nuts and move the locks up and down as necessary. On Volvo 66 models the adjustable rubber plugs should be screwed in or out as necessary.
8 Longitudinal adjustment of the bonnet is possible on both the front hinges and rear catches.

22 Bonnet (Volvo 343 models) – removal and refitting

1 Fully open the bonnet and mark the position of the hinges on the bonnet.
2 While an assistant holds the bonnet, prise the retaining clips from the pivot pins and remove the washers.
3 Disconnect the hinge levers from the pivot pins and lift off the bonnet, at the same time disconnecting the stay.
4 Refitting is a reversal of removal.
5 Adjustment of the bonnet is possible by loosening the hinge and catch mounting bolts and moving them as necessary within the limits of the elongated holes.
6 Access to the bonnet catch retaining bolts is gained by removing the front grille. To do this, unscrew and remove the two central retain-

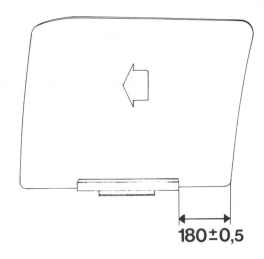

Fig. 10.12 Door window channel setting (Volvo 343 models)

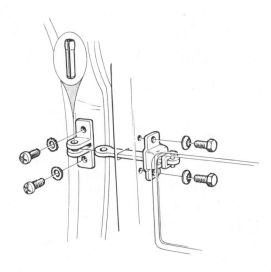

Fig. 10.13 Door check arm components (Volvo 343 models)

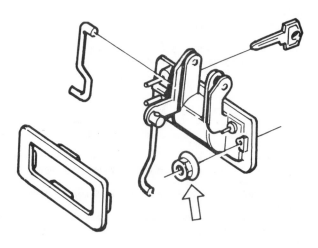

Fig. 10.14 Door outside handle components (Volvo 343 models)

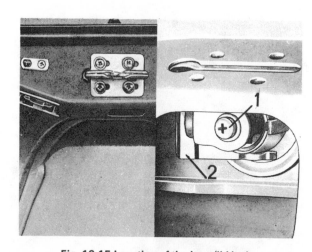

Fig. 10.15 Location of the boot/lid lock

1 Retaining screw   2 Retainer

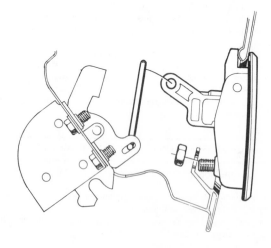

Fig. 10.16 Location of the tailgate lock

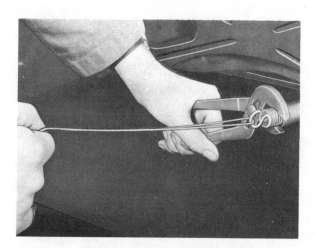

Fig. 10.17 Refitting the boot lid tension springs

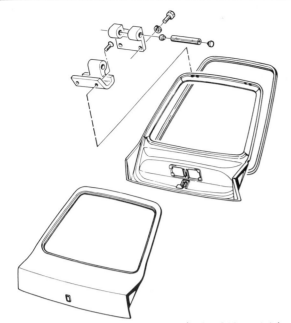

Fig. 10.18 Tailgate hinge components (Volvo 343 models)

Fig. 10.19 Location of the lower bonnet hinge adjustment bolts (Volvo 66 models)

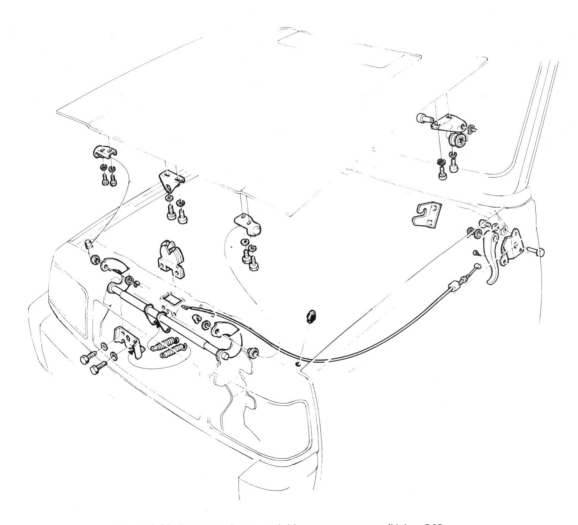

Fig. 10.20 Bonnet release and hinge components (Volvo 343 models)

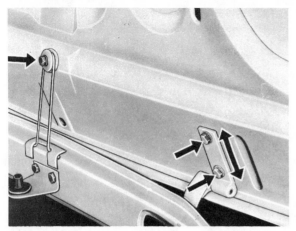

Fig. 10.21 Location of the upper bonnet hinge adjustment bolts and check spring bolt

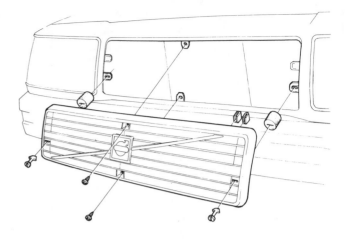

Fig. 10.22 Front grille panel retaining screw locations (Volvo 343 models)

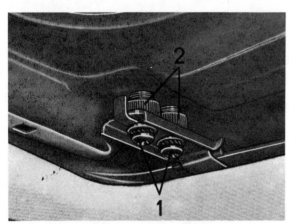

Fig. 10.23 Sliding roof front adjustment

1 Lock screws   2 Milled adjustment nuts

Fig. 10.24 Sliding roof rear adjustment

1 Adjustment bolt

ing screws and turn the outer retaining clips through 90°. Note the location of the two rubber buffers.

23 Sliding roof (Daf 55, Daf 66 and Volvo 66 models) – adjustment

1   Move the roof to its half open position and push back the front lining.
2   Close the roof and loosen the front adjustment crosshead screws.
3   Turn the milled adjustment nuts until the front edge of the sliding roof is flush with the surrounding roof panel, then tighten the screws.
4   The rear height of the sliding roof is adjusted by turning back the springs, loosening the adjustment bolt and moving the roof as necessary until the rear edge is flush with the surrounding roof panel. Some late models are fitted with a rear adjustment cam.
5   Refit the roof lining.
6   If the sliding roof leaks even when adjusted correctly, the drain hoses should be checked for blockage and closed as necessary.

24 Bumpers – removal and refitting

1   The bumpers are secured by brackets to the body and removal and refitting is straight forward.

2   On Volvo 66 models the front indicator leads must be disconnected before removing the front bumper.
3   On Volvo 343 models, access to the front bumper retaining bolts is gained by prising out the plugs from the rubber moulding. An Allen key will also be required to loosen the bolts.

25 Fascia panel (Daf 55, Daf 66 and Volvo 66 models) – removal and refitting

1   Disconnect the battery negative lead.
2   On Daf 55 models, remove the windscreen puller trim on the driver's side.
3   Remove the steering column as described in Chapter 9.
4   On late Daf 66 models disconnect the cigar lighter and spotlight switch wiring and remove the console.
5   Reach under the fascia panel and disconnect the cable from the speedometer head. To do this on Daf 55 and Daf 66 models, unscrew the union nut; on Volvo 66 models press the attachment in, turn it, and release the cable.
6   Remove the instrument cluster from the fascia panel and disconnect the wires, noting their locations.
7   On Daf 55 models remove the windscreen wiper and light switches and disconnect the wiring. On all models disconnect the engine brake switch and windscreen washer hose.

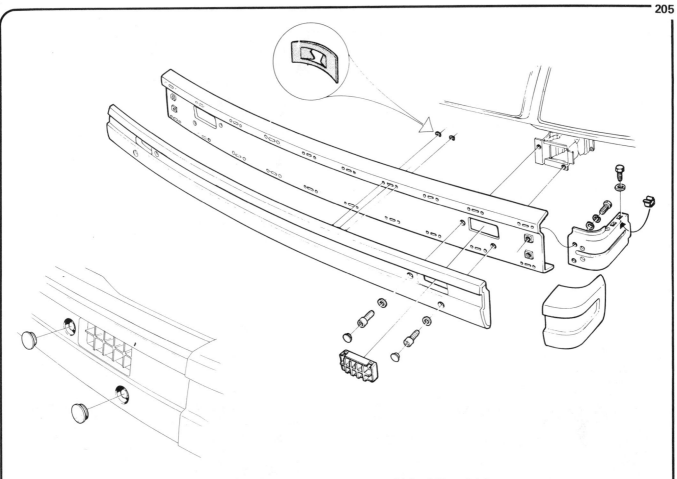

Fig. 10.25 Front bumper components (Volvo 343 models)

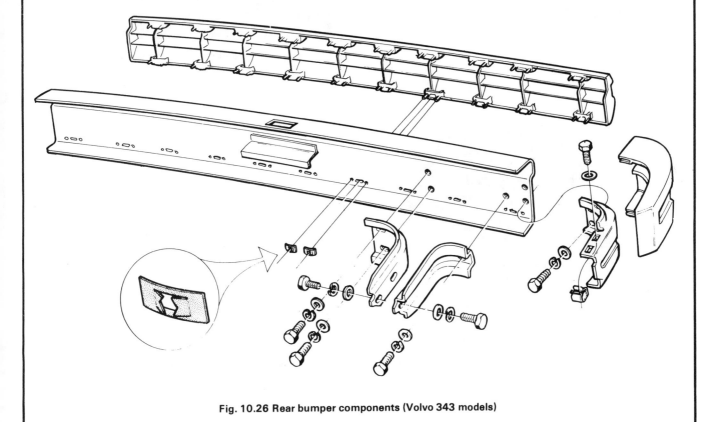

Fig. 10.26 Rear bumper components (Volvo 343 models)

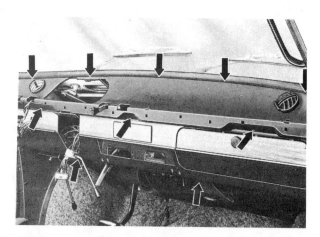

Fig. 10.27 Location of the fascia panel retaining screws (Volvo 343 models)

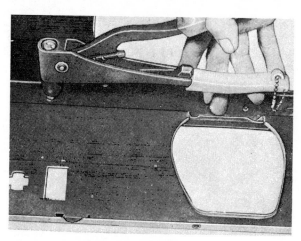

Fig. 10.28 Rivetting the protection strip to a new fascia panel (Daf 55 models)

Fig. 10.29 Location of the heater retaining screws (except Volvo 343 models)

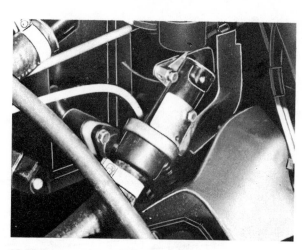

Fig. 10.30 Heater valve and thermostat location (Volvo 66 models)

Fig. 10.31 Separating the two halves of the heater (except Volvo 343 models)

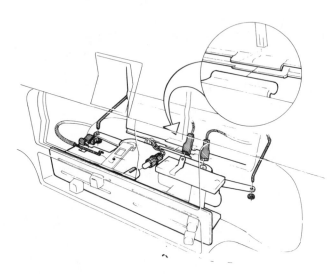

Fig. 10.32 Heater control panel components (Volvo 343 models)

25.11 Fascia panel (Daf 66 models)

8 Disconnect the heater panel control cables at the heater and withdraw the heater panel on Daf 55 and Daf 66 models.
9 On Daf 55 and Daf 66 models, unscrew and remove the fascia panel retaining screws and withdraw the fascia panel. The upper retaining screws have rubber covers and these must be prised out. If it is required to remove the fascia panel frame, disconnect the bonnet lock pull rods then unscrew and remove the retaining bolts.
10 On Volvo 66 models, remove the air vent hoses and on the passenger's side remove the glove compartment. Unscrew and remove the fascia padding retaining bolts, withdraw the fascia padding and disconnect the switch wiring on the driver's side. Unscrew and remove the fascia panel retaining bolts and withdraw the fascia panel, noting that the upper bolts have rubber covers which must be prised out. The fascia panel frame may also be removed by disconnecting the bonnet lock pull rods and removing the retaining bolts.
11 Refitting is a reversal of removal but if a new fascia panel is being fitted to Daf 55 models the protection strip must be transferred by drilling out the pop rivets and riveting the strip to the new panel (photo).

26 Fascia panel (Volvo 343 models) – removal and refitting

1 Disconnect the battery negative lead.
2 Remove the steering wheel (see Chapter 9).
3 Unscrew and remove the choke control knob and steering column shrouds.
4 Unscrew and remove the retaining screws and withdraw the direction indicator and wiper switch stalks.
5 Disconnect the ignition switch wiring plug and the choke cable wire.
6 Detach the ashtray, then unscrew and remove the retaining bolts and withdraw the compartment below the heater control levers.
7 Disconnect all wiring and plugs from the fascia panel noting their locations.
8 Press in the speedometer cable connection, turn it, and withdraw it from the speedometer head.
9 Pull the hoses from the two outer air vents.
10 Using a screwdriver, prise the defroster vents from the fascia panel.
11 Unscrew and remove the retaining screws and withdraw the fascia panel: note that the upper screws are fitted with covers which must be prised out with a screwdriver.
12 Refitting is a reversal of removal.

27 Heater and ventilation system – description

1 The system is of the fresh air type, the air entering through the grilles located at the base of the windscreen. Heat is provided from the engine cooling system through an adjustable water flow valve.
2 Levers on the instrument panel control the temperature and the adjustment of the air deflectors for interior heating or screen demisting or defrosting.
3 Air is drawn over the heater matrix by an electric fan and most models have a *Boost* position on the heater controls whereby the fan is turned at a higher speed.
4 The temperature control valve on Volvo models is fitted with a thermostat which keeps the car interior at a constant temperature.

28 Heater (Daf 55, Daf 66 and Volvo 66 models) – removal and refitting

1 Disconnect the battery negative lead.
2 Partially drain the cooling system with the heater vent nipple loosened (refer to Chapter 2 if necessary).
3 Loosen the hose clips and pull the hoses from the heater unit.
4 Disconnect the control cables from the heater, and remove the throttle cable support.
5 Disconnect the two supply wires from the heater motor noting their locations.
6 Remove the heat distribution box by first loosening the bulkhead trim and then unscrewing the five retaining screws.
7 On Daf 66/1300 and Volvo 66 GL models disconnect the cigar lighter and spotlight switch wiring and remove the console.
8 Working inside the car, unscrew and remove the four retaining screws and then lift the heater assembly out vertically from the car.
9 Refitting is a reversal of removal, but it will be necessary to top up the cooling system as described in Chapter 2.

29 Heater matrix (Daf 55, Daf 66 and Volvo 66 models) – removal and refitting

1 Remove the heater assembly as described in Section 28.
2 Unscrew and remove the retaining bolts and remove the air inlet unit from the heater.
3 Unscrew and remove the retaining bolts and withdraw the fan and motor unit.
4 Unscrew and remove the mounting bolts and remove the heater valve (and thermostat on Volvo 66 models).
5 Prise the clamps from the heater assembly and separate the two halves.
6 Withdraw the heater matrix.
7 Refitting is a reversal of removal, but it will be necessary to top up the cooling system as described in Chapter 2.

30 Heater (Volvo 343 models) – removal and refitting

1 Disconnect the battery negative lead.
2 Partially drain the cooling system with the heater unit nipple loosened (refer to Chapter 2 if necessary).
3 Loosen the hose clips and pull the hoses from the heater unit.
4 Move the heater controls to *Maximum*.
5 Unscrew and remove the retaining bolts and withdraw the small compartment below the control levers.
6 Disconnect the wiring and remove the transmission tunnel console switches.
7 Prise out the console retaining bolt covers, remove the bolts and withdraw the console.
8 Remove the heater bracket from below the control levers.
9 Reach under the fascia panel and detach the speedometer cable, then remove the speedometer.
10 Prise out the defroster vents and remove the ashtray.
11 Disconnect the hoses from the vents and heater, press out the locking clamps, and remove the vents.
12 Disconnect the heater control panel wires and remove the lamp.
13 Detach the two rods from the control levers.
14 Release the heater control cable while bending the fascia outwards, lower the rear of the panel and withdraw the control panel.
15 Disconnect the throttle cable wire at the pedal.
16 Disconnect the bleed hose from the top of the heater unit, and the water hoses from the bottom of the unit.

17 Unscrew and remove the lower heater retaining bolts, and disconnect the motor connecting plug.
18 Working in the engine compartment disconnect the bleed hose and return hose from the air inlet chamber. Turn the nipple a quarter of a turn and pull it from the inlet chamber.
19 Lift the cover from the air inlet chamber, unscrew and remove the four retaining bolts and withdraw the air inlet chamber. Note that on some early models, the upper retaining bolts are fitted from inside, and access if then gained by removing the fascia instruments and clock.
20 Withdraw the heater unit from the car.
21 Refitting is a reversal of removal but it will be necessary to top up the cooling system as described in Chapter 2.

31 Heater matrix (Volvo 343 models) – removal and refitting

1 Remove the heater unit as described in Section 30.
2 Prise the clamps from the heater and carefully withdraw one half of the housing making sure that the flap is not disconnected from the mechanism.
3 Remove the heater matrix and gasket.
4 Refitting is a reversal of removal, but check that the flap and mechanism are correctly installed.

Index

Printed by
Haynes Publishing Group
Sparkford Yeovil Somerset
England